The foreign exchange market

Theory and econometric evidence

D1111878

The foreign exchange market

Theory and econometric evidence

RICHARD T. BAILLIE

Professor of Economics
Michigan State University

and

PATRICK C. McMAHON

Senior Lecturer in Economics
University of Birmingham

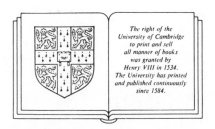

The right of the
University of Cambridge
to print and sell
all manner of books
was granted by
Henry VIII in 1534.
The University has printed
and published continuously
since 1584.

CAMBRIDGE UNIVERSITY PRESS
Cambridge
New York   Port Chester   Melbourne   Sydney

Published by the Press Syndicate of the University of Cambridge
The Pitt Building, Trumpington Street, Cambridge CB2 1RP
40 West 20th Street, New York, NY 10011, USA
10 Stamford Road, Oakleigh, Melbourne 3166, Australia

© Cambridge University Press 1989

First published 1989
First paperback edition 1990

Printed in Great Britain
at the University Press, Cambridge

British Library cataloguing in publication data

Baillie, Richard
The foreign exchange market : theory and
econometric evidence.
1. Foreign exchange. Rates. Variation.
Econometric models.
I. Title.   II. McMahon, Patrick
332.4'56'0724

Library of Congress cataloguing in publication data

Baillie, Richard.
The foreign exchange market.
Includes index.
1. Foreign exchange – Econometric models.
I. McMahon, Patrick.   II. Title.
HC3823.B34 1988   332.4'5   88-2820

Any views expressed in this book are those of the authors and
should in no way be construed as representing the views on
policies, past or present, of the Bank of England.

ISBN 0 521 30761 9 hardback
ISBN 0 521 39690 5 paperback

MC

Contents

Contents

Figures

Tables

Preface

This book is concerned with applying recent developments in economic theory and econometrics to problems in the foreign exchange market. Since 1973 many of the world's major currencies have been floating and the period has been marked by extreme exchange rate volatility, substantial and persistent trade imbalances, and severe Third world debt which has made the understanding of the foreign exchange market of central importance. The last fourteen years has also coincided with a considerable growth of economic theory of relevance to floating exchange rates. Many of these theoretical developments have been closely related to work in finance and concern the properties of efficient markets, the insights provided by the rational expectations revolution, the appropriate modelling of risk, etc. The study of exchange rates is also considerably aided by the availability of high quality data observed at frequent intervals of time. These facts have made it an attractive and challenging field with which to develop and apply econometric techniques. Such methods have been extensively applied to testing various forms of market-efficiency, interest and purchasing power parity, the modelling of risk premia and the development and testing of models to explain nominal exchange rate movements.

In this book we have tried to present a balanced account of the relevance of new economic theory in understanding aspects of the foreign exchange market and the application of new econometric methodology. Chapter 1 is concerned with a background of institutional details and presents a recent history of the movements in some of the major exchange rates. The second and third chapters set out the economic and finance theory required for an understanding of the asset market approach. Chapter 2 considers different definitions of market efficiency, the foundations of the martingale and random walk model and some theoretical models of time varying risk premia. Chapter 3 then develops the macro models from asset market theory to explain the determinants of nominal exchange rates. The chapter provides an initial discussion of purchasing power parity, the basic monetary model, and various extensions of the monetary model such as the Dornbusch sticky price model and Woo's extensions under rational expectations. There is a short appendix to the chapter which attempts to provide a self-contained introduction to rational expectations models.

Chapter 4 then turns to the econometric and statistical evidence of the concepts introduced in Chapter 2. A fairly detailed statistical analysis is given of the time series characteristics of nominal exchange rates using recent and fairly high level econometric techniques such as tests of unit roots in autoregressive models, tests for cointegration, autoregressive conditional heteroskedasticity (ARCH) models, etc. The econometric techniques are described without excessive detail in order to make the concepts understandable to non-specialist econometricians. Where necessary, references are given to more detailed accounts of the methods. Chapter 5 is largely self-contained, and describes interest rate parity, the modern theory of forward exchange and discusses some statistical evidence.

Chapter 6 considers tests of the proposition that the forward rate is an unbiased and efficient predictor of the future spot exchange rate. The chapter deals with tests based on vector autoregressions and the use of limited information type methods. Chapter 7 considers econometric approaches at quantifying the effects of new information on market fundamentals and their relationship to the spot and forward markets. The chapter also examines some models of time varying risk premia in these markets and whether or not simple term structure relationships describe the different forward premia.

The final chapter considers the estimation and testing of various models to explain the determination of nominal exchange rates. The so-called real interest rate differential model, the pure monetary model and its various extensions are all discussed so that empirical context is given to the theoretical models described in Chapter 3.

Although this book is primarily written as a research monograph it is at an appropriate level for it to be accessible to North American students beginning their graduate programs and also to British third year under-graduate specialists in economics who have a reasonable familiarity with econometrics; (i.e. acquaintance with the linear model in matrix notation, plus some knowledge of simultaneous equations, dynamic models and time series analysis). References are given to the more detailed texts where necessary. The book could also conceivably be used as an applied econometrics text with the applications being concentrated in the foreign exchange and financial markets.

The writing of the book developed out of our own research interests and work, some of which is discussed in Chapters 4, 6 and 7. During the course of preparing the manuscript we became aware of the extraordinary growth of research in virtually all of the aspects covered in the text. We may well not have given sufficient weight to some recent developments, such as modelling 'bubbles', to name but one topic. Other topics may have received too great an emphasis. However, research is moving so rapidly in many of the areas discussed in the book, that a revision in future years could conceivably come to quite different conclusions on what material was worth including.

As previously mentioned, the book developed out of various research projects we have been involved with over the last few years. We would like to express particular gratitude to two of our colleagues, Ralph Bailey and Bob Lippens who were our coauthors on some related articles. In different ways they have both had a great impact on our work and our approach to dealing with issues in this book. Many colleagues have also provided some valuable suggestions and contributed to improvements of this book. Without, in any way, implicating them for the remaining inadequacies in the text, we wish to thank Tim Bollerslev, Henri Bourguinat, Marcus Miller, Peter Schmidt, and Uli Schlieper. We would also like to acknowledge Francis Brooke and Anne Rix of the Cambridge University Press. Francis provided considerable help in the initial outline of the project and Anne's careful editorial work was invaluable in the final preparation of the manuscript. Finally, for different types of encouragement and tolerance, we wish to acknowledge our wives, Anne and Trudy.

CHAPTER 1

Exchange rate concepts, historical development and institutions

1.1   Introduction

On December 27, 1945, the Bretton Woods conference of representatives from the major economic industrialised countries agreed to begin a period of pegged, but adjustable exchange rates. Prior to World War II, the 1930s had been a period of flexible exchange rates, characterised by extreme volatility and competitive exchange rate policies adopted by many countries. The Bretton Woods delegates believed that a more stable system of foreign exchange rates would promote the growth of international trade. They also expected that making countries defend agreed parities would prevent the manipulation of exchange rates for purely domestic policy objectives.

The par-value obligation under Article IV of the Bretton Woods Agreement stated that the par value of each member should be expressed in terms of gold as a common denominator or in terms of the U.S. dollar. Furthermore, maximum and minimum rates should not differ from parity by more than one per cent, and national central banks maintained reserves to buy or sell dollars for their domestic currency. The dollar therefore effectively became the official intervention currency.

Under the Bretton Woods system of adjustable par values all countries signing the treaty had to adhere to the declared par values for their currencies which could only be altered to correct a fundamental disequilibrium, and only after consultation with the International Monetary Fund (IMF).

Although the Bretton Woods conference had many goals, its basic aim was to provide a stable monetary framework for international trade and this concern was emphasised by simultaneously founding an International Trade Organisation (ITO) and the IMF. In fact a weaker version of the ITO was set up through the General Agreement on Tariffs and Trade (GATT) in 1947.

1

At this time there was common agreement among the four major western countries that a reduction of trade barriers was essential to post-war prosperity. The desired framework consisted of four basic components:

1 Fixed exchange rates.
2 Policy discipline, i.e. abandoning any sort of 'beggar thy neighbour' policy.
3 Policy coordination, i.e. domestic policies should be consistent with the economic policy of the country which provided the international reserve money.
4 Capital controls; international liquidity should mainly come through the channels incorporated in the IMF.

In terms of the rate of growth of output, international trade and general economic performance, the Bretton Woods system initially worked well. However, changes in exchange rates were generally too infrequent to prevent substantial current account imbalances occurring. Following such an imbalance, the central bank would generally make a step adjustment in the parity and resume its support for the new pegged rate. The appropriate parity was usually calculated from some measure of relative purchasing power; and, although such changes in exchange rate parities were generally synonymous with large current account imbalances, the ultimate decision to alter the peg and its timing was often motivated by political factors.

In general, countries did not show the expected policy discipline; deficit countries took the easier way of deflating demand to correct their balance of payment deficits and surplus countries, like Japan and West Germany, could not be compelled to revalue their currencies or expand domestic demand more rapidly.

To summarise the main features of the international monetary system as it appeared at the end of the 1950s, five points seem to be important.

1 The par-value system was in operation. Most countries were observing par values and prescribed margins except for the special case of the Canadian dollar, which floated from 1950 to 1962.
2 The dollar had also become the major reserve currency.
3 Par-value changes occurred infrequently.
4 Although it took longer than expected, when the Bretton Woods Agreement was reached, the currencies of the industrial countries were convertible.
5 The Fund, after the Marshall Aid period, began to exercise its lending functions as envisaged in the Articles.

But during the early 1960s several weaknesses of the Bretton Woods monetary arrangement became visible.

One alternative to increased central banks holdings of gold was increased foreign holdings of short-term assets denominated in dollars,

Table 1.1 *Money in international exchange*

Official gold holdings and external dollar liabilities of the United States
(billions of dollars)

Year	Official world gold holdings[a]	Official U.S. gold stocks[a]	Outstanding dollar claims on U.S. held by foreign banks
1951	$33.5	$22.9	$ 8.9
1956	35.7	22.1	15.3
1960	37.7	17.8	21.0
1964	40.5	15.4	29.4
1968	38.7	10.9	38.5
Closing of the U.S. gold window			
1972	38.5	10.5	82.9
1974	43.3	11.8	119.1
1976	41.3	11.2	144.7

Source: International Financial Statistics.
[a] Gold is evaluated at official dollar prices through time. After 1968, the open-market price for gold was two or three times this official price. Nevertheless, no major country could sell all of its official gold in the market without driving the price down quite drastically. Therefore, choosing a correct price for evaluation was difficult.
Source: McKinnon (1979, p. 260).

sterling and other major currencies. Foreign countries accumulated liquid dollar assets and as a group achieved balance of payments surpluses, while the United States incurred payment deficits. From Table 1.1 it can be seen that between 1950 and 1970 U.S. gold holdings declined from $23 billion to $10 billion. Whereas the supply of U.S. dollars was potentially without limit, the ability of the Federal Reserve to supply gold to foreign central banks was restricted by its own declining reserves (Aliber 1973).

The so-called 'Triffin-Paradox' became increasingly obvious. The world was dependent on U.S. deficits for growth of reserves; if this process continued, U.S. reserve liabilities would increase relative to the stock of U.S. reserve assets. The stability of the monetary system would be endangered as holders of U.S. dollars began to fear that the value of their reserves might deteriorate in terms of gold. If the U.S. deficits could be eliminated, the world would be deprived of its major source of reserve growth, with depressing effects on world trade and economic activity.

The growth in volume of internationally mobile funds that occurred during the 1950s and 1960s together with the increasing freedom of capital movements became an additional source of pressure on established parities. The measures required to resist undesired exchange rate changes became a significant cost of preserving the system. Such measures were intended to place restrictions on trade and capital mobility 'for balance of payment purposes' or alternatively were part of domestic demand management policies.

The mobility of international funds was partly reduced by later U.S. governments adopting measures to restrict capital outflows brought about by the Kennedy and Johnson administrations such as:

1 The interest – equilisation tax on foreign securities sold in the United States.
2 Restrictions on banks lending to foreigners.
3 Pressure on multinational companies to increase their overseas funding for foreign operations.

Several events also occurred that led to the questioning of the desirability of the pegged exchange rate system. Some controversy centred on the Deutschmark being raised in value by 5 per cent in March 1961 and more particularly on the apparent overvaluation of the U.S. dollar. In all but three of the years between 1950 and 1971 the United States experienced a balance of payments deficit on reserve transactions, mainly on account of outflows of private capital, military expenditure abroad and governmental loans, and grants to foreign countries which were not matched by a sufficient amount of exports. The resulting deficit was primarily financed by the sale of Treasury bills and notes, and by sales of stocks of gold. This led to several central banks setting up a 'gold pool' to stabilise the international price of gold. The problems increased after 1964 when the U.S. trade balance declined from an export surplus of $6.8 billion in 1964 to an import surplus of $6.9 billion in 1972. It was therefore clear that, given the rapid reduction of U.S. gold reserves, the unlimited convertibility of the U.S. dollar into gold could not be maintained indefinitely. The revaluation of the U.S. dollar was strongly opposed by a number of countries and the alternative of restricting U.S. domestic demand was also avoided. However, on August 15, 1971, the U.S. government suspended the convertibility into gold of dollar holdings of other countries. The system of fixed exchange rates anchored in the IMF agreement was in principle questioned by this act, but it formally existed until the beginning of 1973.

The final collapse of the Bretton Woods system really began at the end of 1967 with the devaluation of the pound sterling from $2.80 to $2.40. The ensuing run on gold led to the abolition of the gold pool in March 1968 and to the development of a two-tier gold market. Further difficulties accumulated when the French franc was devalued (against the U.S. dollar) by 11.1 per cent on August 10, 1969, and there followed a one month period of floating. On October 27, 1969 the Deutschmark was upvalued by 9.3 per cent and the Swiss frank upvalued by 7.1 per cent on May 9, 1971. On June 1, 1970, Canada returned to the system of flexible exchange rates, practised by them between 1950 and 1962, and the Deutschmark was floated in May the following year. The speculation against the dollar increased until the Nixon administration suspended the purchase and sale of gold and imposed a 50 per cent import tax as part of their new economic policy.

The major western trading partners of the United States agreed to negotiate the international monetary system and stopped pegging their exchange rates against the U.S. dollar. An attempt was made to realign the exchange rates of the major currencies in a collective bargaining session at the Smithsonian Institute in Washington in December 1971. Following this meeting the Smithsonian Agreement restored the fixed parity exchange rate system and the U.S. dollar became the standard currency. The dollar was devalued and allowed to float within wider bounds. The yen was revalued by 7 per cent from its May 1971 parity, the mark was upvalued by 4 per cent and the dollar remained inconvertible into gold. Therefore, the Smithsonian Agreement did not solve the gold problem or include any provision to ensure a greater harmonisation of domestic economic policies. This led to a brief period of stability until June 23, 1972 when the Bank of England elected to lift all currency ties for the pound sterling and on January 23, 1973 the Swiss National Bank renounced all intervention in favour of the U.S. dollar which was again devalued on February 13, 1973 and simultaneously the Japanese yen began floating.

From March 1973 onwards, the six EEC countries allowed the market to determine the value of their currencies against the U.S. dollar, but preserved the bilateral exchange rates between themselves in a fixed wide band. This attempt at joint floating was hindered by the different rates of inflation and uncoordinated monetary policies within the six countries. At this juncture the Bretton Woods system had finally collapsed and a transition to a period of floating became inevitable.

One reason for the failure to maintain the agreed parities was the large funds which could be invested by speculators against central banks. Some sources estimated the revaluation profits earned by speculators to amount to $2 billion between 1967 and 1973. These profits were carried at the expense of central banks. The risks and costs of foreign exchange speculation were low compared to those in a free floating system. Furthermore the system helped to transmit inflationary pressures originating in the central economy (i.e. United States) to a number of countries of the system. Intervention had demand effects through increasing monetary liquidity and therefore resulted in higher prices. The maintenance of price stability in terms of the major currencies was therefore crucially important for the working of the system.

1.2   The international monetary system after the failure of Bretton Woods

The ultimate withdrawal of member countries from the Bretton Woods system was characterised by the desire to achieve a greater independence of domestic monetary policy and therefore to reduce the impact of American economic policies on the rest of the world. Also it was thought possible to establish more market related exchange rates which should have supported international trade.

As the float began, there were some discussions over whether flexible exchange rates should be completely determined by market forces in a free or 'clean floating' system; or whether managed or so-called 'dirty floating' should take place. In the latter system authorities intervened in the market or imposed controls with the intention of influencing the exchange rate. It has been claimed that such managed interventions produce 'orderly markets' and prevent extreme exchange rate volatility.

Several varieties of exchange rate management emerged under the present system and the only restriction was that a pegged exchange rate must not be denominated in terms of gold. The various exchange rate linkings of IMF member countries in 1975 are presented in Table 1.2.

According to an IMF report on June 30, 1983, there were ninety three countries who chose to peg their currencies to a single currency or to a specific basket of currencies including the eight European Monetary System (EMS) countries. Seven countries opted for limited flexibility arrangements vis-à-vis single currencies or on a cooperative basis; a further thirty five countries pursued more flexible exchange rate arrangements inclusive of independent floating. The tripartite regions Japan, Western Europe and North America had flexible exchange rates between each other. The various exchange rate linkings of the most important Organisation of Economic Cooperation and Development (OECD) countries are presented in Table 1.3. In the developing countries group there are only a few who do not actively pursue a particular exchange rate strategy.

The major distinguishing feature of the changeover from a pegged to a floating exchange rate system in 1973 has been the dramatic and unexpected increase in the volatility of exchange rates, which has been substantial both in real and nominal terms. To quote from Artus and Young (1979):

flexible rates tend to be unstable in the commonsense meaning of moving up and down a lot from day to day, month to month and year to year. (p. 672)

Exchange rates were sticky for a certain period, then changed suddenly, overshot,

Table 1.2 *The exchange rate practices of International Monetary Fund members* (*As of June 30, 1975*)

	Number of currencies	Percentage share of trade of fund members
Currencies that were independently floating	11	46.4
Currencies pegged to a single currency; in particular:	81	14.4
Pegged to U.S. dollar	54	12.4
Pegged to French franc	13	0.4
Pegged to pound sterling	10	1.6
Pegged to Spanish peseta	1	—
Pegged to South African rand	3	—
Currencies pegged to a composite of other currencies; in particular:	19	12.4
SDR	5	5.0
Other	14	7.4
Currencies pegged according to some varying formula	4	2.0
Currencies that were jointly floating	7	23.2
	122	98.4

Source: International Monetary Fund, *Annual Report* (1975).

Table 1.3 *The exchange rate policy of the major OECD countries*

Independent floating	Block-floating EMS membership	Tied to a basket of currencies	Diverse
United Kingdom	West Germany	Australia	Austria
United States	France	Sweden	(linked to
Switzerland	Netherlands	Finland	the German
Japan	Belgium	Norway	mark)
Canada	Luxembourg		
	Denmark		
	Ireland		

Source: IMF International Financial Statistics OECD Country Reports (Various).

and finally moved back to some extent, a pattern that is alien to the gradual adjustment expected by the advocates of flexible rates. (p. 676)

One of the most important lessons gleaned from the current floating exchange rate regime is that the international transmission of growth, inflation and unemployment has not been eliminated with flexible exchange rates, but rather has changed. Under the fixed exchange rate regime, the transmission mechanism of divergent macroeconomic policies was indirect, operating through the balance of payments and changes in official reserves. Under the present system, macroeconomic interdependence has markedly increased and, as a result, transmission mechanisms are often direct, making themselves felt through changes in relative prices, real wages and real capital costs. Today, domestic economies appear to be more vulnerable, not less vulnerable, to external shocks, such as oil crises, wars, bank failures, debt defaults, etc. Such events which often lead to excessive nominal exchange rate movements, are known as 'bubbles' and frequently cause substantial changes in real terms of trade and international competitiveness. The presence of bubbles has given rise to an exchange rate that is unrelated to its fundamentals or determinants and can lead to dislocations of real and financial resources. The apparent omnipresent disequilibrium in exchange rates seems to have resulted from the range of divergent policy mixes used by different countries, and threatens the growth of world trade and gains in welfare experienced over the past forty years. One particularly important aspect of policy interdependence which will be frequently discussed in this book is the role of interest rates. Changes in interest rate differentials instantaneously affect expectations in the foreign exchange market and other asset markets and, through the interrelatedness of markets, affect commodity and factor markets and hence many important macroeconomic variables. This problem was particularly prevalent in 1983 and 1984 when the U.S. policy of maintaining high interest rates led to conflict with many other countries. The over valued dollar associated with the tight U.S. monetary policy and loose fiscal policy caused problems for other countries by raising the cost of imports, including petroleum, whose prices were denominated in dollars. The effect was to increase inflationary pressures in addition to the drain on investment funds as foreign financial capital sought higher returns and lower risk elsewhere.

Extreme exchange rate volatility, the rising tide of protectionism and the apparent turmoil in the international monetary system are also of great concern to multinational corporations. In practice a firm faces both short-term and long-term risks associated with unanticipated changes in exchange rates. Short-term transaction risk emanates from commercial dealings and dividend flows over periods of time that are too short to allow for compensating changes in foreign goods prices. Such risk is typically dealt with by selective hedging as firms enter the foreign exchange market in a defensive rather than speculative manner. After examination of cross border trade accounts, a multinational will generally evaluate the cost of cover available from the relevant interest rate differential and the forecast for a currency in terms of the forward premium. Additional measures to deal with very short-term risk will typically include the leading and lagging of import and loan commitments, changing the currency of invoicing and the existence of third party 'barter' companies. All these measures help reduce the level of direct investment exposure. Other commonly used approaches are back-to-back loans, currency swaps and foreign currency denominated debt instruments. In general, this represents attempts to match financial assets denominated in a particular currency with liabilities denominated in the same currency; or at least to keep the discrepancy between the asset and liability side to a minimum. Unbalanced positions are often created by constraints onshore, and may necessitate offshore borrowing in international markets. However, matchings of this type are often limited by legal or other institutional constraints, by prohibitive transaction costs, and by the underlying operating requirements of the business. Whitman (1984) sets out some of the operational details for one multinational corporation in particular.

Insurance against exchange rate risk can be obtained through the forward market. Such transactions will have a cost; but examination of the bid-ask spread in forward markets, which is probably a good proxy for transactions costs, shows that it is generally small, although it increases in periods of great uncertainty and turbulence. Forward quotations are available for most of the major currencies and for periods of up to a year ahead. Longer-term uncertainty can be hedged by borrowing and lending transactions in different currencies. Long-term movements, of a year or more, can also be problematic to plan for, despite the fact that exchange rates may eventually adjust to relative prices. The persistent overvaluation of the U.S. dollar in 1984 and 1985 resisted the frequently expressed view that a reversal would occur. McKinnon (1981) has noted that such a phenomenon was completely unanticipated in the move to floating exchange rates in 1972. At that time it was felt that short-term volatility might be a problem, but over longer periods, market forces would move exchange rates so as to produce balance of payments equilibria and offset inflation differentials in the major industrialised countries. Williamson (1983) has considered the impact of long-run exchange rate movements on trade, arguing that exchange rate swings generate costly misalignments and that policy should be directed towards limiting departures from the 'fundamental equilibrium exchange rate'. These long-term swings are critically important for many multinationals in their longer-term location and investment decisions.

1.3   The historical debate over floating

There was general concensus between economists and governments that the move to floating in March 1973 was essential if the world economy was to cope with the problems arising from the substantial differences in inflation and growth rates between the industrialised countries. As stated earlier, the introduction of floating was expected to remove the need for policies that were designed to deal with unwanted movements in the exchange rate. While short-term deviations might occur, it was generally expected that exchange rates would in the long run achieve some form of equilibrium. The IMF (1975) report expressed a similarly optimistic view after the system had been operating for two years.

On the whole, exchange rate flexibility appears to have enabled the world economy to surmount a succession of disturbing events, and to accommodate divergent trends in costs and prices in national economies with less disruption of trade and payments than a system of par values would have been able to do.

The ultimate desire of the member countries of the Bretton Woods Agreement, to provide a stable framework for the international economy favourable for international trade and division of labour remained unchanged. There is a substantive question as to whether the floating exchange rate system is inherently stable. Persistent large trade imbalances and the apparent over or under valuation of currencies have emphasised this concern.

Much of the debate concerning the desirability or otherwise of flexible exchange rates arose from Friedman's (1953) seminal paper, and hinged on whether private speculation would stabilise or destabilise foreign exchange markets. Since some discussion centred on stock markets and non-monetary markets it is important to note that these markets are essentially different to a monetary market in the sense that individual commodities have intrinsic value to which private speculation can adjust. Conversely fiat money does not have any intrinsic value other than the backing of its local government; furthermore, for fiat currencies there are no inherent fundamentals that determine equilibrium exchange rates. Without some binding restrictions on asset holdings it has been suggested that demand for different currencies is determined entirely by speculation. For a critical review of the arguments, see Wallace (1979).

Over fourteen years experience of the current float has produced evidence of the surprisingly large fluctuations in exchange rates which have far exceeded that justified by the fundamental determinants of interest rates, inflation rates, etc. Exchange rate movements seem to be characterised by relatively small and continuous price changes that occur in response to new information which arrives randomly. The central thrust of theoretical and empirical research during this period has been to search for a rational explanation of exchange rate behaviour in the context of an integrated international financial market. It has been realised that exchange rate movements can be influenced for long periods of time by capital account changes and that shifts in trade flows have tended to be the result of, rather than the cause of, exchange rate movements. Thus the favourable experience of floating obtained by Austria in the nineteenth century seems a largely irrelevant example given the enormous growth in international capital movements that has occurred. Given the floods of funds which can quickly inundate a country in response to new information, a resulting extreme change in the exchange rate has always seemed likely in a perfectly free market. The alternative view was that exchange rates can rapidly respond to market forces and hence nullify any potentially destabilising movement of capital.

One major theoretical development that has occurred in the present period of floating is the so called 'asset market approach' to exchange rate determination. In this view of the world, the exchange rate is perceived as the relative price of two currencies and the price is determined by the relative demand for them *vis-à-vis* other currencies. This demand is based on the currency's utility as a medium of exchange, store of value and unit of account, and hence has a broader range of determinants than a typical security which depends on return and risk relative to a market index.

A central feature of the asset market approach is the notion of rational expectations which implies that all relevant and currently available information is used by agents (in a market) when making economic decisions. In the context of an asset market with an almost infinite number of traders the price of an asset can be expected to reflect all relevant and available information known to market participants. This gives rise to the idea of an efficient market and will be discussed more rigorously in Chapter 2.

The asset market approach is closely related to the monetary model of exchange rate determination where the current spot exchange rate can be shown theoretically to be a function of the discounted rational expectations of future exogenous variables that determine the exchange rate. A key to this theory is uncovered interest rate parity and the notion of efficient financial markets. Since the expectations of market participants dominate short-run price movements in the asset market approach, volatility of exchange rates is entirely to be expected and is due to new information being made available to the market. Such news is received on an almost continuous basis by financial markets and important pieces of news can be expected to rapidly change expectations and to only change fundamentals over a much longer time period. While volatility conforms with the asset market approach, it is of course at odds with the more traditional flow models.

Apart from the arrival of new information to financial markets the observed instability of exchange rates is probably due to the relatively uncoordinated monetary and exchange rate policies pursued by different countries. Market participants may well be confused when distinguishing the permanent from the transitory components of such policies and this will lead to an increased uncertainty in the formation of expectations. Related to this is the idea that the exchange rate can overshoot its equilibrium value due to some markets (e.g. the goods market) being slower to adjust or process information than financial markets.

The observed short-run instability of floating exchange rates is often viewed as an inherent weakness of the system. The suspicion that foreign exchange markets may not process information efficiently has also been expressed by central banks and monetary authorities to justify intervention in the market for the purpose of smoothing short-term fluctuations and to influence the course of exchange rates. From the asset market perspective however, such intervention is an indefensible attack on an efficient market and will only serve to destabilise the market. To quote from Dooley and Shafer (1976, p. 5): 'At worst, central bank intervention would introduce noticeable trends into the evolution of exchange rates and create opportunities for alert private market participants to profit from speculating against the central bank.'

The core of the debate on the desirability of intervention essentially hinges on whether or not the market is 'efficient' in some sense and whether agents form expectations rationally. Initial work by Nurkse (1944) maintained that excessive volatility of exchange rates in the 1920s was largely due to psychological factors, rather than changes in fundamentals.

Anticipatory purchases of foreign exchange tend to produce or at any rate to hasten the anticipated fall in the exchange value of the national currency, and the actual fall may set up or strengthen expectations of a further fall ... Exchange rates in such circumstances are bound to be highly unstable and the influence of psychological factors may at times be overwhelming. (Nurkse 1944, p. 118)

Nurkse concluded that the only effective means 'to prevent the disturbing exchange rate movements . . . is direct stabilisation of the exchange market'

(Nurkse 1944, p. 121). The psychological aspect of speculation was also stressed by Keynes (1936, p. 158), when he described speculation as the 'activity of forecasting the psychology of the market'. This is also evident in his famous description of investment.

Professional investment may be likened to those newspaper competitions in which the competitors have to pick out the six prettiest faces from a hundred photographs, the prize being awarded to the competitor whose choice most nearly corresponds to the average preferences of competitors as a whole; so that each competitor has to pick not those faces which he himself finds prettiest, but those which he thinks likeliest to catch the fancy of the other competitors, all of whom are looking at the problem from the same point of view. (Keynes 1936, p. 156)

A contrary view to Nurkse (1944) was taken by Friedman (1953) who felt that destabilising capital movements could not be profitable for the market as a whole, since speculators would purchase at high exchange rates and sell at low exchange rates. Therefore among speculators a natural selection process would occur, whereby destabilising speculators would continuously incur losses and thus leave the market. Friedman's theory was based on assuming that speculative activities depend linearly on the level of the exchange rate. However, counter examples due to Baumol (1957), who assumed agents used adaptive rather than rational expectations; Kemp (1963) and Glahe (1966) have shown that in certain cases destabilising speculation may be profitable. Although Friedman (1953, p. 175) acknowledged that speculation might conceivably be profitable he felt it unlikely and regarded volatility of exchange rates as merely 'a symptom of instability in the underlying economic structure' (Friedman 1953, p. 158)

The substitution of flexible for rigid exchange rates changes the form in which uncertainty in the foreign exchange market is manifested; it may not change the extent of uncertainty at all and, indeed, may even decrease uncertainty. (Friedman 1953, p. 425)

Kindleberger (1976) has considered some periods of volatility to be due to the profitable activities of speculators who destabilise the market. This viewpoint is expressed in a survey of the opinions of specialist bankers undertaken by the Group of Thirty and is described as a bandwagon effect by Bell (1974, p. 27), who writes:

Once a currency begins to fall, then other banks join in the selling pressure, pushing the currency down further. The momentum can gather ground quickly as the market trend becomes self-fulfilling assuming that no institutions are willing to take the opposite view . . .. And many banks have concluded (quite correctly in the short term) that by following the pack it is easy to pick up profits; or if they do not respond to the market movement they are exposed to the danger of serious currency losses. It is only when a currency has fallen (or risen) by a very great amount that the pressure of selling or buying stops and is reversed.

In testimony before the U.S. Congress in 1974 commercial banks in West Germany and Switzerland were particularly criticised for influencing the foreign exchange markets by their combined and coordinated activities. As Katz (1975, p. 40) has noted, 'It is a kind of pooling operation, where they suddenly flood the market with orders, driving up the price . . . a few points – and there is no way you can go against it.'

Niehans (1975) describes a successful intervention by the Swiss National Bank to stabilise the exchange rate in the second half of 1978 based on the target of a fixed money supply. During the period of intervention the stock of foreign exchange reserves of the Swiss authorities increased initially by 50 per cent and was then completely reduced within six months without any serious consequences for money supply and inflation.

In summary the above evidence seems to indicate that periods of time exist when the foreign exchange market is not dominated by rational agents. However, successful speculation certainly presupposes extraordinary talents as far as forecasting exchange rates is concerned. Friedman's (1953) notion of a natural elite of speculators is not sufficiently strong to exclude *a priori* the destabilising influences of speculators on the exchange rate. Even when destabilising speculation is accompanied by losses for most speculators, it can still prove highly profitable for a minority and is the basis of the bandwagon theory where it is assumed that a group of powerful market leaders are better informed about future changes in the exchange rate rather than other market participants.

The purchase or sale of foreign exchange by this group is a signal for other market participants to follow them and may ultimately lead to the exchange rate overshooting its equilibrium value. Such a process may occur within hours as information is typically processed and transmitted very rapidly.

An alternative view expressed by McKinnon (1976) is that there has been insufficient speculation in the current float to smoothen exchange rate changes. McKinnon attributes this mainly to the unwillingness of banks to take open positions following the collapse of the Herstatt Bank in June 1974. Also the increased exchange risk and probability of insolvency resulted in regulatory controls being imposed on banks by the monetary authorities. McKinnon has argued that this has led to an inadequate supply of capital for banks to take positions in either the spot or forward markets. In particular, McKinnon (1976) notes that 'once an exchange rate starts to move because of some temporary perturbation, no prospective speculator is willing to hold an open position for a significant time interval in order to bet on a reversal ... whence the large daily and monthly movements in the foreign exchanges and bid-ask spreads'.

Bandwagon psychologies result from the general unwillingness of participants to take net positions against near-term market movements. Keynes (1924, p. 113) held a similar view on the 1920s floating period and wrote that, 'The wide fluctuations in the leading exchanges over the past three years, as distinct from their persisting depreciation, have been due, not to the presence of speculation, but to the absence of a sufficient volume of it relatively to the volume of trade'. Since the intervention by monetary authorities is generally secret it is extremely difficult to empirically examine whether or not intervention is destabilising.

1.4   Exchange rate concepts

The exchange rate is the price at which one national money can be exchanged for another. The most common currency value notion is the *bilateral* exchange rate quoted by a foreign exchange trader or reported in a newspaper. This is a *nominal* exchange rate because it is the number of units of one currency offered in exchange for a unit of another (i.e. $0.4/DM or 2.5 DM/$). The spot exchange rate and the forward exchange rate are particular examples of nominal bilateral exchange rates. A nominal bilateral exchange rate translates flows in one unit of account say Deutschmarks, into their equivalent in another unit, say U.S. dollars.

Assessing a currency's *value* on the foreign exchange market by examining one or several bilateral exchange rates can be misleading in much the same way as judging the general price level by looking at the prices of only one or a selection of commodities. As with any price index individual bilateral rates of a particular currency can be combined in different ways to construct an effective exchange rate index.

The effective exchange rate is a term applied to a weighted average of trading partners' exchange rates with the country in question. Multilateral rates measure the overall nominal value of a currency in the foreign exchange markets. The construction of the effective exchange rate indices can be illustrated by considering the effective exchange rate of the U.S. dollar and is illustrated in Table 1.4. It is an average of the dollar's exchange rate against the currencies of ten major industrial countries, which as a group, account for about two-thirds of total world trade and are very important in terms of international financial flows. Before averaging, appropriate weights must be assigned to the individual countries. Several

Table 1.4 *Effective exchange rate indices*

Currency	Multilateral weight	Bilateral weight
Deutschmark	208	101
Japanese yen	136	207
French franc	131	047
Pound sterling	119	080
Canadian dollar	091	401
Italian lira	090	048
Netherlands guilder	083	046
Belgian franc	064	034
Swedish krona	042	016
Swiss franc	036	020
Sum	1,000	1,000

Source: Hooper and Morton (1978).

types of trade weights, such as a country's share of international trade, are used in order to simplify construction procedures. The most frequently used trade weights are bilateral and multilateral. In the case of the dollar, bilateral weights measure each country's share of total U.S. exports plus imports. The multilateral rates, in contrast, are the shares of each country in the combined total trade of all the foreign countries included in the index. Bilateral weights do not capture the effects of trade competition in third markets whereas multilateral weights allow for such competition. Thus in an exchange rate index for the dollar based on bilateral weights, a decline in the U.S. demand for German cars following a depreciation of the dollar against the mark would be allowed for, but it would ignore a shift in demand towards Japanese cars. Thus the effective U.S. dollar exchange rate uses a weighting scheme that reflects the importance of each country's trade with the United States. Effective exchange rates are regularly calculated and reported by various institutions such as the IMF, Federal Reserve Board, etc., and each institution may use a slightly different currency coverage and choice of weights. The effective exchange rate is a useful statistic for gauging the overall supply and demand for a currency on the foreign exchange market, but by its nature it conceals price behaviour in individual bilateral markets.

1.5   Purchasing power parity (PPP) theory and real exchange rates

This theory was developed by the Swedish economist Cassel (1919, 1922) who asserted that the exchange rate would tend to fall in exactly the same proportion as the price level rose. Thus if prices in the U.K. doubled while foreign prices remained unchanged the value of the pound would be just half what it was previously. Regarded as a theory, PPP is subject to important qualifications such as modifications to tariff policy. It is also necessary to define what we mean by the price level for obviously all prices do not enter into the calculations of those engaged in foreign trade. There is the problem of tradeable and non-tradeable goods. Houses may be much cheaper in France than Switzerland but this will not induce people to import houses from France. The other extreme that assumes that the exchange rate is influenced only by the prices of tradeable goods is also incorrect. Account must also be taken of the goods which might move since between any pair of countries there are a number of non-traded goods which could easily be traded with a slight alteration in relative prices.

This point raises a practical difficulty of calculating real exchange rates based on PPP. Alterations in the general price level can only be approximated by means of index numbers and the composition of the index number will determine the proportionate effect on the exchange rate. The choice of an inappropriate price index can systematically affect judgements on the scope and direction of movements in real exchange rates. The use of cost of living indices include diverse commodities such as rent, which have no influence on international trade. At the other extreme the wholesale prices index ignores not only all forms of manufactured goods and products but the whole range of services and other invisible exports. It is generally argued that the index used should attempt to measure the costs of production of tradeable goods rather than actual prices which the forces of competition tend to equalise among countries through changes in profit margins.

One solution is to use an index of wage rates, for wages enter into every form of manufactured and non-manufactured goods and services. Unless wages are lower in the export trades than in the rest of industry, movements of the index number of wages will be a good guide to the movements of the price level of those goods and services which move in international trade. Even here allowance must be made for changes in the relative efficiency of labour in different countries.

One important concept is the real bilateral exchange rate, which allows for differentials in inflation rates between the domestic and the foreign country. Many bilateral exchange rates have been associated with changes in relative domestic price levels over extended periods of time. The real bilateral exchange rate can be calculated on the basis of absolute purchasing power parity. The real bilateral DM/$ exchange rate is calculated by dividing the DM/$ bilateral nominal exchange rate by the ratio of the German consumer price index P^* to the U.S. consumer price index P to give

$$S_t = S_t^{\text{PPP}} P_t / P_t^*$$

where the term S_t^{PPP} represents the real bilateral exchange rate in units of U.S. market basket per unit of the German market basket.

On strict PPP grounds this ratio should be independent of the nominal bilateral exchange rate. Frequently the real exchange rate at time $t + n$ is expressed as an index of the actual exchange rate relative to the PPP exchange rate

$$S_{t+n}^{\text{real}} = S_{t+n} / S_{t+n}^{\text{PPP}},$$

where

$$S_{t+n}^{\text{PPP}} = S_t \frac{P_{t+n} / P_{t+n}^*}{P_t / P_t^*}$$

and the period t denotes an equilibrium base period. This version assumes that *relative* purchasing power parity is maintained so that S_t^{PPP} is a constant. Relative purchasing power parity requires that the *percentage* change in the exchange rate equals the difference between the percentage changes in the prices of the market basket of goods in the two countries. Relative PPP might hold, even when absolute PPP does not, if the factors that cause absolute PPP to fail, such as tariffs and non-traded goods, are constant overtime. Values of S_t^{real} greater (less) than unity indicate real depreciation (appreciation) of the domestic currency; that is more (less) U.S. goods are required to purchase one unit of the Germany market basket. Values of S_t^{real} equal to unity indicate that the real exchange rate and relative purchasing power parity were maintained.

The nominal effective exchange rate of a currency can also be price adjusted to obtain a *real effective exchange rate*. It is calculated by dividing the domestic country's nominal effective exchange rate by an index of the ratio of average foreign prices to home prices. It attempts to measure the overall competitiveness of the home country in international markets. However, it is still only a partial and inexact measure of international competitiveness and should be interpreted with caution.

The choice of a particular measure will depend upon the purpose for which it is required and there is no clear cut answer to this. In some cases trade has a very short-term horizon and all costs and prices are known except the nominal exchange rate. Thus one should focus on nominal magnitudes when short-term variability in exchange rates is being considered. Once the time period concerned is lengthened other prices and costs as well as the exchange rate become variable. From such a perspective the real exchange rate is the most appropriate measure for examining the effects of exchange rate swings on trade flows and resource allocation. It is clear that shifts in nominal exchange rates that merely offset inflation differentials would not affect resource allocation directly; it is changes in real rates that are of significance. Furthermore, since the bulk of trade in the major industrial countries is undertaken by diversified enterprises, effective exchange rates are probably more appropriate. In general the concept of the real exchange rate is more prominent in recent international economic discussions because there is now widespread belief that purchasing power parity is not relevant. For example, the substantial increase in the value of the dollar against most other currencies in the period 1980–1985 occurred despite only slight narrowings in inflation differentials.

1.6   Recent exchange rate behaviour

After more than fourteen years of experience under floating rates it is clear that exchange rate variability has been more substantial than expected by the advocates of the system. Nominal exchange rates have strayed over a wide range since 1973. The Deutschmark, Swiss franc and Japanese yen demonstrated a strong tendency to appreciate over the period, while the Canadian dollar and Italian lira generally weakened. The pound sterling depreciated sharply until late 1976 and appreciated thereafter. The cyclical pattern of exchange rate movements between 1973 and 1976 observed in particular for the Deutschmark and Swiss franc suggested exchange rates overshooting their equilibrium values. Between mid-1975 and mid-1977 exchange rate movements were relatively flat but the strong appreciation of the Deutschmark, Swiss franc and Japanese yen began again in mid-1977. During 1980–81 the U.S. dollar appreciated against most currencies with the exception of the pound sterling and since then its appreciation against almost all currencies has been one of the most outstanding features of the entire floating period. (See Figures 1.1 to 1.6 in the appendix to this chapter.)

Since 1985 the trend has been reversed and the dollar has depreciated against all major currencies. Between the first quarter of 1985 and the second quarter of 1986 the depreciation of the U.S. dollar against the Deutschmark amounted to over 40 per cent. These sharp changes in the direction and level of exchange rate movements appear to have significant implications for world trade, by reviving protectionist sentiment in certain countries.

Table 1.5 below gives an account of the overall shifts of the level of exchange rates in the medium term. Whereas short-term fluctuations create

Table 1.5 *Changes in relative value of individual currencies against U.S. dollar*

Period	7/80–7/81	7/81–10/81	10/81–2/85	2/85–8/85
Currency				
DM	−30%	+14%	−34%	+60%
Yen	−4%	+2%	−13%	+68%
Pound	−21%	+3%	−34%	+36%

Source: OECD, Main Economic Indicators, Paris (1986).

additional uncertainty for single business transactions, sharp medium-term shifts put additional stresses on the financial system as a whole. Compared to the goals of the Bretton Woods Agreement, which tried to provide an international monetary arrangement tailored to supporting the international flow of goods and services and the international division of labour, it remains doubtful if the regime of flexible exchange rate has been any more successful in achieving this goal.

These above shifts are substantial enough to severely disrupt most domestic economies. Since the so-called 'Plaza Accord' of the finance ministers of the five major economic countries in 1985, the relative value of the dollar has shifted particularly dramatically. Furthermore, the successful 'talking down' of the dollar demonstrated the strong influence of political signals on the foreign exchange market. These effects have appeared stronger than any physical intervention by central banks during the last few years. Recent experience shows that intervention either by means of political signalling and/or by market intervention has the highest leverage when it points in a direction which is generally in accord with market perceptions.

The variability of nominal exchange rates has also substantially exceeded that implied by inflation differentials across countries, thereby also yielding sizeable changes in real exchange rates. This has been particularly marked over the short to medium term when purchasing power parity clearly failed to hold. Developments in real exchange rates are presented in Figures 1.7 to 1.12 of the appendix. These graphs also give some indication of the performance of PPP since the real exchange rates presented have experienced substantial fluctuations which appear to be systematically associated with movements in the corresponding nominal exchange rate. An illustration of this is that in mid-1975 the dollar appreciated relative to the Deutschmark by nearly 10 per cent and an associated increase can be seen in the real exchange rate. The depreciation of the dollar in late 1977 and early 1978 is reflected in a declining real exchange rate.

The record of effective exchange rates is illustrated in Figures 1.13 to 1.19 inclusive. Whatever statistical ambiguities arise from measuring effective exchange rates these fluctuations should be considerably smaller than fluctuations in bilateral rates since most currencies will appreciate against those of some of their trading partners and depreciate against others. An exception is the Swiss franc which appreciated against every currency and the Italian lira which depreciated against all other currencies by about 60 per cent by 1985. The effective value of the U.S. dollar changed very little between 1973 and 1980 largely because the U.S. dollar depreciated against the Deutschmark, the Swiss franc and Japanese yen but it appreciated against the Canadian dollar. Between 1980 and 1985 however, the U.S. dollar's effective rate has appreciated by about 50 per cent.

The charts presented above illustrate that the year 1979 can be viewed as a form of watershed. Since then there has been an upward movement in the U.S. dollar of about 50 per cent whereas between 1973 and 1979 it moved down by about 12 per cent on average with an intermediate upward movement in 1976. There has also been more pronounced movements in other currencies in recent years than in the immediate period after floating began. Hence it is not surprising that exchange rate movements in the past six years has prompted serious questions about the functioning of the system. The real external value of the pound sterling fluctuated within a band of about 10 per cent during the first five years of floating, then appreciated by over 50 per cent over four years before declining by about 20 per cent from its 1981 peak. Between 1973 and 1979 the range of fluctuations in the annual average real rate was about 10 per cent for West Germany but has been almost twice as large since then. A similar picture is evident for other countries such as France, Belgium, the Netherlands and Sweden. This phenomenon is less apparent for Japan, Canada and Italy who have increased domestic savings throughout the floating period. For example, in the case of Japan, the appreciation of the yen from 1976 to 1978 and its subsequent depreciation from 1978 to 1980 exceeded 20 per cent, approximately double the size of the swings that have taken place during the 1980s.

Thus, within the floating rate period itself there has not been a tendency for exchange rate variability to decline over time and the prediction that the large variability experienced at the onset of floating would diminish as traders and policy makers learned how to cope with the new regime has proved incorrect. On most measures exchange rate variability peaked in 1973, was on a declining trend until about 1978 and then rose sharply again during the late 1970s and the 1980s.

The recognition of the overshooting property of exchange rates gives rise to the prospect of unilateral currency manipulation and therefore an unwelcome return to a 'beggar-thy-neighbour' policy. The United States which, under the Reagan administration favoured a non-interventionalist attitude towards the exchange rate, suffered most under the apparent 'overvaluation' of the currency which caused problems for the export industry and gave rise to protectionist pressure.

Since the meeting of central banks and Treasury representatives of the five economically most important western countries, attempts were made to induce a 'soft landing' for the dollar. These attempts towards a more coordinated foreign exchange (i.e. interventionist) policy were further promoted by the so-called Balier Plan which was announced in October 1985 at the Annual IMF meeting. The proposal dealt with several problem areas of the international monetary system and suggested the establishment of reference zones for three or more key international currencies. This probably indicated a change in attitude of the U.S. government towards greater economic policy coordination at least in the field of intervention in the foreign exchange markets.

However, the variability of nominal exchange rates under floating has still been smaller than the variability of some other asset prices. For example in Table 1.6 it can be seen that the average absolute monthly changes in nominal bilateral exchange rates for the seven major currencies over the 1973–80 period were typically smaller than changes in national stock market prices. This result was confirmed by Bergstrand (1983) for the period 1973–83 who also found that the exchange rate fluctuated less than changes in either short-term interest rates or in long-term bond yields, or changes in either commodity prices or prices of commodity baskets. The recognition that flexible exchange rates behave similarly to share prices or commodity prices led to the development of the asset market approach of the exchange rate which attempted to explain theoretically the observed phenomenon of exchange rate volatility.

The similarity in the movement of exchange rates and other financial asset prices has resulted in more empirical studies of the foreign exchange markets. Since Figures 1.7 to 1.12 can be interpreted as showing deviations from PPP for various currenties; it can be observed that short-run changes in exchange rates displayed little relationship to short-run differentials in notional inflation rates, at least as measured by consumer price indices. It can also be seen in Table 1.6 that on average the index of relative inflation rates fluctuates four to five times less than the exchange rate. Thus exchange rates appear to fluctuate more strongly than their fundamental economic determinants.

It should also be noted that statements that exchange rate fluctuations

Table 1.6 *Mean absolute percentage changes in prices and exchange rates. Monthly data: June 1973–February 1979*

Variable	WPI	COL	Stock market	Exchange rate against the dollar
Country				
U.S.	0.009	0.007	0.038	—
U.K.	0.014	0.012	0.066	0.020
France	0.011	0.008	0.054	0.020
Germany	0.004	0.004	0.031	0.040

Note: All variables represent the absolute values of monthly percentage changes in the data. WPI denotes the wholesale price index and COL denotes the cost of living index. Data on prices and exchange rates are from the IMF tape (May 1979 version). The stock market indices are from *Capital International Perspective*, monthly issue.
Source: Frenkel and Mussa (1980).

have been excessive or unwarranted are often made within a relatively narrow framework. Ideally variability of a currency should be measured relative to the equilibrium exchange rate over time and this raises several conceptual problems. Usually one focuses mainly on short-run deviations from purchasing power parity but there are also a host of factors that influence purchasing power parity over the longer run, such as energy and natural resource developments, labour market events and changes in the economic and policy environments and management. These factors have to be evaluated by market participants and policy makers in a world environment of shocks and rapid changes and so a high degree of exchange rate flexibility is necessary and desirable.

Simple analysis of the development of exchange rates since 1973 reveals that two types of exchange rates movements can be discerned: (i) short-run fluctuations and (ii) long-run shifts in the level of exchange rates. Exchange rates have a tendency during longer periods of time to consolidate very considerable short-run fluctuations to a specific level. Regular fluctuations in exchange rates, in particular the Deutschmark and Swiss franc between 1973 and 1976, led many commentators to speak of cyclical fluctuations and even to calculate the length of such fluctuations. Later it turned out under more careful inspection that these cycles were temporary phenomena. The movement from an old to a new exchange rate plateau did not follow in a smooth process, but generally in a stepwise discontinuous manner. Most nominal exchange rate series are well represented by martin gale or random walk models. The statistical properties of the series are described in chapter four.

Concluding comments on exchange rate movements since 1973

The above brief history of the floating period clearly illustrates the varied and complex nature of exchange rates. The foreign exchange markets also appear to respond to the arrival of new unanticipated information in a rather chaotic manner. Turbulent phases with massive interventions by central banks alternate with periods of relative calm. Daily changes in the spot exchange rate often exceed 2 per cent or over 700 per cent on an annual basis.

The development of individual spot exchange rates can only be partly explained in the short run by movements in the fundamental determinants, such as international interest rate differentials, relative inflation rates, the balance of payments and its various components, foreign exchange reserves, the supply of money, etc. Neither can most exchange rate volatility be ascribed directly to changes in the fundamental determinants, which show a relatively slight variance. Since the transition to flexible exchange rates, the observed high volatility has led to controversies concerning the appropriateness of such a system for an optimal allocation of international factors and resources. A related issue concerns whether the foreign exchange markets efficiently use all the relevant information when determining the current exchange rate.

The presence of volatility has given rise to substantial differences of interpretation. Kindleberger has attributed volatility to the activities of destabilising speculation whereas McKinnon assumed that it was due to too little speculative capital being available to guarantee the efficiency of the foreign exchange markets.

The suspected presence of destabilising speculation has been frequently used to justify massive intervention by central banks. Subsequently, it was decided at the Rambouillet Conference in November 1975 to attempt to avoid erratic exchange rate movements and that the currency authorities should aim to minimise uncertainty in foreign trade and hence reduce the welfare losses induced by erratic exchange rates.

However, central banks intervened not only for the purpose of smoothing daily exchange rate movements, but also to achieve a particular exchange rate target. Obvious examples of this are the massive interventions by the Bank of England in 1977, in order to prevent an appreciation of the pound sterling, and the formulation of an exchange rate target by the Swiss National Bank in 1978. Furthermore, attempts by officials and central bankers to *talk down* a particular currency (i.e. the United States before 1978) through official or semi-official statements, thus influencing the formation of expectations so as to induce a depreciation of their own currency and achieve a competitive advantage have also been pursued. Thus the current exchange rate system is certainly not compatible with the text book system of flexible exchange rates but is more like a system of regulated floating. Note that in the Bretton Woods system the exchange rate was an instrument of balance of payments adjustment whereas since 1973 it was employed as an instrument of internal stabilisation and employment policy. Such an employment policy involves extremely large risks for price stability associated with the *vicious circle* hypothesis. According to this a depreciation feeds quickly through import prices to increases in domestic costs and prices. The resulting inflationary tendencies induce a further depreciation of the currency, since the balance of payments only reacts very slowly and initially even anomalously (J curve effect). Examples of such a *vicious circle* are the developments in the United States, Italy and the U.K. since 1973. For stability prone countries there exists a so-called *virtuous circle* associated with an appreciation of the currency and a reduction in inflation rates without reducing aggregate demand. Typical examples of this phenomena are Switzerland, Japan and the Federal Republic of Germany. See the Annual Report of the Bank of International Settlements, (1976, 1977); Bilson (1979).

In several instances turbulent movements in exchange rates can be directly traced back to the arrival of new information such as political events and the announcement and unexpected implementation of economic policy measures. These strongly suggest the important role of expectations in the short-run behaviour of exchange rates. These expectations may not be firmly based so that revisions in expectations occur frequently leading to bandwagon effects. Such patterns can also result from the interventions of central bankers, who cannot maintain or do not wish to continue their intervention strategies.

The functioning of the system of flexible exchange rates since 1973 has also been evaluated by practitioners in two comprehensive worldwide surveys of bankers conducted by the Group of Thirty. The Group of Thirty is an association of international financial experts founded in December 1978, in order to explore the basic problems in the functioning of the international economic system. The survey conducted in 1978 included fifty six banks, of which twenty were in London, sixteen in Switzerland,

France and the Federal Republic of Germany, ten in Tokyo and Singapore and ten in U.S.A. In the following some of the results of this survey are given. The survey summarises many broad views, which in some cases provide conflicting assessments. See Group of Thirty (1980).

1 Most respondents believed that the foreign exchange markets successfully determined the medium- and long-run trends in equilibrium exchange rates for the leading currencies. In the short run, however, the market over-reacted to new information.

2 Some respondents expressed the opinion that amateur speculators dominated periods of turbulent exchange rate movements. In these situations professional speculators no longer based their actions on fundamental determinants. In the short run changes in the terms of payment through leading and lagging of foreign trade contributed to the destabilising speculation.

3 Since the Herstatt collapse both official and self-imposed restrictions, by banks on the holding of open positions, led to a reduction in speculation below that required for achieving a stabilising effect. Another reason for the insufficient degree of speculative activity was the increased uncertainty surrounding the extent and unpredictability of central bank intervention and monetary policy.

4 Changes in currency preferences led to diversification in the international portfolios of large capital investors, such as the OPEC countries, which mainly affected the Deutschmark and the Swiss franc.

5 The activities of central banks on the foreign exchange markets with regard to reducing the variability and stabilising exchange rates was often described as unsuccessful, although central bank intervention on the foreign exchange market was not fundamentally opposed. Central banks were partly blamed for having at times contributed to magnifying extreme fluctuations in the exchange rates, because they attempted through intervention to prevent an adjustment of the exchange rate which the market then ultimately implemented. Examples of this phenomenon were the sterling crisis of 1976 and the dollar crisis of 1978. Central banks were furthermore accused of being *inconsistent*, *unprofessional* and *poor at reading the market* (Group of Thirty (1980, p. 30)) and of intervening with the *wrong* quantities at the *wrong* times. Some banks reported that the larger portion of their profits from exchange market business resulted, not from business with the private sector, but from business with central banks. One bank reported that 80 per cent of its profit from foreign exchange business since 1973 arose from transactions with central banks.

6 Some banks maintained that the foreign exchange market had declined in efficiency in more recent years. The most frequently cited reasons for

Table 1.7 *Reasons for the suspected decline in efficiency on the foreign exchange markets*

Reason	Efficiency decline	No efficiency decline
a	Z	F, L
b	F	L, Z
c	F	L, Z
d	Z	F, L
e	F, L	Z

Key to Notation
a = More intensive banking control and regulation by the currency authorities.
b = Capital mobility controls.
c = Intervention by the central banks on the foreign exchange markets.
d = More strict internal guidelines by the banks themselves with respect to foreign exchange business.
e = Increased risk aversion.

this in London (L), Frankfurt (F) and Zurich (Z) are presented in Table 1.7 above. It should, however, be noted that the majority of the banks interviewed in New York, London, Frankfurt, Singapore and Tokyo did not ascertain any decline in efficiency, although the majority of them assumed that the foreign exchange markets were subject to short-run adjustments (overshooting).

These results demonstrate that there existed considerable differences in the interpretation of the factors determining the development and behaviour of exchange rates. Above all there were widespread differences in opinion on the extent to which foreign exchange markets process information efficiently. On the one hand it was maintained that the observed behaviour was at least partly dominated by destabilising speculation and on the other hand this was attributed to discretionary intervention by central banks and to an unsystematic economic policy. An additional interpretation of the observed exchange rate behaviour was that it was typical of a speculative auction market with uncertain expectations and was not due to an inefficient processing of information by market participants.

In order to explore the views of market participants on the functioning of the foreign exchange market and the changes that had taken place since the first survey the 'Group of Thirty' conducted a second survey in May–August 1985 based on the replies of forty international banks, fifteen securities houses, fifty large international companies and seven international money managers.

According to this study, the foreign exchange market doubled in size between 1979 and 1984 when the last survey was carried out. The daily volume had risen from an estimated $75 billion in 1979 to $150 billion. This rise far outstripped the annual increase in world exports from $1,531.5 billion in 1979 to $1,661.8 billion in 1983. The 'Group of Thirty' suggested that new participants tended to take large risks, and that this combined with the trading in new instruments, e.g. options and futures, had particularly contributed to greater volatility.

The main views of the different groups of market participants can be summarised as follows.

1 A majority of banks perceived a loss of depth and resilience in the market – the size of transactions that could be absorbed without affecting the rate was often smaller – and there was evidence of decline in the competence of dealers. The volatility of exchange rates had worsened since 1979 because of increased attention to short-term economic and financial fluctuations and the market behaviour of new participants. There was some doubt expressed about the value of official interventions to stabilise exchange rates unless accompanied by harmonising monetary and fiscal policies.

2 The replies given by companies were broadly in line with the findings of the Group's 1980 survey, which aimed to assess the impact of floating exchange rates, and reflected the opinion of corporate treasurers that floating had not materially impeded international trade and investment. Overall there seemed to be no general effect of increased volatility on the level of economic activity. The effectiveness of official interventions without any policy changes was regarded as being weak. Overall, the present survey of the business impact of exchange rate behaviour gave the impression that increased volatility had not generally affected the level of economic activity, but had led to more financial transactions of a protective nature and an approach to financing that was markedly conditioned by foreign exchange risk.

3 Fund managers claimed that volatility had a mostly negative effect on the overall return on investment. Official interventions were generally not regarded as being successful.

Appendix: Graphical display of recent exchange rate behaviour

Figure 1.1 Nominal exchange rate: Canadian dollar per U.S. dollar

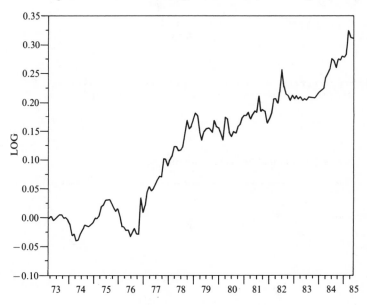

Figure 1.2 Nominal exchange rate: franc per dollar

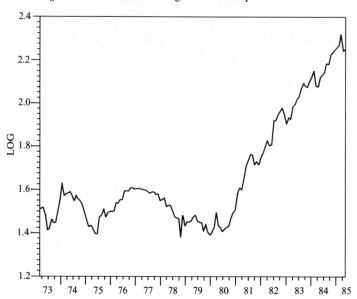

Figure 1.3 Nominal exchange rate: lira per dollar

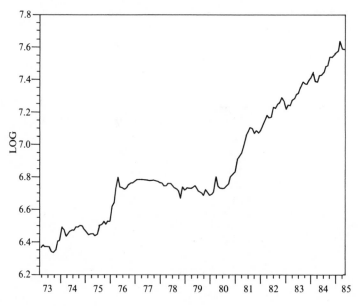

Figure 1.4 Nominal exchange rate: yen per dollar

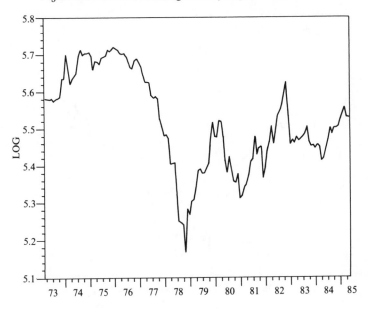

Figure 1.5 Nominal exchange rate: pound per dollar

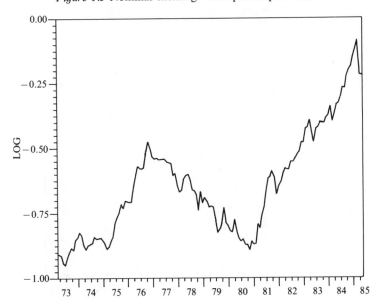

Figure 1.6 Nominal exchange rate: Deutschmark per dollar

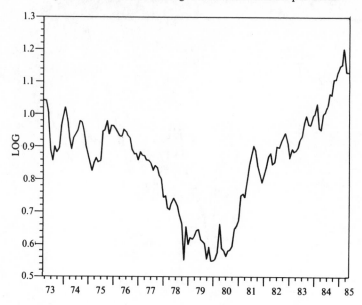

Figure 1.7 Real exchange rate: Canada–United States (March 1973 = 100)

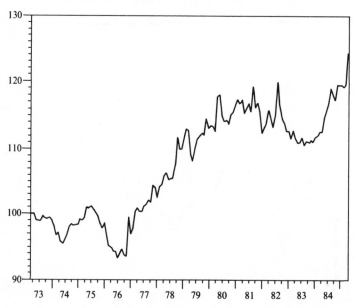

Figure 1.8 Real exchange rate: France–United States (March 1973 = 100)

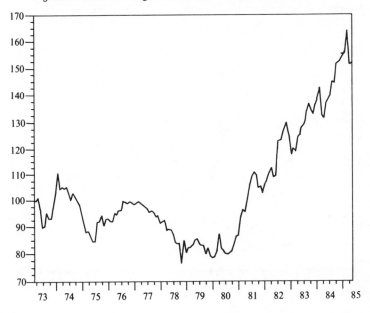

Figure 1.9 Real exchange rate: Italy–United States (March 1973 = 100)

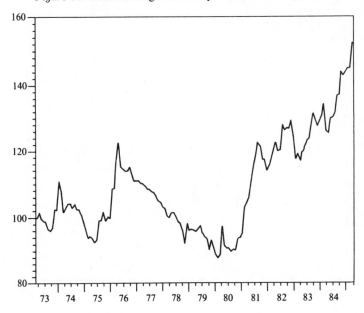

Figure 1.10 Real exchange rate: Japan–United States (March 1973 = 100)

Figure 1.11 Real exchange rate: United Kingdom–United States (March 1973 = 100)

Figure 1.12 Real exchange rate: West Germany–United States (March 1973 = 100)

Figure 1.13 Trade weighted Canadian dollar (March 1973 = 100)

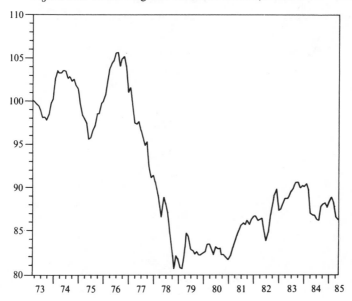

Figure 1.14 Trade weighted French franc (March 1973 = 100)

Figure 1.15 Trade weighted lira (March 1973 = 100)

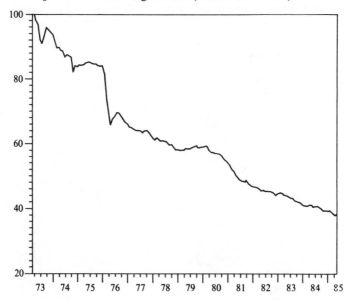

Figure 1.16 Trade weighted yen (March 1973 = 100)

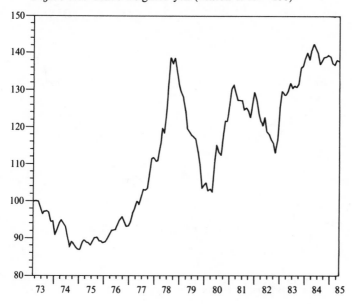

Figure 1.17 Trade weighted pound (March 1973 = 100)

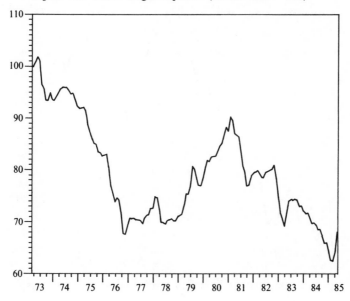

Figure 1.18 Trade weighted U.S. dollar (March 1973 = 100)

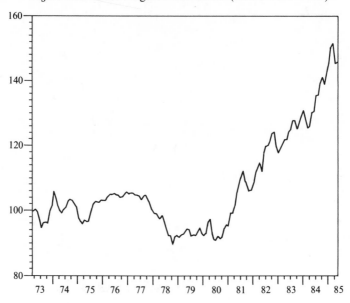

Figure 1.19 Trade weighted Deutschmark (March 1973 = 100)

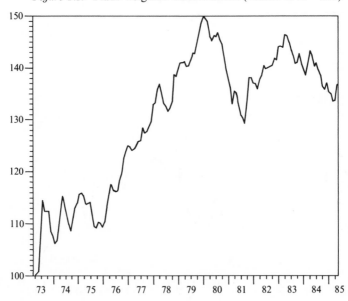

CHAPTER 2

The theory of efficient markets

2.1   Introduction

This chapter discusses some of the background theory behind the efficient markets hypothesis (EMH) and its application to the foreign exchange market. The first section deals with the different definitions of efficiency, which have been primarily developed in the context of asset markets. The concept of efficiency is seen to be inextricably linked with the assumption concerning the mechanisms used by agents in the market to form expectations. As many of the key ideas concerning efficiency have been developed for asset markets, there are inevitably some problems in translating the theory to the foreign exchange market. These issues are addressed in Section 2.4 where the practical implications and limitations of the theories are discussed. Although many of the assumptions appear erudite, it does seem that they can be fairly closely satisfied by the foreign exchange market. This conclusion is important since many of the models concerning exchange rate determination depend on the existence of market efficiency. In some ways there are many similarities between asset markets and foreign exchange markets, since they can both be viewed as well organised forward looking financial markets that adjust to expectations of future developments rather than merely providing a mechanism for balancing various current international transactions.

The asset market theory of exchange rate determination as developed by Branson (1977), Dornbusch (1976a and b), Frenkel (1976) and Mussa (1976), typically places considerable emphasis on the importance of expectations, which are unobservable and may be difficult to model empirically. According to this theory exchange rates are merely the relative prices of assets determined in organised markets where prices can be adjusted on an instantaneous basis to whatever 'the market' regards as the currently appropriate price. In this respect 'exchange rates are similar to stock prices, long-term bond prices and the prices of commodities traded on organised exchanges' (Frenkel and Mussa 1980, p. 375). Some writers, e.g. Kohlhagen (1978) and Levich (1979) have expressed doubts as to whether this theory can be successfully applied to the foreign exchange market. Their main criticism is that these models ignore the activities of central banks on the foreign exchange market, which in contrast to the activities of arbitrageurs, speculators and hedgers, can have a decisive effect upon the development of exchange rates and the efficiency of the market. These effects will be especially strong when they are unanticipated by other market participants. Before considering these points in more detail, it is first necessary to examine some of the theories regarding efficient markets.

2.2   Alternative definitions of efficiency

The original concept of an efficient market is due to Fama (1965) who described such a market as consisting of a 'large number of rational, profit maximisers actively competing with each other to predict future market values of individual securities and where important current information is almost freely available to all participants'. Thus if asset prices are to serve their function as signals for resource allocation they must successfully process and transmit all relevant information about future market developments to the suppliers and demanders of the asset. Hence for a foreign exchange market to be efficient, exchange rates must always fully reflect all relevant and available information.

It is important to note that the concept of market efficiency is quite distinct from economic efficiency and perfect markets, since market efficiency does not imply that the resulting equilibrium prices are optimal in any sense. The criterion of market efficiency is thus much narrower than that which is utilised in economic theory when referring to the conditions required for Pareto optimality. In an efficient market prices must fully reflect all relevant and available information and hence no profit opportunities are left unexploited.

These prices are established at equilibrium and are conditional on all information being available at the time they are formed. Thus the market is considered to be a sensitive processor of all new information with prices fluctuating in response to such information. The hypothesis of an efficient foreign exchange market is in principle merely the theory of informationally efficient financial markets extended to the international money markets arena. The literature in modern finance usually refers to the efficient market hypothesis instead of the theory of informationally efficient markets. The concept is concerned with the capacity of the market to process information and extends the classical perfect competition equilibrium model to incorporate the formation of expectations.

In effect a dynamic model of the exchange rate requires the introduction of expectations. However, there is no theory of expectations formation that can be derived from the basic principles of economic behaviour. To quote Hahn (1982, p. 3)

Clearly expectations must be based on the agent's observations, which of course is meant to include the history of such observations. But ... the transformation of observation into expectations requires the agent to hold a theory, or, if you like, requires him to have a model. This model itself will not be independent of the history of observations. Indeed, learning largely consists of updating of models of this kind. Although we have Bayes theorem, very little is known about such learning in an economic context. There is thus a great temptation to short-circuit the problem, at least in a first approach, and to consider only economic states in which learning has ceased. There will be states in which the realization of an expected variable provides no disconfirmation of the theory and the beliefs held in the light of that theory and the past realisation of the variables. Thus, in such states, the probability distribution over economic variables that agents hold cause them to take actions which in turn generate just this probability distribution. This is the idea of a rational expectations equilibrium.

Coming to the question of empirical testing it is necessary to be a little more specific about the formation of expectations. A rational expectations equilibrium has the property that there are no systematic errors in the forecasts. This implies that price changes must be random in the sense that such changes cannot be predicted from past realizations.

Three types of market efficiency are generally distinguished:

i)   *The weak form:* where a current price is considered to incorporate all the information contained in past prices.

ii)   *The semi-strong form:* where a current price incorporates all publicly known information, including its own past prices.

iii) *The strong form:* where prices reflect all information that can possibly be known. Therefore the activities of investment analysts and other insiders make it impossible for any class of investor to consistently earn above average returns. The strong form of the EMH is probably unlikely to hold since secret non-random intervention by central bankers takes place in exchange markets.

The semi-strong form has been divided by Geweke and Feige (1979) into two further categories:

a   *Single market efficiency* where all publicly available information which is important for a single exchange rate is contained in the information set.

b   *Multi market efficiency* where the information set includes information available on all other exchange rates and/or all available international economic information.

While the weak form of the EMH is highly conducive to statistical testing, the semi-strong form is generally taken to be implied when reference is made to the EMH in an unqualified way.

It is now convenient to define efficient markets in a more formal manner. Suppose at a given point in time t, market participants have available a given information set Ω_t^m, which is assumed to be produced without cost. This given information set, must, in an efficient market, be equal to the information set Ω_t, which contains all relevant information required for price formation, so that $\Omega_t^m = \Omega_t$.

Since all available information at time $t-j$ for $(j=1,2,\ldots)$, is also available at time t; it follows that $\Omega_{t-j} \subseteq \Omega_{t-j+1} \subseteq \cdots \Omega_t$, so that the information set Ω_t includes the current and past values of the recent variables and details of how they are interrelated. Thus Ω_t contains the probability distribution of future prices conditional on the information contained within Ω_t, so that moments can be readily calculated. Participants in an efficient market not only know Ω_t but also fully understand the implications of such information. Hence

$$f^m(p_{t+n}|\Omega_t^m) = f(p_{t+n}|\Omega_t) \tag{2.2.1}$$

where f^m denotes the market participants specification of the density function of future prices. No special assumptions are made at this stage about the properties of the density function. A breakdown of equation (2.2.1) can occur if market participants either do not have all the necessary information or else do not fully understand its implications. This idea is connected to the way agents or market participants form expectations. For (2.2.1) to hold, it is clear that market participants form rational expectations so that they are assumed to know the true economic model and use all relevant and available information to form their expectations regarding the future development of prices. In this situation the price becomes a sufficient statistic of the distribution of information.

For weak form efficiency, agents form expectations in an optimal manner conditional on the fact that Ω_t only contains past prices. Thus agents make the best of their limited set of information. These ideas are defined in more detail in Chapter 3, where the optimal information expectations from a set of information only containing past prices is defined as an optimal extrapolative expectation. An important implication of the EMH is that no investor is in a position to make unexploited profit opportunities by forecasting future prices on the basis of the available information. In the slightly different situation where expectations are uncertain, no investor can expect to find unexploited profit opportunities which exceed the normal market rate of return. This means that *ex ante* available information cannot be used to make unexploited profits. Since in this case future prices are not known with certainty and are therefore stochastic, it is possible for individual market participants to make extraordinary *ex post* profits.

In an efficient market however, the expectation of such profits are zero, so that the *ex post* profit or loss of an investment of an n period maturity is given by

$$Z_{t+n} = R_{t+n} - E(R_{t+n} | \Omega_t^m) \qquad (2.2.2)$$

where R_{t+n} is the actual rate of return and $E(R_{t+n} | \Omega_t^m)$ is the expected rate of return. In an efficient market

$$E(Z_{t+n} | \Omega_t^m) = 0$$

so that Z_t is a fair game with respect to the sequence Ω_t^m. It should be noted that this condition assumes the investors to be risk neutral. Risk averse investors will of course require a risk premium for undertaking risk. This means that the equilibrium model used must specify the relationship between the expected yield and the risk of the particular investment. This is one of the aspects of portfolio models. This definition of an efficient market is very general and for empirical testing requires knowledge of the information set Ω_t^m and the current equilibrium model of pricing behaviour. Hence the hypothesis of market efficiency is a joint test of the equilibrium model of pricing and the efficient use of information. Rejection of the hypothesis could be due to the inappropriateness of either or both of the joint assumptions; while failure to reject, implies support for both the assumptions. To quote Levich (1979, p. 247): 'For studies that reject this simultaneous test, it is impossible to determine whether an incorrect specification of equilibrium expected returns is responsible for the rejection or whether, in fact, investors were inefficient information processors. And for studies that cannot reject market efficiency, it can be argued that the wrong equilibrium expected return process was assumed.' A practical problem in empirical testing which will be returned to later, concerns the specification of Ω_t^m. Given an Ω_t^m it is possible to test to see if this information is completely incorporated into current prices. Once again it can be seen that there is a natural linkage between information sets and the standard definitions of market efficiency as applied by Fama (1965, 1970).

Fama (1970) also argued that efficiency requires that actual prices, or rates of return follow a 'fair game' process relative to expected equilibrium prices. Since expected equilibrium prices need not be constant or display constant linear growth, efficiency does not require that prices (or rates of return) follow a random walk with zero mean or constant drift. Levich (1979) applied this argument to the foreign exchange market noting that many equilibrium exchange rate models necessarily implied serial correlation in the differences of exchange rates.

2.3   Martingale, sub-martingale and random walk models

One approach to testing market efficiency is based on the assumption that the equilibrium value of the security rate can be written in terms of the expected return on the security. At time t, the expected yield at time $t + 1$ given Ω_t, can be interpreted as the expected relative change in the price of the security, that is

$$E(R_{t+1} | \Omega_t) = \frac{E(p_{t+1} | \Omega_t) - p_t}{p_t}$$

where R is the one period rate of return and p is the price of the security. The expected price in the next period is then given by

$$E(p_{t+1} | \Omega_t) = [1 + E(R_{t+1} | \Omega_t)] p_t \qquad (2.3.1)$$

In the context of the foreign exchange market p_t can be interpreted as the spot rate S_t, so that

$$E(S_{t+1} | \Omega_t) = [1 + E(R_{t+1} | \Omega_t)] S_t$$

The term $E(R_{t+1} | \Omega_t)$ can be interpreted as the expected yield from a spot market speculation, that is the speculator purchases currency at the spot exchange rate S_t in anticipation of making a profit later when selling at the rate of $E(S_{t+1} | \Omega_t)$. Thus the expected future exchange rate essentially depends on assumptions about the expected yield. To test market efficiency a specification of the equilibrium yield is thus necessary. In order to produce such a model it is generally necessary to assume that financial and foreign exchange markets are perfect. This implies that there are no transaction costs, capital controls, taxes, default risk, or constraints with respect to availability of credit. Nor any other market imperfections. Information is also assumed to be freely available, and furthermore domestic and foreign assets and liabilities are assumed identical with respect to maturity and risk, the only difference being the currency of denomination. It is also necessary for there to be no intervention by the monetary authorities, and for market participants to form expectations rationally and to be risk neutral.

The martingale–random walk model

If it is assumed that the expected return is equal to zero, so that

$$E(R_{t+1} | \Omega_t) = 0$$

Then from equation (2.3.1)

$$E[(S_{t+1} - S_t) | \Omega_t] = 0$$

which implies that the sequence S_t is a martingale with respect to the information set Ω_t. Thus all information about the future development of the spot rate is incorporated in S_t by the actions of market participants. The use of other information, such as the past history of the spot exchange rate will not improve the forecast. Hence the spot rate at time t is the best forecast of the spot rate at period $t + 1$ and for all future periods $t + j$. This implies that the probability of an appreciation or depreciation are both equal, so that

$$P(\Delta S_t > 0) = P(\Delta S_t < 0) = 0.5$$

An implication of martingale theory is that changes in the exchange rate are serially uncorrelated, so they appear random. The term random in this context does not imply that exchange rate movements are chaotic. In fact the theory means that since exchange rates respond to new information which arrives randomly, the spot rate will move in an unpredictable manner, which is a rational response to the new information. Also the sequences Z_{t+1} and X_{t+1} where

$$Z_{t+1} = R_{t+1} - E(R_{t+1} \mid \Omega_t) \quad \text{and}$$

$$X_{t+1} = S_{t+1} - E(S_{t+1} \mid \Omega_t)$$

are both fair games, which means that

$$E(Z_{t+1} \mid \Omega_t) = E(X_{t+1} \mid \Omega_t) = 0,$$

which can alternatively be expressed, that for the given information sets the expected profit of a speculator will be zero. In particular, this implies that extrapolation of past price changes of S_t, do not lead to *ex ante* profit opportunities.

Ever since the paper by Working (1958), it is generally accepted that the random pattern of prices observed on speculative auction markets are determined on the basis of expectations of rational market participants possessing exceptional talents in the processing and dissemination of market information. When the market receives new information this leads in turn to an alteration of price expectations, which in an efficient market is instantaneously reflected in prices which will obviously eliminate any unexploitable profit opportunities. New information can only arrive randomly, since anticipated information is neither new nor random. Since new information is defined to be independent of all previous information it follows that price changes are also independent of past price changes.

The martingale model has grown in popularity ever since the work of Samuelson (1965) and Mandelbrot (1966), who considered the martingale property of prices in speculative auction markets. In earlier work the random walk model has been used to model the observed behaviour of prices in speculative markets, especially the security market. Whereas the martingale model postulates that market equilibrium can only be described in terms of expected yield or expected price changes, the random walk model implies that yields or price changes are independently and identically distributed. This means that not only the equilibrium expected value, but also the entire distribution must be considered in describing equilibrium. However, it is only necessary for the distribution to be stationary, so that the random walk model is a special case of the more general martingale model. The history of random walk models can be traced back to Bachelier (1900), and was later revived by the works of Kendall (1953), Working (1958) and Osborne (1959). A brief survey is given by Fama (1970) and Granger and Morgenstern (1970).

Formally the random walk can be written as

$$S_{t+1} = S_t + \varepsilon_{t+1} \tag{2.3.2}$$

where

$$E(\varepsilon_t) = 0 \quad \text{and} \quad E(\varepsilon_t \varepsilon_s) = \begin{cases} \sigma^2 & s = t \\ 0 & s \neq t \end{cases}$$

Also ε_t is assumed to be a sequence of independent, identically distributed random variables so that the joint density $f(\varepsilon_t \varepsilon_s) = f(\varepsilon_t) f(\varepsilon_s)$ for $s \neq t$.

In contrast, the martingale model only requires ε_t and ε_s to be uncorrelated rather than independent.

It can easily be seen that the random walk model implies several testable restrictions of S_t, the spot exchange rate. Firstly, from equation (2.3.2) it follows that

$$S_{t+1} = S_t + \sum_{j=1}^{l} \varepsilon_{t+j} \tag{2.3.3}$$

and hence the conditional expectation based on information available at time t and denoted by E_t is

$$E_t S_{t+l} = S_t$$

The forecast error is then given by

$$e_{t,l} = \sum_{j=1}^{l} \varepsilon_{t+j}$$

has mean zero and variance $l\sigma^2$ so that the forecast variance is proportional to the forecast horizon, or lead time l. Even ignoring all the problems associated with the existence of perfect markets, the pure random walk and martingale models can only be derived under very stringent conditions for the foreign exchange market. Since spot market speculation requires capital, a rational speculator will consider not only the interest obtained abroad but the opportunity costs of a domestic investment. The speculator is indifferent when the expected return is equal for both the domestic and foreign investment, that is when

$$E[(1 + r_t^d) | \Omega_t] = E[(1 + r_t^f)(S_{t+1}/S_t) | \Omega_t], \tag{2.3.4}$$

where r_t^d = domestic interest rate and r_t^f = foreign interest rate. Assuming that r_t^d, r_t^f and S_t are known with certainty at time t it follows that

$$\frac{E(S_{t+1} | \Omega_t) - S_t}{S_t} = \frac{r_t^d - r_t^f}{1 + r_t^f} \tag{2.3.5}$$

$$E(S_{t+1} | \Omega_t) = \frac{1 + r_t^d}{1 + r_t^f} S_t \tag{2.3.6}$$

The pure random walk and martingale models are derived under the assumption that the expected yield is zero. In the above situation the expected yield is given by

$$E(R_{t+1} | \Omega_t) = \frac{r_t^d - r_t^f}{1 + r_t^f} \tag{2.3.7}$$

and this is only zero when $r_t^d = r_t^f$ so that domestic and foreign interest rates are equal.

Assuming the more realistic situation that domestic and foreign interest rates of similar securities are unequal, then

$$E(S_{t+1} | \Omega_t) \gtrless S_t, \quad \text{or} \quad E(R_{t+1} | \Omega_t) \gtrless 0. \tag{2.3.8}$$

Under the above inequalities S_t is known as a sub-martingale given the information set Ω_t. Furthermore, the sequence $(-S_t)$ which occurs when $E(R_{t+1} | \Omega_t) < 0$, is known as a super martingale.

The forecasting model implied by equation (2.3.6) is very simple since in general only three available explanatory variables are required, namely the spot exchange rate S_t and the corresponding interest rates r_t^d and r_t^f. As pointed out by Levich (1979) 'the cost is that we no longer see how underlying economic variables affect the exchange rate. Implicitly we are acting as though the equation is the reduced form equation for the spot rate in a correctly specified structural model. In effect we rely on markets to be efficient processors of information.'

In the literature on stock and securities markets it is generally assumed that risk neutral utility maximising investors require a positive yield from an investment as compensation for undertaking non-diversifiable risk. This form of statement is probably too strong a restriction when applied to foreign exchange markets. In the case of speculation on the foreign exchange spot market, the strategy of a speculator expecting a negative yield from the purchase of spot foreign exchange, (i.e. expecting an appreciation of the domestic currency), is to take up a one period credit in the foreign currency. The expected yield from this variety of spot market speculation can alternatively be assumed to be positive, so that the expected yield from a purchase of spot foreign exchange is negative.

A testable implication of the assumption that the expected return in a given period is non-zero is based upon the fact that in an efficient market no strategy based on the information set Ω_t can deliver more than a normal market return, based on a buy and hold strategy. The hypothesis does not imply that in an efficient exchange market the exchange rate follows a pure random process, but only that the deviations of the exchange rate from their expected values are random. It is not *a priori* excluded, that the expected yield based on some systematic determinants (e.g. relative money supplies or rates of inflation) follows a process which is not white noise.

The crucial point for the existence of market efficiency is only that the deviation of the realised yields or exchange rates from their corresponding expected values are random, that is, that the sequence $R_{t+1} - E(R_{t+1}|\Omega_t)$ or $S_{t+1} - E(S_{t+1}|\Omega_t)$ represents a fair game. This is equivalent to stating that in an efficient market the expected value of supernormal profits is zero. This again emphasises the importance of the specification of the equilibrium exchange rate process for testing the efficiency hypothesis.

A special case which has played an important role in the literature is the so-called random walk model with a drift or trend parameter. This is based on the assumption that the expected yield is constant over time, so that

$$E(R_{t+1}|\Omega_t) = c \tag{2.3.9}$$

where c is a constant. This assumption implies that the expected relative change in the exchange rate is also a constant

$$\frac{E[(S_{t+1}|\Omega_t) - S_t]}{S_t} = c \tag{2.3.10}$$

As is clear from equation (2.3.6) this assumption implies a constant difference in equilibrium between domestic and foreign interest rates. Given the existence of market efficiency the relative changes in the exchange rate fluctuates randomly about a fixed value determined by the interest differential as follows

$$\frac{S_{t+1} - S_t}{S_t} = c + \varepsilon_{t+1} \tag{2.3.11}$$

where ε_{t+1} is a white noise disturbance as defined in (2.3.2).

The logarithmic transformation of equation (2.3.11) provides, using the approximation $\log(1 + c) = c$, the following model used frequently in the empirical literature

$$\log S_{t+1} - \log S_t = c + \zeta_{t+1} \tag{2.3.12}$$

where ζ_t is lognormal. The sequence S_t is according to the above definition a sub, or super martingale, depending on whether $c > 0$ or $c < 0$. If in addition it is assumed that the random variable ζ_{t+1} is identically distributed, then the above equation is the random walk model with a trend parameter.

2.4   Practical problems with the concept of an efficient market

The assumption of a perfect market discussed in section 2.3 requires some fairly erudite assumptions which appear to remove it somewhat from reality. In particular according to Fama's (1970) definition there is a frictionless world where information is freely available to all agents and there are no transaction costs. Traders are assumed to have homogeneous expectations and evaluate new information in an identical manner. These are unrealistic assumptions, but Fama (1976, p. 168) defends the EMH on the grounds that even though market participants possess different expectations and make different evaluations:

the force of common judgements is sufficient to produce an orderly adjustment of prices to new information. Such an intuitively appealing statement is however too unspecific to be the basis of formal tests. Formal tests require formal models with their more or less unrealistic structuring of the world.

The question still arises, however, as to what effect the non-existence of these conditions have on the EMH. Fama (1970, p. 387) has stated that these conditions are sufficient but not necessary.

For example, as long as transactors take account of all available information even large transactions costs that inhibit the flow of transactions do not in themselves imply that when transactions do take place, prices will not 'fully reflect' available information. Similarly ... the market may be efficient if 'sufficient numbers' of investors have ready access to available information. And disagreement among investors about the implications of given information does not in itself imply market inefficiency unless there are investors who can consistently make better evaluations of available information than are implicit in market prices.

More recent research has examined these implications more thoroughly and derived some important new theorems relevant for a reformulation of the EMH. These results also highlight the difficulties inherent in empirical tests of the EMH. Recent research by Grossman and Stiglitz (1976) and (1980), has introduced an explicit cost for information, and demonstrated that the Fama concept of market efficiency is incompatible with competitive equilibrium in the presence of information costs. It follows that prices in competitive markets do not perfectly reflect all available information, since otherwise there would be no reward for those investing resources in the acquisition of new information. The logic of their argument is as follows: if market prices always fully reflect all relevant information then there is no incentive for individuals to acquire new information which can be obtained costlessly from the price system. In a competitive market prices are a given set of data for all market participants who are assumed identical. Thus if any large group of market participants invest resources in the acquisition of new information an equilibrium cannot result. The other extreme case where no traders have resources to invest in the acquisition of new information also implies the non-existence of equilibrium, since all market participants can realise profits at given market prices by producing information. The existence of information costs thus implies that no equilibrium exists where prices fully reflect all available information.

Grossman and Stiglitz (1980) solve the problem by extending the wider concept of market efficiency to incorporate the concept of informational efficiency. The link between the transmission of information and the informational efficiency of markets has been established by the Grossman-Stiglitz (1980) impossibility theorem discussed above. The theorem is basically the result of a free-rider problem which leads to an erosion of futures markets as a means of processing and disseminating information. This also highlights the difficulties faced by comparative static equilibrium analysis in attempting to capture the salient features of speculative markets. If the conditions are such that prices convey all information which informed traders collect, other traders can get the information freely by just observing market prices. Hence speculative markets can only exist if they are not informationally efficient. To quote Grossman and Stiglitz, 'If information is costly, prices cannot perfectly reflect the information which is available, since if it did, those who spent resources to obtain it would receive no compensation' (Grossman and Stiglitz 1980, p. 405). In the Grossman-Stiglitz model those who chose to be informed earn higher profits than those who remain uninformed. The greater profit however is only to compensate for the cost of information. As long as the information collection industry is competitive with free entry and exit there will be no excess returns earned by acquiring new information. In equilibrium the marginal revenue from additional information is equal to the marginal cost of acquiring the information.

However, if the information industry is not fully competitive, information takes on insider characteristics and excess returns are possible.

An interesting extension of the analysis by Grossman and Stiglitz is provided by Verrechia (1982), whose model has the same basic structure but uses a differential information assumption and a continuous information cost function. Verrechia demonstrates that the information each agent acquires is a decreasing function of the informativeness of the price system and that the informativeness of the price is non-decreasing as information costs decrease. These results are similar to the results derived in the more simple model by Grossman and Stiglitz (1980) but Verrechia also shows that an increase in noise implies that the informativeness of the price system decreases. Thus the increase in the acquisition of information by agents arising from an increase in noise does not in equilibrium outweigh the decrease in information revealed by the price due to the increased noise. In the Grossman-Stiglitz model both effects exactly balance each other and hence an increase in noise has no effect on the informativeness of the price systems. Both Grossman and Stiglitz (1980) and Verrechia (1982) have shown that the informativeness of the price system increases as the market tends to be dominated by less risk-averse agents.

Friedman (1979) is also concerned with the cost of acquiring information by market participants, and how this affects the definition of rational expectations. In Friedman's view rational behaviour may well correspond to agents basing their expectations on a limited set of information, since the cost of a more 'inaccurate' error may be outweighed by the cost of acquiring extra information. However, in virtually all empirical work rational expectations are taken to mean agents forming expectations on the basis of knowledge of a complete information set Ω_t which includes knowledge of the past history of all the relevant variables and exact knowledge of the equations and parameter values in an econometric model linking the relevant variables. This is known as Muthian rational expectations following Muth (1960, 1961).

A further problem concerns the dynamics of the situation and has been addressed by Stiglitz (1983). Given the time structure of transactions the information externality created via trading can only endanger the existence of a speculative market, if an informed trader has no opportunity of trading before he shares his informational advantage with others. Speculative markets cannot be completely efficient at every point in time. Inefficiency in the dynamic sense is part of the process of discovery and transmission of information and is the result of some traders being able to trade at a temporary informational advantage. The profit derived is a premium for being faster in the acquisition and correct interpretation of new information and also for reinterpreting already available information. This competition for a temporary informational monopoly not only determines the informational quality of prices but also the speed at which changes in beliefs and underlying information are disseminated. The structure of the market is also important. Private speculators are less willing to undertake stabilising speculation in the presence of market distortions. In the case where the central bank intervenes in the foreign exchange market, speculators may believe that this market power will be used to manipulate the market so as to generate profits for the intervention authorities at the expense of the speculators.

A further interesting model which attains an equilibrium solution in a speculative market where prices do not fully reflect all available information, has been developed by Figlewski (1978). Figlewski assumes that market participants possess heterogeneous information, price expectations and different wealth endowments. Since the market values information not according to its intrinsic value, but according to the financial wealth it can generate, the exceptional information of a market participant, with limited wealth can result in the market price being undervalued by the market, and hence the market appears inefficient. Alternatively it is possible that less valuable information be overvalued. Market participants whose information is undervalued by the market price obtain a profit whereas those whose information is overvalued incur a loss. Over time this process leads to a redistribution of wealth in favour of the better informed with increasing informational content of market prices, while of course the condition for market efficiency in the Fama sense is not reached. This process of wealth redistribution was also suggested by Cootner (1964, p. 80) for explaining the informational content of stock prices.

If any group of investors was consistently better than average in forecasting stock prices, they would accumulate wealth and give their forecasts greater and greater weight. In the process they would bring the present price closer to the true value. Conversely, investors who were worse than average in forecasting ability would carry less and less weight. If this process worked well enough, the present price would reflect the best information about the future in the sense that the present price, plus normal profits, would be the best estimate of the future price.

The point is made by Figlewski as follows (1978, p. 581).

In the short run the market tends toward increased efficiency but neither in the short nor the long run is full efficiency likely...
When there is a wide range of forecasting ability or diversity of expectations among the participants the market may deviate relatively far from efficiency. (p. 597)

An interesting result from the model is that a market participant with inferior information is not completely crowded out of the market, since he only incurs losses to the extent that his information is overvalued by the market; '... once his wealth drops below the efficient market level, his information becomes undervalued, and he begins to recoup some of his losses' (Figlewski 1978, p. 591).

This process of wealth reallocation has also been discussed by Feiger (1978) in a simple two period model with spot markets at date t and $t + 1$ and a forward market at date t for delivery at date $t + 1$. The market is assumed to be dominated by informed agents and hence the forward price reflects their information and consequently uninformed agents have access to the information of the informed agents. In this case there is no wealth redistribution since all agents have the same information. In contrast if uninformed agents with homogeneous but erroneous information dominate the market and determine the price, this prevents the price from revealing the information available to informed agents. Thus, imperfect information persists in equilibrium implying a transfer of wealth from uninformed to informed agents. This wealth reallocation process runs until the wealth of the informed agents has increased and they come to dominate the market.

The existence of transaction costs also provides an argument for the case that in general prices in equilibrium do not contain all available information, since in this case it would not be profitable for profit maximising, rational speculators to bring about through arbitrage a complete correspondence between the market price and the expected price as required by the martingale model. However the magnitude of transaction costs connected with foreign exchange business is relatively small and would only give rise to small deviations from the martingale model.

Since the return on risky assets depends on the market's valuation of the asset in the future it is necessary to consider the problem of sequential trading. Consider a simple speculative market for a single risky asset where the current price in period t depends on the expected spot price in period $t + 1$. Given rational expectations agents will also realise that the $t + 1$ period price depends on the expected price in period $t + 2$ and so on. It is well known from macromodels with rational expectations that a sequence structure implies that spurious variables or sunspots may influence the solution. This may occur even under homogeneous expectations. Thus, totally irrelevant variables may influence the equilibrium and as a result an infinity of equilibria may exist (see Gourieroux et al. 1982). This demonstrates that purely speculative manias or bubbles are consistent with the assumption of rational expectations, see Blanchard (1979) and Flood and Garber (1980). Furthermore, it is consistent with rational expectations that the bubble bursts and the market returns to being determined by fundamentals. In Andersen (1984) it is shown that if the market is informationally efficient, the expectations of future asset prices become indeterminate. It follows that asset prices which depend on price expectations are also indeterminate and hence become determined in an arbitrary way similar to Keynes' analogy between a beauty contest and the operation of financial markets. This indeterminacy implies that it becomes impossible to define precisely the information relevant for the pricing of financial assets because any information which agents conjecture to be relevant comes in a self-fulfilling way to be reflected in the equilibrium prices of the assets.

2.5   Consideration of risk

So far we have only examined the expected yield of an investment and have not dealt with the variability. The equilibrium condition given in equation (2.3.1) is only correct if the future spot rate is known with certainty, so that risk becomes irrelevant. If the risk of an investment can be measured by the unconditional variance of the yield (ignoring more complicated portfolio measures for the present), then the following equation must hold

$$\text{Var}(1 + r_t^d) = \text{Var}(1 + r_t^f)(S_{t+1}/S_t)$$

so that the variance of the revenue from a domestic investment, must be equal to that of a foreign investment. Since r_t^d, r_t^f and S_t are known with certainty, this condition only holds if

$$\text{Var}(S_{t+1}) = 0.$$

Otherwise a risk premium must be introduced into the equilibrium condition. In that case, the expected yield from an investment of K units of domestic currency invested domestically would be equal in equilibrium to the expected yield from a similar foreign investment where the risk premium depended upon the variance of the yield of the foreign investment.

Assuming that the risk premium is proportional to the variance of the yield the equilibrium condition then becomes

$$E\left[\frac{K(1 + r_t^d) - K}{K}\,\bigg|\,\Omega_t\right] = E\left[\frac{K(1 + r_t^f)S_{t+1}/S_t - K}{K}\,\bigg|\,\Omega_t\right]$$
$$-\rho_t\,\text{Var}\left[\frac{K(1 + r_t^f)(S_{t+1}/S_t) - K}{K}\right] \quad (2.5.1)$$

where ρ_t can be interpreted as the proportionality factor of such a yield, so that the market is prepared to pay for undertaking one more unit of risk. It then follows that

$$(1 + r_t^d) = (1 + r_t^f)E(S_{t+1}|\Omega_t)/S_t$$
$$- \rho_t \operatorname{Var}(1 + r_t^f)(S_{t+1}/S_t) \tag{2.5.2}$$

Since

$$\operatorname{Var}(1 + r_t^f)S_{t+1}/S_t = \frac{(1 + r_t^f)^2 \operatorname{Var}(S_{t+1})}{S_t^2} \tag{2.5.3}$$

it follows that the expected spot rate is

$$E(S_{t+1}|\Omega_t) = \frac{1 + r_t^d}{1 + r_t^f}S_t + \frac{(1 + r_t^f)}{S_t}\rho_t \operatorname{Var}(S_{t+1}) \tag{2.5.4}$$

Thus the expected spot exchange rate is a weighted average of the current spot exchange rate and its variance.

Similarly, the expected yield for the expected exchange rate is

$$\frac{E(S_{t+1}|\Omega_t - S_t)}{S_t} = \frac{r_t^d - r_t^f}{1 + r_t^f} + (1 + r_t^f)\rho_t \operatorname{Var}\left(\frac{S_{t+1} - S_t}{S_t}\right) \tag{2.5.5}$$

For small values of r_t^f the expected change in the exchange rate is approximately equal to the international interest differential plus a risk premium. The martingale or pure random walk model is then only valid when the risk premium as well as the interest differential is equal to zero. Furthermore, the random walk model with a trend parameter only exists when in addition to the interest differential the risk premium is also a constant. This is approximately the case, for small values of r_t^f and only when the price of risk ρ as well as the variance of exchange rate changes are constant. In addition to the interest differential the risk premium can also be the source of an autoregressive pattern of equilibrium exchange rate changes without implying that the market is inefficient, although the existence of a risk premium, even in equilibrium, is often taken to mean that the market is inefficient, Geweke and Feige (1979).

Consider

$$E[(1 + r_t^d)|\Omega_t] = E[(1 + r_t^f)(F_t^{t+1}/S_t)|\Omega_t]$$

where r_t^f, r_t^f, S_t and F_t^{t+1} are all known with certainty at time t. Then

$$(1 + r_t^d) = (1 + r_t^f)(F_t^{t+1}/S_t)$$

where F_t^{t+1} is the forward rate determined at time t for delivery of a foreign unit of currency in domestic currency units at maturity date $t + 1$. From this well-known equation, the interest rate parity theory (IRPT) equilibrium condition can be derived and is expressed as

$$\frac{F_t^{t+1} - S_t}{S_t} = \frac{r_t^d - r_t^f}{1 + r_t^f} \tag{2.5.6}$$

Deviations from this condition imply that under the given assumptions unexploited profit opportunities exist which are not compatible with profit maximising behaviour on the part of market participants and hence with market efficiency. Any such unexploited profit opportunities that exist would in this model be eliminated by the activities of pure interest arbitrageurs with perfectly elastic excess demand functions for foreign exchange. The speculative activities of uncovered interest arbitrageurs would lead to the conclusion that in equilibrium the expected change in spot exchange rates would be approximately equal to the international interest rate differential and this in turn implies that in equilibrium both on the spot and on the forward market the forward rate would be equal to the expected spot exchange rate, so that

$$F_t^{t+1} = E(S_{t+1} \mid \Omega_t)$$

This condition can also be derived directly from the activities of risk neutral pure speculators possessing rational expectations, where pure speculators are viewed as being market participants who hold open positions on the forward market in order to make profits from the expected development of the spot exchange rate.

The unbiasedness proposition has become part of economic folklore and the intuitive reasoning behind it is as follows. If $F_t > E(S_{t+1})$, where the exchange rates are defined as DM/\$ then a risk-neutral speculator will sell \$ forward and buy \$ spot in the future. If all speculators have the same information then no one would be willing to buy \$ forward and therefore, $F_t > E(S_{t+1})$ cannot be an equilibrium. Should $F_t < E(S_{t+1})$, then a speculator will buy \$ forward and sell \$ spot (in the future), and the same reasoning as above applies. The argument appears to be valid; however consider the following simple example. Let $S_{t+1} = 2$ DM/\$, $S_{t+1} = 3$ DM/\$ each occurring with probability 0.5. If $F_t = 2.45$ DM/\$ and a German speculator buys 1000 \$, his expected profit (in DM) is

$$E(R_{DM}) = (2000-2450)0.5 + (3000-2450)0.5 = 50 \text{ DM}$$

Obviously, a sale of 1000 \$ forward would yield a negative expected profit. But consider an American speculator who calculates his wealth in \$. He would indeed be willing to sell 1000 \$ forward as the following calculation shows:

$$E(R_\$) = \left(\frac{2450}{2} - 1000\right)0.5 + \left(\frac{2450}{3} - 1000\right)0.5 = 21 \text{ \$}$$

Thus, the *German* speculator having a linear risk–neutral utility function in DM and the American speculator having a linear risk neutral utility function in $ both find it profitable to agree on the following forward contract:

The German promises to pay mF DM for delivery of $m$$

The American promises to pay $m$$ for delivery of mF DM.

Now the argument that $F_t = E(S_{t+1})$ is the only possible equilibrium position, has collapsed. A general argument can be made out as follows.

Let m be the engagement in $ of a speculator in the forward market, $m > 0$ is a purchase of $m$$, $m < 0$ is a sale of $m$$. The expected return is

$$\text{in DM:}\quad E(R_{DM}) = m[E(S_{t+1}) - F_t]$$

$$\text{in \$:}\qquad E(R_S) = m[1 - F_t E(1/S_{t+1})]$$

The following outcomes are possible:
(a) If all speculators calculate in DM and have the same expectations, then $E(S_{t+1}) = F_t$ is the only possible equilibrium as

$$m \to +\infty \quad \text{for} \quad E(S_{t+1}) > F_t \quad \text{and} \quad m \to -\infty \quad \text{for} \quad E(S_{t+1}) < F_t.$$

(b) If all speculators calculate in $ and have the same expectations then $F_t = 1/E(1/S_{t+1})$ is the only possible equilibrium.
(c) If there are speculators on both sides of the market then they are able to make profitable contracts. This requires $E(R_{DM}) > 0$ for $m > 0$ and $E(R_S) > 0$ for $m < 0$, or $E(R_{DM}) > 0$ for $m < 0$ and $E(R_S) > 0$ for $m > 0$.
The required condition is sign $E(S_{t+1} - F_t) = $ sign $(F_t E(1/S_{t+1}) - 1)$ which holds if

$$\text{either}\quad E(S_{t+1}) > F_t \quad \text{and} \quad F_t > 1/E(1/S_{t+1})$$

$$\text{or}\qquad E(S_{t+1}) < F_t \quad \text{and} \quad F_t < 1/E(1/S_{t+1})$$

It is known from Jensen's inequality that $E(S_{t+1}) > 1/E(1/S_{t+1})$. This inequality can easily be verified if $E(.)$ is interpreted as a linear combination of different values of the argument and noting that $1/S_{t+1}$ is a convex function in S_{t+1}. Any F_t satisfying $E(S_{t+1}) > F_t > 1/E(1/S_{t+1})$ allows profitable contracts between both types of speculators.

However, in case (c) an equilibrium cannot be determined since for the DM speculator $m \to +\infty$ and for the $ speculator $m \to -\infty$. One escape from this situation is by including risk. One would argue that although forward speculation does not require any initial endowment the partner in a forward contract wants to ensure that his/her counterpart can honour any loss resulting from the speculation. Therefore, in one way or another risk considerations have to be included.

The previous example will now be extended to illustrate some further considerations. Assume that there are investors in two countries with currencies DM and $ and that commodity prices are constant. Both representative individuals have initial endowments of m_tDM and n_t\$ respectively. They consume c_tDM and b_t\$ in the present period and save the rest. Savings $m_t - c_t$ and $(n_t - b_t)$ can be invested:

(a) in DM-bonds with interest rate r_t^d.
(b) in \$-bonds with interest rate r_t^f.

The present exchange rate is S_tDM/\$, the forward rate is F_t and the future spot rate is S_{t+1}. Then the DM-investor has the following options:

(c) exchange \$ bonds at S_{t+1} or at F_t
(d) buy/sell \$ at F_t and sell/buy at S_{t+1} (forward speculation)
(e) borrow/lend at home at r_t^d, lend/borrow abroad at r_t^f and cover risk by a forward contract (interest arbitrage).

Let $\alpha(m_t - c_t)$ be investment in (a), $(1 - \alpha)(m_t - c_t)$ in (b) of which $\beta(1 - \alpha)(m_t - c_t)$ is covered on the forward market, μ (in \$) the engagement in forward speculation and, ε the engagement in interest arbitrage.

The consumable wealth in the next period is then

$$W_{t+1} = \alpha(m_t - c_t)(1 + r_t^d) + \beta(1 - \alpha)(m_t - c_t)(1 + r_t^f)\frac{F_t}{S_t}$$

$$+ (1 - \beta)(m_t - c_t)(1 - \alpha)(1 + r_t^f)\frac{S_{t+1}}{S_t} + \mu(S_{t+1} - F_t)$$

$$+ \varepsilon\left[(1 + r_t^d) - (1 + r_t^f)\frac{F_t}{S_t}\right]$$

The utility function is

$$U = u(c_t) + \delta u(W_{t+1}); \quad 0 < \delta < 1.$$

and the assumption of rational behaviour requires: max $E(U)$.

Risk neutrality requires U to be linear so that we can simply write

$$U = c_t + \delta W_{t+1} \quad \text{and} \quad E(U) = c_t + \delta E(W_{t+1})$$

$$E(U) = c_t + \delta\left\{(m_t - c_t)\left[\alpha(1 + r_t^d) + \beta(1 - \alpha)(1 + r_t^f)\frac{F_t}{S_t}\right.\right.$$

$$\left. + (1 - \beta)(1 - \alpha)(1 + r_t^f)\frac{E(S_{t+1})}{S_t}\right] + \mu[E(S_{t+1}) - F_t]$$

$$\left. + \varepsilon\left[(1 + r_t^d) - (1 + r_t^f)\frac{F_t}{S_t}\right]\right\}$$

Differentiation yields

$$\frac{\partial E(U)}{\partial c_t} = 1 - \delta\left[\alpha(1+r_t^d) + \beta(1-\alpha)(1+r_t^f)\frac{F_t}{S_t}\right.$$

$$\left. + (1-\beta)(1-\alpha)(1+r_t^f)\frac{E(S_{t+1})}{S_t}\right]$$

$$\frac{\partial E(U)}{\partial \alpha} = \delta(m_t - c_t)\left[(1+r_t^d) - \beta(1+r_t^f)\frac{F_t}{S_t}\right.$$

$$\left. - (1-\beta)(1+r_t^f)\frac{E(S_{t+1})}{S_t}\right]$$

$$\frac{\partial E(U)}{\partial \beta} = \delta(m_t - c_t)(1-\alpha)(1+r_t^f)\left[\frac{F_t}{S_t} - \frac{E(S_{t+1})}{S_t}\right]$$

$$\frac{\partial E(U)}{\partial \mu} = \delta[E(S_{t+1}) - F_t]$$

$$\frac{\partial E(U)}{\partial \varepsilon} = \delta\left[(1+r_t^d) - (1+r_t^f)\frac{F_t}{S_t}\right]$$

If interest arbitrage and forward speculation are not profitable, then $E(S_{t+1}) = F_t$ and $(1+r_t^d) = (1+r_t^f)\dfrac{F_t}{S_t}$. Then $E(U)$ would not be changed by any μ, ε. This would also imply that $\dfrac{\partial E(U)}{\partial \beta} = 0$ and $\dfrac{\partial E(U)}{\partial \alpha} = 0$. Finally,

$$\frac{\partial E(U)}{\partial c_t} = 1 - \delta(1+r_t^d)$$

which gives

$$c_t = \begin{cases} 0 & \text{if } \delta > (1+r_t^d) \\ 0 \leqslant c_t \leqslant m_t & \text{if } \delta = (1+r_t^d) \\ m_t & \text{if } \delta < (1+r_t^d) \end{cases}$$

Therefore, in the linear case there are corner solutions or no definite solutions.

However, if the \$-investor is taken into account, it is obvious that $E(S_{t+1}) > F_t$ is likely. On assuming that $(1+r_t^d) = (1+r_t^f)\dfrac{F_t}{S_t}$; $\varepsilon = 0$ leads to

(a) $\mu \to \infty$

(b) $\dfrac{\partial E(U)}{\partial \beta} < 0$, hence $\beta = 0$

(c) $\dfrac{\partial E(U)}{\partial \alpha} < 0$, hence $\alpha = 0$.

If the \$ investor behaves in a similar way since he has the same stochastic information then both will engage excessively in forward market speculation and both will buy only foreign bonds.

Thus, the combination of rational expectations (agents have the same information) and risk neutrality on both sides of the market, yields unlikely results. Introducing risk aversion, however, allows one to determine finite optimal amounts of α^*, β^* and μ^*.

In order to simplify assume that $1 + r_t^d = (1 + r_t^f)\dfrac{F_t}{S_t}$ holds because of interest arbitrage.

Introducing $\gamma = 1 - \alpha$ and $\omega = (m_t - c_t)\gamma \dfrac{1 + r_t^f}{S_t} + \mu$, it is possible to write

$$W_{t+1} = (m_t - c_t)(1 + r_t^d) + \omega(S_{t+1} - F_t);$$

$$E(U) = u(c_t) + \delta E[u(W_{t+1})]; \quad \frac{\partial u}{\partial(.)} > 0; \quad \frac{\partial^2 u}{\partial(.)^2} < 0.$$

$$\frac{\partial E}{\partial c_t} = \frac{\partial u}{\partial c_t} - \delta E\left[\frac{\partial u}{\partial W_{t+1}}(1 + r_t^d)\right] = 0$$

$$= > 1 + r_t^d = \frac{\partial u/\partial c_t}{\partial E(\partial u/\partial W_{t+1})} \tag{2.5.7}$$

$$\frac{\partial E}{\partial \omega} = \delta E \frac{\partial u}{\partial W_{t+1}}(S_{t+1} - F_t) = 0,$$

$$\Rightarrow E\frac{\partial u}{\partial W_{t+1}}S_{t+1} = F_t E\frac{\partial u}{\partial W_{t+1}} \tag{2.5.8}$$

From (2.5.7) and (2.5.8) one can obtain $\omega^* = h(F_t)$ where ω^* is the optimal speculative engagement, be it strict forward speculation or investment in foreign bonds without risk coverage. Obviously, $\omega^* = 0$ if $F_t = E(S_{t+1})$, since W_{t+1} is then a constant and (2.5.7) only holes for $F_t = E(S_{t+1})$. It can be established that at least in the neighbourhood of $F_t = E(S_{t+1})$ the slope of $h(F_t)$ is negative. The appropriate calculation for the representative American investor results in a supply function of forward $

$$\zeta^* = g(F_t) \quad \text{with} \quad \zeta^* = 0$$

if $F_t = 1/E(1/S_{t+1}) < E(S_{t+1})$, and a positive slope

in the neighbourhood of $\zeta^* = 0$.

Equilibrium in the forward market can be described by the graph in Figure 2.1:

Figure 2.1 Forward Market Equilibrium

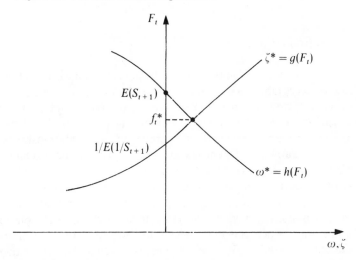

Having established $E(S_{t+1}) > f_t^* > 1/E(1/S_{t+1})$ it can also be demonstrated that another well-known equation of interest arbitrage does not hold. Let $E(S_{t+1}) = S_t$ and $(1 + r_t^d) = (1 + r_t^f)\dfrac{f_t^*}{S_t}$. Then the expected rate of depreciation of the domestic currency is zero, and yet domestic and foreign interest rates differ $(r_t^f > r_t^d)$. The explanation is that the expected rate of depreciation of the foreign currency $E[1/(S_{t+1}) > 1/S_t]$ is not zero, which implies the expected rate of depreciation of the $ is not zero.

In conclusion it should be noted that the preceding analysis has implications for recent attempts at measuring foreign exchange market risk. A more detailed discussion is provided in McMahon (1987).

CHAPTER 3

Theoretical models of exchange rate behaviour

3.1   Introduction

One major research goal in the study of flexible exchange rates is the desire to find an acceptable model that explains the movement of the nominal spot exchange rate in terms of other macroeconomic variables. Chapter 1 discussed the long-run concept of purchasing power parity (PPP) and Chapter 2 introduced the short-run interest rate parity relationship and the idea of a fair game or efficient market generating nominal exchange rate changes. These concepts provide some of the basic building blocks for many of the current models of exchange rate determination.

The role of this chapter is to develop some of the theoretical models that have been popularised in recent years to account for the volatility of exchange rates since the float began in 1973. All theoretical models considered are based on the asset market approach with the exchange rate determined by the relative supplies and demands of national monies. A major requirement for the validity of these models is that capital is perfectly mobile internationally so that there are no regulations on international finance and that interest rate parity holds.

A distinguishing feature of alternative asset market models is given by the assumptions concerning the substitutability of domestic and foreign securities and leads to a dichotomy of financial markets into models of the so-called monetary approach and the portfolio approach.

In the monetary models, domestic and foreign securities are assumed perfect substitutes and hence have identical risk; the forward rate is the unbiased, efficient expectation of the future spot rate. In order to avoid riskless profits being made the interest rate differential must equal the expected change in the spot rate. The implication of the assumption of the perfect substitutability of capital is that the exchange rate is completely determined by the equilibrium on the corresponding money markets.

In contrast, portfolio models treat domestic and foreign securities as imperfect substitutes and changes in the expected yields and risks associated with different securities lead to portfolio diversification, wealth redistribution and hence affect the exchange rate. The stock of wealth also appears in the demand for money functions and allows a more flexible approach to modelling exchange rate fundamentals. For example, deficits in the current account lead to a redistribution of the world's wealth, while budgetary deficits lead to an increase in the stock of private wealth. Furthermore, sterilised central bank intervention, which leaves the money supply unaltered, still leads to a change in private wealth and hence to a change in the equilibrium exchange rate.

This chapter considers the theoretical derivation and economic interpretation of some of the basic and important models. After a short section describing some of the theory behind PPP, the monetary model is considered in detail, followed in the next section by the Dornbusch sticky price model. Whereas the monetary model assumes that disequilibrium on the goods and financial markets is eliminated instantaneously by an adjustment of goods prices, the Dornbusch model drops the short-run validity of PPP and distinguishes between short and long-run equilibrium. The adjustment to long-run equilibrium depends on a price adjustment process where price is a function of excess demand on the goods market. The overshooting property of the Dornbusch sticky price model is considered and the rational expectations solutions of the monetary and Dornbusch models are derived. The next section considers a portfolio model which allows domestic and foreign securities to be imperfect substitutes and implies that overshooting of the exchange rate will not necessarily result following a monetary shock. The chapter concludes with a discussion of currency substitution models and a brief review of more recent models that attempt to link current account and capital account transactions.

The concept of rational expectations was introduced in the previous chapter and was motivated in terms of the properties such an expectation must possess when generated as a fair game sequence. Many of the models considered in this chapter involve the rational expectations of certain variables appearing within the model. The inclusion of such variables gives rise to many special problems both in terms of solution and estimation of the model. Some of the appropriate techniques for dealing with these models are discussed in the appendix to this chapter. It should be noted that the appendix is merely an introduction to the use of expectations models and gives a survey of some particular solutions. A more general treatment is provided by Whiteman (1983) and Pesaran (1988).

The models discussed in this chapter are purely theoretical. Subsequent chapters consider the empirical evidence for various relationships and properties that have been hypothesised to exist between variables in the foreign exchange market and Chapter 8 considers the estimation and testing of many of the models introduced within this chapter.

3.2 Purchasing power parity

In its absolute form purchasing power parity (PPP) theory posits the nominal exchange rate S to be determined by the ratio of domestic and foreign prices P and $P*$ respectively, so that

$$S_t = P_t/P_t^* \qquad (3.2.1)$$

The theory thus assumes the existence of a price index. On denoting p_i as the price in the domestic currency of the ith good, and p_i^* as the price in the foreign currency of the same good in the foreign country, then the two indices can be defined as

$$P = \prod_{i=1}^{N} (p_i)^{\alpha_i}; \qquad P* = \prod_{i=1}^{N} (p_i^*)^{\alpha_i^*}$$

where it is assumed that the same N goods exist in both countries and α_i and α_i^* represent a system of weights with $\sum \alpha_i = \sum \alpha_i^* = 1$. These indices are usually justified using consumer theory by assuming that the consumer devotes a constant fraction α_i of his or her budget to the ith good which is given independently of relative prices. Hence the level of welfare or utility between consumers depends only on their purchasing power.

In the relative version of PPP it is no longer necessary for the exchange rate to be equal to the ratio of price indices instantaneously but to simply remain at a constant ratio as

$$S_{t+1}/S_t = (P_{t+1}/P_{t+1}^*)/(P_t/P_t^*) \qquad (3.2.2)$$

Since the behaviour of consumption in both countries is reflected in the composition of the indices P_t and P_t^* it is possible to rewrite (3.2.2) in terms of the inflation rates π_t and π_t^* in each country. Since

$$\pi_t = \frac{P_{t+1} - P_t}{P_t} = \frac{dP_t/dt}{P_t} \qquad (3.2.3)$$

$$\pi_t^* = \frac{P_{t+1}^* - P_t^*}{P_t^*} = \frac{dP_t^*/dt}{P_t^*}$$

and $(S_{t+1} - S_t)/S_t = \dfrac{\pi_t - \pi_t^*}{1 + \pi_t^*} \qquad (3.2.4)$

and in the case where the foreign inflation rate π_t^* is low this can be further simplified to

$$(S_{t+1} - S_t)/S_t = \pi_t - \pi_t^* \tag{3.2.5}$$

Hence, the rate of change of prices, or inflation differentials, is balanced by a corresponding change in the exchange rate.

Both the absolute and relative versions of PPP can be expressed in terms of the real exchange rate S_t^{PPP} as

$$S_t^{PPP} = S_t P_t^*/P_t \tag{3.2.6}$$

which defines the real exchange rate in terms of the purchasing power between two consumption baskets. It is easy to verify that absolute purchasing parity can be expressed as

$$S_t^{PPP} = 1 \tag{3.2.7}$$

and relative parity as

$$S_{t+1}^{PPP} = S_t^{PPP} \tag{3.2.8}$$

Furthermore, even if relative purchasing power parity is not verified, differentiation of equation (3.2.6) allows the change in the exchange rate to be decomposed into three components

$$\frac{dS_t/dt}{S_t} = \pi_t - \pi_t^* + \frac{dS_t^{PPP}/dt}{S_t^{PPP}} \tag{3.2.9}$$

In macroeconomic models that do not assume the validity of relative PPP the first two components of

$$\frac{dS/dt}{S}$$

are associated with an increase in the monetary stock in each country and the third component is linked to a modification in relative prices.

There are three ways in which purchasing power parity can be justified. The most traditional approach has been called the Law of One Price, the second requires the invariance of relative prices and the third is based on the Fisherian hypothesis concerning the real interest rate. These shall now be considered in turn.

The Law of One Price
If the behaviour of consumers is the same in both countries then the system of weights will also be identical, so that

$$\alpha_i^* = \alpha_i \quad i = 1 \ldots N \tag{3.2.10}$$

Thus, the real exchange rate can be written as

$$S_t^{PPP} = \prod_{i=1}^{N} (P_{it}^* S_t / P_{it})^\alpha \qquad (3.2.11)$$

and is equal to 1 if the price of each of the N goods does not vary between one country and another, so that

$$P_{it} = P_{it}^* S_t \qquad i = 1 \ldots N \qquad (3.2.12)$$

The last condition characterises the Law of One Price in its absolute version. If only the relative version of this law applies then by definition

$$P_{i,t+1}^* S_{t+1} / P_{i,t+1} = P_{i,t}^* S_t / P_{i,t} \qquad i = 1 \ldots N \qquad (3.2.13)$$

a condition which clearly implies that the real exchange rate is stable over time. Hence when the price indices in both countries are identical the Law of One Price justifies purchasing power parity.

It is also obvious that the Law of One Price can be verified if internationally produced goods are perfect substitutes. Then simple arbitrage by market participants will establish uniformity of price in closely integrated markets, and the Law of One Price is sometimes known as 'global monetarism' e.g. Whitman (1975). The theory is probably only correct for raw materials, commodities and food, since a number of market imperfections such as transport costs, taxes, tariffs and other duties violate the required arbitrage conditions. Also since there is the opportunity for product differentiation, especially in the short-run, price adjustment becomes a question of substitution and no longer a matter of arbitrage.

A country that becomes more price competitive would expect demand to shift towards its goods and, in full employment, would exert upward pressure on costs and prices. This process of price adjustment is certainly not instantaneous but depends on the pressure of demand and on expectations concerning the persistence of real price changes. This suggests that deviations from PPP are probable and likely to persist for some time. Accordingly the Law of One Price can only be verified approximately even for the goods which are traded internationally. In the case of non-traded goods these imperfections prevent international trade from being profitable and the Law of One Price has virtually been demonstrated to be defective.

The invariance of relative prices

If the composition of the indices P and P^* differ, relative PPP can be verified providing that the relative version of the Law of One Price holds for all the N goods and that relative goods prices are not modified during the period. These assumptions are quite restrictive but, in a number of macroeconomic models, it is assumed that purely monetary disturbances do not have any effect upon relative prices. Thus relative purchasing power parity can be justified in models where money is assumed to be neutral and where the exchange rate is not subject to disturbances of a purely monetary character.

However, in the short run the hypothesis of the neutrality of money is quite difficult to accept. For instance a devaluation can have real effects on the economy and, through the terms of trade, affect the real exchange rate. In addition monetary disturbances usually have short-term effects upon relative prices and the real exchange rate, since goods prices are not entirely flexible due to institutional rigidities and imperfect dissemination of information.

The Fisher hypothesis

The Fisher hypothesis postulates that real rates of interest r and r^* are equalised between two countries through the following relationship between domestic and foreign nominal rates i and i^* and price levels. Then

$$1 + r_t \equiv \frac{1 + i_t}{P_{t+1}/P_t} = \frac{1 + i_t^*}{P_{t+1}^*/P_t^*} \equiv 1 + r_t^* \qquad (3.2.14)$$

To move to purchasing power parity, it is sufficient to appeal to the uncovered interest rate parity relationship

$$(1 + i_t)S_t = (1 + i_t^*)S_{t+1} \qquad (3.2.15)$$

which indicates how the hypothesis of relative purchasing power parity is verified. When the future is uncertain the relationship between the Fisher hypothesis and relative purchasing power parity is more complex but it is possible using the equality between the real interest rates to deduce the result that the real exchange rate follows a martingale.

Chapter 1 considered the development over time of various exchange rates and their deviations from PPP. The extent to which exchange rates deviate from PPP is an important issue in trade theory and the basic empirical evidence presented in Chapter 1 has shown these deviations to be quite substantial. In fact the distortions introduced into the theory by the existence of non-traded goods parity explains systematic deviations from PPP. One explanation centres on the comparative technologies of two countries, for a high income country is generally technologically more advanced than a low income country and productivity is thus greater. However, the advantages in terms of efficiency are not the same in different industries. It is more important in the industrial and agricultural traded goods sector than in the non-traded services sector. Since wages are higher in higher income countries and in any given country are roughly equalised between different industries, it follows that the prices of non-traded goods are relatively higher in a high income country. The use of the general PPP index in this situation will result in an underestimation of the value of money in the wealthier country. The extent of the underestimation depends on the technological gap that exists between countries.

Both Balassa (1964) and Samuelson (1965) have argued that since services are generally non-traded, labour intensive and show relatively low productivity growth, it follows that the real price level in fast growing, innovative economies will increase over time. This would imply that wages in the non-traded sector grow less rapidly than wages in the open, traded sector. However, the prices of traded goods should be equalised through arbitrage so that productivity growth in the traded sector will raise wages in both sectors and hence raise the relative price of non-traded goods and the real price level in the fast growing countries.

The following example illustrates the point raised by Balassa and Samuelson. Consider a two country model in which the U.S. and a developing country produce non-traded goods in addition to traded goods. Assume that wages and labour productivity are the only elements in the cost of producing these goods; in addition wages are equalised within a country between the traded and non-traded goods sectors but may differ across countries. Furthermore there is assumed to be a positive relationship between prices and wages and an inverse relationship between productivity and prices. It is also assumed that the behaviour of consumers in both countries is the same, so that $\alpha_i = \alpha_i^*$ for $i = 1 \ldots N$. The number of hours required to produce good i is given by c_i in the U.S. and c_i^* in the developing country; the respective productivities b_i, b_i^* corresponding to these goods are given by

$$b_i = \frac{1}{c_i} \quad \text{and} \quad b_i^* = \frac{1}{c_i^*}$$

The price of each good can then be deduced from its costs of production by applying a profit margin, which is assumed the same in every sector, as

$$p_i = (1 + m)c_i L; \quad \text{and} \quad p_i^* = (1 + m^*)c_i^* L^* \tag{3.2.16}$$

where L and L^* represent the hourly cost of labour in each country.

Consider the case where there exists only two commodities, commodity 1 which is traded and commodity 2 which is non-traded. Then $S = P_1/P_1^*$ where P_1 is the price of commodity 1 in dollars and P_1^* the price in pesos so that S measures \$/pesos. The real exchange S^{PPP} is given from (3.2.6) as

$$S^{PPP} = SP^*/P \quad \text{and} \quad P = P_1^{1-\alpha}P_2^\alpha, \quad P^* = P_1^{*1-\alpha}P_2^{*\alpha}$$

$$S^{PPP} = \frac{P_1 P_1^{*1-\alpha}P_2^{*\alpha}}{P_1^* P_1^{1-\alpha}P_2^\alpha} = \left[\frac{P_2^* P_1}{P_2 P_1^*}\right]^\alpha$$

Using (3.2.16) one can rewrite the real exchange rate in a particularly simple form as

$$S^{PPP} = \left(\frac{b_1^*/b_2^*}{b_1/b_2}\right)^\alpha = \left(\frac{b_2/b_1}{b_2^*/b_1^*}\right)^\alpha = \left(\frac{b_2 b_1^*}{b_2^* b_1}\right)^\alpha \tag{3.2.17}$$

The real exchange rate can thus deviate from 1 if the productivity conditions differ between one country and another. On this basis if $b_2 \cong b_2^*$ and $b_1 > b_1^*$ (productivity is similar in the non-traded goods sector and higher in the U.S. in the traded goods sector) the real exchange rate $S^{PPP} < 1$. In a similar way if productivity increases more rapidly in the U.S. in the traded goods sector the rate of change in the real exchange rate $\hat{S}^{PPP} < 0$, where $\hat{}$ denotes rate of change. Thus if

$$\hat{b}_2 = \hat{b}_2^* \quad \text{and} \quad \hat{b}_1^* < \hat{b}_1 \tag{3.2.18}$$

then

$$\hat{S}^{PPP} = \alpha[\hat{b}_2 - \hat{b}_2^* + \hat{b}_1^* - \hat{b}_1] < 0 \tag{3.2.19}$$

Consequently, in this case, a relative increase in the nominal exchange rate must be less than the differential in inflation rates. This can be demonstrated assuming PPP:

$$\hat{S} = \hat{P}_1 - \hat{P}_1^*$$

Let the inflation rates be denoted by

$\pi = (1-\alpha)\hat{P}_1 + \alpha\hat{P}_2$ and $\pi^* = (1-\alpha)\hat{P}_1^* + \alpha\hat{P}_2^*$. Let L and L^* change by $\hat{L}$ and $\hat{L}^*$ respectively. Then it follows that $\hat{P}_i = \hat{L} - \hat{b}_i$ which implies that $\pi = \hat{L} - (1-\alpha)\hat{b}_1 - \alpha\hat{b}_2$

Since $\hat{S} = \hat{L} - \hat{b}_1 - \hat{L}^* + \hat{b}_1^*$ and

$$\pi - \pi^* = \hat{L} - \hat{L}^* + (1-\alpha)(\hat{b}_1^* - \hat{b}_1) + \alpha(\hat{b}_2^* - \hat{b}_2).$$

If $\hat{b}_2 = b_2^*$ and $\hat{b}_1 > b_1^*$ then

$$\hat{S} - (\pi - \pi^*) = (\hat{b}_1^* - \hat{b}_1) + (1-\alpha)(\hat{b}_1 - \hat{b}_1^*)$$

$$\hat{S} - (\pi - \pi^*) = \alpha(\hat{b}_1^* - \hat{b}_1) < 0$$

Thus $\hat{S} < \pi - \pi^*$ where $\hat{S} < 0$ means that the dollar appreciates against the peso.

This type of analysis has been used to try to explain the disparity in purchasing power between developed and non-developed countries. If it is the traded goods which have registered the most important gains in productivity and if these gains have been higher in the more developed countries, then the preceding model predicts that the depreciation in purchasing power in the less developed countries must exceed the inflation differential, which is generally the case. By a similar argument, the increase in real wages is greater in the developed country than in the less developed country if $b_1 > b_2$.

A further explanation for deviations from PPP concerns countries that have a current account deficit and finance an increase in aggregate demand by borrowing. Then the current account deficit would raise the relative price of non-traded goods and hence the real price level.

As it stands PPP specifies a final equilibrium relationship between exchange rates and prices without specifying the precise details of the process. An integral part of the theory as developed by Cassel (1919, 1922) was that movements in price levels caused changes in exchange rates but that changes in exchange rates exercised no influence over price levels. Clearly this part of the theory is not always true. Suppose for instance that heavy, speculative capital movements depress the value of the pound for several months. The immediate effect will be to make imports into the U.K. more expensive and British exports cheaper in foreign currencies. British industries depending upon imported raw materials may consequently be forced to raise prices and British exporters will be tempted to raise their prices for, if they raise them by less than the pound has fallen, they will increase their profits. Their goods will still be cheaper in foreign currencies than they were and will enjoy a larger share of the foreign market. Thus the British price-level will be raised by the fall of the pound. At the same time the increased competitive power of British export industries may compel other countries to lower their prices in order not to lose their trade. Thus the fall of the pound will tend not only to raise British prices but also to lower foreign prices.

The relationship between prices and exchange rates dates back to the older quantity theory of money and is best described by assuming a completely fixed exchange rate. The existing balances in the balance of payments will be financed by just one international medium of reserve, say gold, by the central banks. Since the change in the domestic money supply adjusts completely to the change in reserves, the central bank is unable to control the money supply in such a system. In addition, if the domestic economy is small in comparison with the rest of the world then it cannot influence the external price level. From PPP, inflation will be imported from abroad by means of the relationship

$$P = P^*S$$

which is the well-known Fisher quantity equation and links money supply, and real income to the velocity of circulation. For a full description of fixed exchange rate theory, see for example, Frenkel and Mussa (1980). Some further econometric evidence on the validity of PPP is discussed in Chapter 8.

3.3   The monetary model

An extremely important and influential model of exchange rate determination is the so-called monetary model which is a logical extension of the quantity theory of the demand for money in an open economy. Before discussing the model in detail it is important to note that the following assumptions are made: (i) all goods prices are completely flexible, (ii) domestic and foreign assets are perfect substitutes, (iii) there is perfect capital mobility, (iv) the money supply and real income are determined exogenously, and (v) domestic money is demanded only by domestic residents, and foreign money only by foreign residents.

The model requires the following five basic equations

$$s_t = p_t - p_t^* \tag{3.3.1}$$

$$m_t - p_t = k + \phi y_t - \lambda r_t \tag{3.3.2}$$

$$m_t^* - p_t^* = k^* + \phi^* y_t^* - \lambda^* r_t^* \tag{3.3.3}$$

$$r_t - r_t^* = f_t - s_t \tag{3.3.4}$$

$$f_t = E_t s_{t+1} \tag{3.3.5}$$

where s is the spot exchange rate, f is the forward exchange rate, y is real income, p is the price level, m is the money supply; and all are in natural logarithms. The variable r is nominal interest rates; and asterisks denote foreign quantities. The variable s_t is defined as the price of the foreign currency in units of the domestic currency. The first equation represents an assumption of short and long-run validity of PPP in its absolute form so that no terms of trade effect exists and that the goods market is in short-run equilibrium. Equations (3.3.2) and (3.3.3) are the conventional demand for money functions due to Cagan (1956) and provide the central behavioural parts of the model since domestic and foreign price levels are determined by equilibrium on the relevant money markets.

On assuming that the real income elasticities and semi-interest rate elasticities for money demand are identical in both countries, it follows that

$$s_t = -(k - k^*) + (m_t - m_t^*) - \phi(y_t - y_t^*) + \lambda(r_t - r_t^*) \qquad (3.3.6)$$

This relationship may be modified by assuming non-instantaneous adjustment of the exchange rate according to the following partial adjustment mechanism

$$s_t - s_{t-1} = \theta(\bar{s}_t - s_{t-1}) \qquad (3.3.7)$$

where $\bar{s}_t = p_t - p_t^*$.

Introducing the equilibrium exchange rate from (3.3.6) into this gives

$$s_t = -\theta(k_t - k_t^*) + \theta(m_t - m_t^*) - \theta\phi(y_t - y_t^*)$$
$$+ \theta\lambda(r_r - r_t^*) + (1 - \theta)s_{t-1} \qquad (3.3.8)$$

The exchange rate can be interpreted as the relative price of two currencies, determined by equilibrium on the money market. Hence an increase in the domestic money supply will lead to a depreciation of equal proportion and an increase in the relative domestic real income leads to an appreciation. It is particularly interesting to note than an increased interest rate differential will also lead to a depreciation. This occurs since an increase in the domestic rate of interest will decrease the real demand for money; and given a fixed nominal money supply, this will be achieved by a rise in the domestic price level and hence a depreciation of the exchange rate. Hence the predicted effect is the opposite to that in the standard Keynesian Model with incorporated capital mobility, as described by Mundell (1968) and Fleming (1962). In their model a relative increase in the domestic interest rate led to capital imports, and hence to an appreciation of the exchange rate.

The nominal interest rate differential in the monetary model is generally interpreted in terms of differences of inflationary expectations. This interpretation follows from the assumption of perfect substitutability of assets and perfect capital mobility, which imply that real interest differentials cannot exist in equilibrium. Thus the instantaneous adjustment of all financial markets precludes the existence of short-run liquidity effects. An increase in the money supply does not lead to a decline in the interest rate, but indeed to an increase in the nominal interest rate through anticipated price changes. In contrast the Mundell–Fleming model uses the assumption of fixed prices which implies that nominal and real interest differentials are always the same.

Another interesting conclusion arising from the monetary model is that a policy of monetary expansion cannot have any real effects due to perfect price flexibility. However, an increase in domestic real income leads to an increase in the real demand for money, a corresponding decline in the price level to obtain money market equilibrium and hence an appreciation of the exchange rate. The alternative Mundell–Fleming analysis generally regards an increase in domestic real income as leading to a worsening trade balance and therefore to a depreciation of the exchange rate. However, if the increase in real income results purely from increased exports, which are exogenous, then an appreciation of the exchange rate will follow.

The above treatment of the monetary model has assumed the interest rate differential exogenous. This assumption does not seem reasonable given the high degree of integration of the security and foreign exchange markets and does not provide any explanation for the high volatility that occurs in the foreign exchange market. By invoking the previously stated assumptions of domestic and foreign assets being perfect substitutes and the existence of perfect capital mobility, it is then possible to close the model from the covered interest parity condition (3.3.4).

$$s_t = (k - k^*) + (m_t - m_t^*) - \phi(y_t - y_t^*) + \lambda(f_t - s_t) \tag{3.3.9}$$

so that the model now includes two endogenous variables, the spot and forward exchange rates. Either of these variables can adjust to clear the foreign exchange market and there will be an infinite number of (s_t, f_t) points in a locus to maintain equilibrium for given m, m^*, y and y^*. The particular combination that clears the market can be obtained by introducing (3.3.5), i.e. the condition that the forward rate is the unbiased efficient expectation of the future spot exchange rate. Equations (3.3.4) and (3.3.5) give

$$r_t - r_t^* = E_t s_{t+1} - s_t \tag{3.3.10}$$

which is the uncovered interest parity condition already encountered in Chapter 2. The condition states that the interest differential must be equal to the expected rate of change of the exchange rate in equilibrium, otherwise uncovered interest arbitrage or spot market speculation would lead to riskless profit. On elimination of the interest rate differential, equation (3.3.6) then becomes

$$s_t = -(k - k^*) + (m_t - m_t^*)$$
$$- \phi(y_t - y_t^*) + \lambda(E_t s_{t+1} - s_t) \tag{3.3.11}$$

and hence

$$s_t = z_t + \left(\frac{\lambda}{1 + \lambda}\right) E_t s_{t+1} \tag{3.3.12}$$

where

$$z_t = \left(\frac{1}{1+\lambda}\right)(m_t - m_t^*) - \left(\frac{\phi}{1+\lambda}\right)(y_t - y_t^*) + c \qquad (3.3.13)$$

and

$$c = -\left(\frac{1}{1+\lambda}\right)(k - k^*)$$

Equation (3.3.12) is the usual way of expressing the monetary model. The exchange rate is defined in terms of its expected value next period and the current variables z_t which are known as the 'fundamentals'. As shown in the appendix to this chapter there are many solutions to equation (3.3.12) under rational expectations. In particular forward and backward solutions exist and if we are prepared to assume that z_t follows an ARMA process, the results of Gourieroux, Laffont and Monfort (1982) can be used. Generally the forward solution is taken, so that (3.3.12) is solved out to give

$$s_t = \left(\frac{1}{1+\lambda}\right) \sum_{j=0}^{\infty} \left(\frac{\lambda}{1+\lambda}\right)^j E_t z_{t+j} \qquad (3.3.14)$$

and the current exchange rate is a function of the rational expectations of discounted future exogenous fundamentals. One attractive feature of the above is that the observed volatility of exchange rates can to some extent be explained by the instability in the expectations of the future fundamentals. Substantial revisions to expectations may be made in successive periods following unanticipated shocks and will thus make the path of the exchange rate extremely volatile.

A satisfactory empirical analysis of the monetary model requires specifying the process for z_t so that future expectations can be generated. As will be seen in Chapter 8, in many empirical applications this can be a problem. Under the highly simplistic assumption of the fundamentals following a random walk

$$z_t = z_{t-1} + a_t$$

where a_t is a white noise process; then $E_t z_{t+j} = z_t$ and the model (3.3.14) collapses to the rather uninteresting static solution of

$$s_t = c + (m_t - m_t^*) - \phi(y_t - y_t^*)$$

Subsequent chapters examine the theory and empirical evidence for many of the assumptions required by the model, namely interest parity, an efficient forward market, purchasing power parity, etc. Finally, Chapter 8 sets out details of some attempts at econometric estimation of the model and the general evidence for its validity.

3.4   Dornbusch's sticky price monetary model

The monetary model just analysed contains a number of strong assumptions, particularly with regard to the notion of all markets being in approximate equilibrium and the assumption of perfectly flexible goods prices. One of the most influential papers to deal with generalising the model, is due to Dornbusch (1976a and b), whose analysis allowed different speeds of adjustment for the goods and money markets. Dornbusch's model is able to provide an explanation for the dynamic adjustment process that occurs as exchange rates move towards a new equilibrium. The model develops the idea of price stickiness and shows that following an unanticipated monetary disturbance the exchange rate expectations will deviate from PPP for as long as it takes goods prices to fully adjust to the new monetary conditions. One implication of this is that the exchange rate can overshoot its long-run path.

As in the monetary model, a two country model is considered with identical structural parameters in the domestic and foreign countries; domestic and foreign assets are still assumed to be perfect substitutes, so that risk considerations are avoided. Most controversially perhaps, domestic money and real outputs are still assumed to be exogenous. The major difference with the monetary model is that domestic and foreign goods are no longer considered perfect substitutes, and goods prices only adjust to a new equilibrium with a lag. The lagged response being due to costs of adjustment, or due to lack of complete information. However, the maintenance of long-run equilibrium PPP implies that the long-run effect of a change in money supply is identical to that of the monetary model.

However financial markets are still assumed to adjust instantaneously, and due to the different speed of adjustment in the goods market, a short-run increase in the money supply can have real effects due to the terms of trade. These real effects can have liquidity effects, and similarly to the Mundell–Fleming model can cause a reduction in interest rates in response to a capital inflow resulting in an immediate depreciation of the domestic currency which can be greater than the long-run equilibrium value. Hence during the adjustment process, prices and exchange rates may move in opposite directions. The model is formulated in terms of the following behavioural equations

$$(m_t - m_t^*) - (p_t - p_t^*) = (k - k^*) + \phi(y_t - y_t^*)$$
$$- \lambda(r_t - r_t^*) + \varepsilon_{1t} \tag{3.4.1}$$

$$(d_t - d_t^*) = \gamma(y_t - y_t^*) - \sigma(r_t - r_t^*) - \omega(s_t - p_t + p_t^*) \tag{3.4.2}$$

$$(p_t - p_t^*) - (p_{t-1} - p_{t-1}^*) = \partial[(d_t - d_t^*) - \lambda(y_t - y_t^*)] + \varepsilon_{2t} \tag{3.4.3}$$

$$(r_t - r_t^*) = E_t s_{t+1} - s_t + \varepsilon_{3t} \tag{3.4.4}$$

where d is domestic demand for goods, asterisks denote foreign equivalents, $\varepsilon_{1t}, \varepsilon_{2t}$, and ε_{3t} are mutually uncorrelated white noise disturbances and all other variables are as previously defined.

The first equation represents the standard demand for real balances put in relative form, while the second specifies the relative demand for goods to depend upon the level of relative real incomes, the interest differential and the terms of trade. Equation (3.4.3) implies price adjustment to be proportional to current excess demand and equation (3.4.4) is the uncovered interest parity condition with a white noise disturbance.

It is usual, although not strictly necessary, as will be seen later, to complete the model by specifying the equations

$$\bar{s}_t = \bar{p}_t - \bar{p}_t^* \tag{3.4.5}$$

and

$$E_t s_{t+1} - s_t = \alpha(\bar{s}_t - s_t) \tag{3.4.6}$$

where $\bar{s}_t$, $\bar{p}$ and $\bar{p}^*$ are the long-run equilibrium exchange rate and prices. Thus (3.4.5) implies PPP to hold absolutely in the long run and (3.4.6) specifies next periods expectation of the exchange rate to be proportional to the current periods exchange rate deviation from long-run equilibrium.

From equations (3.4.1), (3.4.2) and (3.4.3) it follows that

$$(p_t - p_t^*) = \beta_0 + \beta_1(p_{t-1} - p_{t-1}^*) + \beta_2 s_t + \tau_t, \tag{3.4.7}$$

where

$$\beta_1 = [1 + \partial(\omega + \sigma/\lambda)]^{-1}$$
$$\beta_2 = \beta_1 \partial \omega$$
$$\tau_t = \beta_3(y_t - y_t^*) + \beta_4(m_t - m_t^*) + v_t \tag{3.4.8}$$

where

$$\beta_3 = \beta_1 \partial(\gamma - 1 - \sigma\phi/\lambda)$$
$$\beta_4 = \beta_1 \partial \sigma/\lambda$$
$$\beta_0 = -\beta_1 \sigma \partial(k - k^*)/\lambda$$

and $\quad v_t = \beta_1 \varepsilon_{2t} - (\beta_1 \partial \sigma/\lambda)\varepsilon_{1t}$

It should be noted that s_t and $(p_t - p_t^*)$ are jointly endogenous variables in (3.4.7) while τ_t is strictly exogenous. The coefficients will be expected to satisfy the restrictions that $0 \leqslant \beta_1 \leqslant 1$, $0 \leqslant \beta_2 \leqslant 1$, $\beta_3 \leqslant 0$ and $0 \leqslant \beta_4 \leqslant 1$.

One interesting property of the model concerns the solution for the long-run exchange rate equilibrium. From equations (3.4.1) and (3.4.4) the price differential can be written as

$$(p_t - p_t^*) = -(k - k^*) + (m_t - m_t^*) - \phi(y_t - y_t^*)$$
$$+ \lambda(E_t s_{t+1} - s_t) + u_t, \tag{3.4.9}$$

where

$$u_t = \varepsilon_{1t} + \lambda \varepsilon_{3t}$$

For a long-run stationary equilibrium the expected change in the exchange rate will be zero, so that $E_t(s_{t+1} - s_t) = 0$ and from (3.4.5), it follows that the long-run exchange rate equilibrium can be found from (3.4.9) to be

$$\bar{s}_t = -(k - k^*) + (m_t - m_t^*) - \phi(y_t - y_t^*) \tag{3.4.10}$$

On elimination of $E_t s_{t+1}$ in (3.4.4) and (3.4.6), the expected depreciation in the exchange rate is given by

$$r_t - r_t^* = \alpha(\bar{s}_t - s_t) \tag{3.4.11}$$

and hence

$$(r_t - r_t^*) = \alpha[-(k - k^*) + (m_t - m_t^*) - \phi(y_t - y_t^*) - s_t] \tag{3.4.12}$$

But from equation (3.4.1) the interest rate differential is also given by

$$(r_t - r_t^*) = \frac{1}{\lambda}[(k - k^*) - (m_t - m_t^*) + (p_t - p_t^*) + \phi(y_t - y_t^*)] \tag{3.4.13}$$

On equating (3.4.12) and (3.4.13) and eliminating $(p_t - p_t^*)$ from (3.4.7) and (3.4.8) a solution for s_t the nominal exchange rate is found to be

$$s_t = b_0 + b_1(m_t - m_t^*) + b_2(y_t - y_t^*) + b_3(p_{t-1} - p_{t-1}^*) \tag{3.4.14}$$

where

$$b_0 = \mu[-(k - k^*)(1 + 1/\alpha\lambda) - \beta_0/\alpha\lambda]$$
$$b_1 = \mu(1 + 1/\alpha\lambda - \beta_4/\alpha\lambda)$$
$$b_2 = -\mu[\phi(1 + 1/\alpha\lambda) + \beta_3/\alpha\lambda], \quad b_3 = -b_1$$
$$\mu = (1 + \beta_2/\alpha\lambda)^{-1}$$

and $\quad v_t = -(\beta_1 \partial\sigma/\lambda^2)\varepsilon_{1t} - (\beta/\lambda)\varepsilon_{2t}$

Hence (3.4.7) and (3.4.14) are the reduced form equations for the endogenous variables $(p_t - p_t^*)$ and s_t, while the long-run exchange rate equilibrium is given by (3.4.10). The celebrated 'overshooting' of the Dornbusch model can be demonstrated in the following manner. Consider just the domestic demand for real balances equation

$$m_t - p_t = \phi y_t - \lambda r_t \tag{3.4.15}$$

Then since the expected depreciation in the exchange rate is given from (3.4.11) as

$$r_t - r_t^* = \alpha(\bar{s}_t - s_t)$$

the domestic interest rate can be eliminated between (3.4.15) and (3.4.11) to give

$$m_t - p_t = \phi y_t - \lambda r_t^* - \lambda\alpha(\bar{s}_t - s_t) \tag{3.4.16}$$

However, in equilibrium $s_t = \bar{s}_t$ and the above equation in equilibrium will be

$$\bar{p}_t = m_t - \phi y_t + \lambda r_t^*$$

On substituting this into (3.4.16) and rearranging

$$s_t = \bar{s}_t - (1/\lambda\alpha)(p_t - \bar{p}_t) \tag{3.4.17}$$

which shows the magnitude by which the exchange rate deviates from its long-run equilibrium given a deviation of domestic prices from its long-run equilibrium.

The main building blocks of the Dornbusch model are given by equations (3.4.1) to (3.4.4) inclusive with the adjustment in expectations mechanism given by (3.4.6) to some extent arbitrary. In fact (3.4.6) can be shown to be the expectations solutions under perfect foresight. A natural extension is to consider the model under rational expectations. From equations (3.4.1) and (3.4.4)

$$s_t = E_t s_{t+1} - (1/\lambda)(p_t - p_t^*) + \eta_t \tag{3.4.18}$$

where

$$\eta_t = -(\phi/\lambda)(y_t - y_t^*) + (1/\lambda)(m_t - m_t^*) - (1/\lambda)(k - k^*)$$

Hence

$$(p_t - p_t^*) = \lambda E_t s_{t+1} - \lambda s_t + \lambda\eta_t$$

and on substituting for $(p_{t-1} - p_{t-1}^*)$ from the above into (3.4.7) gives

$$\lambda E_t s_{t+1} - \lambda s_t + \lambda\eta_t - \beta_1 \lambda E_{t-1} s_t - \beta_0$$

$$+ \beta_1 \lambda s_{t-1} - \beta_1 \lambda\eta_{t-1} - \beta_2 s_t - \tau_t = 0$$

Hence

$$\lambda E_t s_{t+1} - \beta_1 \lambda E_{t-1} s_t - (\beta_2 + \lambda)s_t + \beta_1 \lambda s_{t-1} = x_t \tag{3.4.19}$$

where

$$x_t = \beta_0 + \tau_t - \lambda\eta_t + \beta_1\lambda\eta_{t-1}$$

On taking the rational expectations operator E_{t-1}, conditioned on all information available at time $t-1$ throughout (3.4.19) gives

$$\lambda E_{t-1}s_{t+1} - (\beta_1\lambda + \lambda + \beta_2)E_{t-1}s_t + \beta_1\lambda s_{t-1} = E_{t-1}x_t \qquad (3.4.20)$$

This equation is particularly interesting and is a second order forward rational expectations equation, which is linear in variables. Woo (1985) has considered the solution to a model which is slightly more complicated in dynamic structure and Wickens (1984) has considered the solution of this particular model. General solutions are provided by Whiteman (1983) and Pesaran (1988). The most direct method appears to be to consider the characteristic function of (3.4.20) which is

$$\lambda F^2 - (\beta_1 + \lambda + \beta_2)F + \beta_1\lambda = 0$$

where F is the forward operator, i.e. the inverse of the lag operator L. The solutions to this equation are

$$\zeta = (\beta_1\lambda + \lambda + \beta_2) \pm [(\beta_1\lambda + \lambda + \beta_2)^2 - 4\beta_1\lambda^2]^{1/2}/2\lambda$$

It is easily seen that one root $\zeta_1 < 1$, giving a stable solution, while the other $\zeta_2 > 1$ is unstable and thus implies that a saddlepoint solution exists. Hence (3.4.20) can be expressed as

$$\lambda(F - \zeta_1)(F - \zeta_2)s_{t-1} = E_{t-1}x_t$$

which can be rewritten as

$$-\lambda\zeta_2 F(1 - \zeta_1 F^{-1})(1 - \zeta_2^{-1}F)s_{t-1} = Fx_{t-1}$$

so that

$$(1 - \zeta_1 F^{-1})Fs_{t-1} = -Fx_{t-1}/[\lambda\zeta_2(1 - \zeta_2^{-1}F)]$$

and hence

$$s_t = \zeta_1 s_{t-1} - (\lambda\zeta_2)^{-1}\sum_{j=0}^{\infty}\zeta_2^{-j}E_t x_{t+j}$$

On taking expectations at time $t-1$

$$E_{t-1}s_t = \zeta_1 s_{t-1} - (\lambda\zeta_2)^{-1}\sum_{j=0}^{\infty}\zeta_2^{-j}E_{t-1}x_{t+j} \qquad (3.4.21)$$

and from the definition of rational expectations it follows that

$$s_t = E_{t-1}s_t + \varepsilon_t$$

where ε_t is the usual white noise process. Hence the solution of (3.4.20) is given by

$$s_t = \zeta_1 s_{t-1} - (\lambda\zeta_2)^{-1} \sum_{j=0}^{\infty} \zeta_2^{-j} E_{t-1} x_{t+j} + \varepsilon_t \qquad (3.4.22)$$

Wickens (1984) also writes the solution (3.4.22) as

$$s_t = \zeta_1 s_{t-1} - (\lambda\zeta_2)^{-1} \sum_{j=0}^{\infty} \zeta_2^{-j} E_{t-1} x_{t+j}$$

$$- [\lambda\zeta_2(1-\zeta_1)]^{-1} \sum_{j=0}^{\infty} \zeta_2^{-j}(E_t - E_{t-1}) x_{t+j}$$

so that the error term in (3.4.22) can be interpreted as the aggregate of revisions in expectations following the acquisition of new information. Under perfect foresight, rather than rational expectations, the last term in the above would be zero.

3.5   The Portfolio Balance model

The pure monetary model and Dornbusch's sticky price model are both essentially 'monetary' in their formulation, since they both consider the exchange rate to be determined in the short-run by the demand and supply of money in the two countries.

One of the central assumptions in both models is that domestic and foreign assets are perfect substitutes. However, evidence which will be examined in subsequent chapters, has accumulated to cast doubt on this assumption. Apart from short-run deviations from interest rate parity, the forward rate appears not to be the unbiased efficient expectation of the future spot rate so that uncovered interest rate parity seems to be invalid. Also many nominal exchange rates seem to be influenced by cumulative changes in the current account, while most portfolio managers subscribe to the existence of foreign exchange risk and believe that this risk cannot be completely eliminated by diversification. Hence the exchange rate is considered to be determined as a stock equilibrium on all financial markets, including the money market. The existence of risk implies that the interest rate differential is equal to the expected change in the exchange rate, plus a time varying risk premium. The inclusion of such a risk premium is the distinguishing feature of the Portfolio Balance model. Short-run portfolio equilibrium describes the allocation of a given stock of wealth among alternative securities on the basis of expected yields and exchange rates. Shocks to this portfolio equilibrium are assumed to be eliminated by instantaneous adjustment of exchange rates and interest rates, so that the owners of wealth produce a demand which exactly matches the supply of financial claims, which are fixed in the short run. Since goods prices are assumed fixed, changes in the exchange rate affect the balance of payments, so that the flexible exchange rates lead to changes in net foreign claims and hence wealth.

The role of current account changes is also important in the Portfolio Balance model setting in leading to a redistribution of international wealth. Deviations from the existing portfolio equilibrium are also important so that the interaction of stock and flow variables will explain exchange rate movements. The approach is appealing in the sense that it re-establishes traditional exchange rate analysis which emphasises the importance of the current account. In the Portfolio Balance model, money demand only depends on the domestic interest rate and nominal income. The rest of the world is assumed so large that foreign interest rates, prices, and incomes are taken as being exogenous. Furthermore, domestic and foreign securities are considered similar with respect to maturity and risk; there are no capital controls, no transaction costs nor other market imperfections. The only difference is the currency of denomination and the only risk is due to uncertainty concerning the expected exchange rate. To diversify exchange risk, investors divide their portfolio between domestic and foreign securities according to the expected relative return, given the risk premium. The risk premium is assumed to be a function of domestic and foreign wealth, W and W^*, respectively. The UIP condition then becomes

$$\frac{W_t^*}{S_t W_t} = \exp\{\tau + \beta[(r_t - r_t^*) - (E_t s_{t+1} - s_t)]\} \tag{3.5.1}$$

where $\beta > 0$. In practice wealth is most easily proxied by considering the supplies of domestic and foreign bonds, or securities. Then, as the risk premium increases in (3.5.1) following an increased interest rate differential or a decline in the expected change in the exchange rate, so investors will restructure their portfolio in favour of domestic securities. In the analysis of the Portfolio Balance model it is common to make any one of the following assumptions:

(i)   Domestic and foreign investors have the same portfolio preferences; so that W and W^* represent the supply of domestic and foreign government bonds in the existing currencies;

(ii)   The supply of domestic securities (in domestic currency terms) is only demanded by domestic residents, which as an assumption is only really applicable to a small country. However it is employed in many portfolio models and implies that the flow of capital can be interpreted as an increase or decrease of foreign securities on the domestic market.

(iii)   The foreign country is small and the domestic country is of non-trivial size, so that domestic residents do not hold any foreign securities.

(iv)   Domestic and foreign residents demand securities which have been issued in both countries; then a current account surplus leads to a redistribution of the world's wealth, and an appreciation of the domestic currency only occurs if domestic and foreign residents always wish to hold a higher proportion of their wealth in securities denominated in the domestic country.

The above assumptions are mutually exclusive and all help to simplify analysis of the model; assumption (iv) is probably the most realistic one.

On taking logarithms of equation (3.5.1) and denoting the logarithm of the wealth variables in lower case letters the equation can be incorporated into the Dornbusch sticky price model to give

$$(m_t - m_t^*) - (p_t - p_t^*) = (k - k^*) + \phi(y_t - y_t^*)$$
$$- \lambda(r_t - r_t^*) + \varepsilon_{1t} \qquad (3.5.2)$$

$$(d_t - d_t^*) = \gamma(y_t - y_t^*) - \sigma(r_t - r_t^*)$$
$$+ \omega(s_t - p_t + p_t^*) + (b_t - b_t^*) \qquad (3.5.3)$$

$$(p_t - p_t^*) - (p_{t-1} - p_{t-1}^*) = \partial[(d_t - d_t^*) - (y_t - y_t^*)] + \varepsilon_{2t} \qquad (3.5.4)$$

$$(r_t - r_t^*) - E_t(s_{t+1} - s_t) = \frac{1}{\beta}(-\tau + w_t^* - w_t - s_t) \qquad (3.5.5)$$

$$\bar{s}_t = \bar{p}_t - \bar{p}_t^* \qquad (3.5.6)$$

$$E_t s_{t+1} - s_t = \alpha(\bar{s}_t - s_t) \qquad (3.5.7)$$

Analysis of the above model is very similar to that of the previous section. Again the interest rate differential can be written as

$$r_t - r_t^* = \frac{1}{\lambda}[(k - k^*) - (m_t - m_t^*) + (p_t - p_t^*) + \phi(y_t - y_t^*)] \qquad (3.4.13)$$

and equation (3.4.7) will hold and the long-run solution for the exchange rate is again given by

$$\bar{s}_t = -(k - k^*) + (m_t - m_t^*) - \phi(y_t - y_t^*) \qquad (3.4.10)$$

with the overshooting equation remaining as

$$s_t = \bar{s}_t - (1/\lambda\alpha)(p_t - \bar{p}_t) \qquad (3.4.17)$$

and a slightly more complicated reduced form equation resulting for the spot exchange rate as

$$s_t = c_0 + c_1(m_t - m_t^*) + c_2(y_t - y_t^*) + c_3(p_{t-1} - p_{t-1}^*) + c_4(w_t - w_t^*)$$

where

$$c_j = \Omega b_j, \quad j = 0, 1 \ldots 4$$

$$\Omega = \alpha\beta/(1 + \alpha\beta)$$

and b_j are as defined in (3.4.14).

Various dynamic modifications can be introduced into the Portfolio Balance model and depend upon the assumptions about the degree of asset substitutability, the determinants and speed of adjustment of goods prices, the determinants of aggregate demands and the distribution of demand among goods produced in different countries.

3.6 Other variants of the monetary model

This section considers some simplified versions of the monetary model that replace the rational expectation of the future exchange rate with an observed proxy. This substantially reduces the econometric complexity of the model and has given rise to a wide range of estimated models that are discussed in Chapter 8.

From the PPP condition (3.2.1) the change in the exchange rate can be expressed as

$$s_{t+1} - s_t = (p_{t+1} - p_t) - (p^*_{t+1} - p^*_t)$$

and on taking expectations at time t

$$E_t \Delta s_{t+1} = E_t(\Delta p_{t+1} - \Delta p^*_{t+1}) \tag{3.6.1}$$

and from the uncovered interest rate parity condition (3.3.7), elimination of $E_t \Delta s_{t+1}$ from (3.6.1) gives

$$E_t(\Delta p_{t+1} - \Delta p^*_{t+1}) = (r_t - r^*_t) \tag{3.6.2}$$

Hence the expected currency depreciation in (3.3.7) is now expressed in terms of the expected inflation differential. Substitution of (3.6.2) into (3.3.6) then gives the *Flexible Price Monetary Model*, originally proposed by Frenkel (1976) and Bilson (1978)

$$s_t = (m_t - m^*_t) - \phi(y_t - y^*_t) + \lambda E_t(\Delta p_{t+1} - \Delta p^*_{t+1}) \tag{3.6.3}$$

Bilson (1978, p. 52) has noted that, 'the interest rate differential represents the relative holding cost of the two currencies compared to other real financial assets' and that, 'the Fisher condition may be used to express the nominal interest rate differential as the difference between the expected rates of inflation of the two price indices'. Frankel (1981) has referred to this expected rate of inflation as being equal to 'the rationally expected monetary growth rate'. For estimation purposes, most researchers generally use the long-term government bond rate as a proxy for expected inflation. A rationale for this assumption is that real returns on long-term bonds are equal for all countries so that differences in nominal rates reflect expected inflation rate differentials. The higher nominal rate is required to compensate for currency value erosion. Denoting π_t as the change in the long-term bond rates and π_t^* as the foreign equivalents, then an observable form of (3.6.3) is given by

$$s_t = (m_t - m_t^*) - \phi(y_t - y_t^*) + \lambda(\pi_{t+1} - \pi_{t+1}^*) \qquad (3.6.4)$$

The model also generates an expected positive sign of λ, since given the expected rate of inflation equal to the rationally expected monetary growth rate, an increase in money growth in the home country over the foreign country leads to faster growth of domestic prices. Moreover, ensuing higher inflation expectations will open up an immediate inflation premium on home country long-term bonds equal to the expected depreciation. This leads to an instantaneous depreciation of the domestic currency in order to satisfy PPP and uncovered interest parity.

A further variant of the basic monetary model and the above Flexible Price Model is the *Real Interest Rate Differential* (RID) model of Frankel (1979). The model maintains a sticky price assumption in the short run, similar to the Dornbusch model discussed in section 3.4, and the adjustment of the exchange rate to its equilibrium level depends on the real interest rate differential. The model assumes that PPP only holds in the long run, so that a long-run equilibrium version of (3.6.4) becomes

$$\bar{s}_t = (m_t - m_t^*) - \phi(y_t - y_t^*) + \lambda(\bar{\pi}_{t+1} - \bar{\pi}_{t+1}^*) \qquad (3.6.5)$$

Short-run deviations from the equilibrium exchange rate are determined according to the inflationary gap, so that

$$E_t s_{t+1} - s_t = \alpha(s_t - \bar{s}_t) + (\bar{\pi}_{t+1} - \bar{\pi}_{t+1}^*) \qquad (3.6.6)$$

and from (3.3.6)

$$r_t - r_t^* = \alpha(s_t - \bar{s}_t) + (\bar{\pi}_{t+1} - \bar{\pi}_{t+1}^*)$$

and hence

$$
\begin{aligned}
s_t - \bar{s}_t &= 1/\alpha[(r_t - r_t^*) - (\pi_{t+1} - \pi_{t+1}^*)] \\
&= 1/\alpha[(r_t - \pi_{t+1}) - (r_t^* - \pi_{t+1}^*)]
\end{aligned}
\qquad (3.6.7)
$$

Hence the spot rate departs from its equilibrium depending on the real interest rate differential.

On substituting for $\bar{s}$ from (3.6.5) into (3.6.7) gives

$$s_t = (m_t - m_t^*) - \phi(y_t - y_t^*)$$
$$+ (\lambda - 1/\alpha)(\pi_{t+1} - \pi_{t+1}^*) + 1/\alpha(r_t - r_t^*) \qquad (3.6.8)$$

The previous Flexible Price Model is given by the special case where the adjustment to the long-run equilibrium is instantaneous, so that $\alpha \to \infty$, and the coefficient of the interest rate differential is positive. Frankel's RID model can be written as

$$s_t = (m_t - m_t^*) - \phi(y_t - y_t^*) + \lambda(\pi_{t+1} - \pi_{t+1}^*)$$
$$- 1/\alpha((r_t - \pi_{t+1}) - (r_t^* - \pi_{t+1}^*)) \qquad (3.6.9)$$

where the last RID term represents the effect of overshooting.

This model has generated a large number of empirical investigations by Frankel (1979, 1981), Haynes and Stone (1981), Driskill and Sheffrin (1981), and many others. The econometric work is discussed in detail in Chapter 8.

3.7   Currency substitution models

The models discussed in the previous sections have relied on the implicit assumption that domestic residents do not hold foreign money; thus the elasticity of substitution in demand between national money supplies is assumed to be zero. However, foreign exchange market participants have an incentive, as is usual in portfolio theory, to hold a basket of currencies depending on the risk and expected rates of return of the specific currencies in the portfolio. The lifting of exchange controls in the 1970s by most of the participating countries in the floating regime enhanced the ability of foreign exchange market participants to substitute between different currencies. The implication of currency substitution for the behaviour of exchange rates can be examined in the following simple model.

The model is formulated in terms of the following behavioural equations.

$$m_t - p_t = \theta(w_t') + E_{t-1}[\alpha(i_t - i_t') + \sigma(i_t - i_t^*)] \qquad (3.7.1)$$

$$m_t^* - p_t^* = \theta^*(w_t') + E_{t-1}[\alpha^*(i_t^* - i_t') + \sigma^*(i_t^* - i_t)] \qquad (3.7.2)$$

$$E_{t-1}(i_t - i_t^*) \equiv (r_t - r_t^*) - E_{t-1}(\pi_t - \pi_t^*) \qquad (3.7.3)$$

$$E_t \Delta s_{t+1} = E_{t-1}(\pi_t - \pi_t^*) \qquad (3.7.4)$$

where m_t is the nominal quantity of money, p_t is the price level, i is the real yield on domestic currencies, i' is the real yield for a unique non-monetary asset, r_t is the nominal interest rate and w' is the stock of world wealth or production. All variables are in logarithms and asterisks denote foreign equivalents. The first two equations give the demand for money functions; the difference in real interest rates is given by equation (3.7.3) and equation (3.7.4) expresses PPP in terms of the expected inflation differential. In this type of model arbitrage occurs with money and not commodities. Subtracting (3.7.2) from (3.7.1) and using (3.7.3) and (3.7.4) gives the currency substitution model proposed by Kouri and Macedo (1978)

$$s_t = m_t - m_t^* + \theta^* - \theta - (\alpha + 2\sigma)[r_t - r_t^* - (Es_{t+1} - s_t)]$$

To complete the model it is again necessary to formulate a hypothesis on the formation of exchange rate expectations, which Kouri and Macedo assumed to be adaptive or rational. If the quantities of money are assumed to be exogenous, the model has the same implications for the exchange rate as in monetary models. An interesting feature of currency substitution models concerns the influence of the term $(\alpha + 2\sigma)$. The higher the coefficient of substitution σ between two currencies, then the higher the variation given by $Es_{t+1} - s_t$. At the limit when σ is infinite, the currencies are perfect substitutes, and the exchange rate is no longer defined or is extremely unstable.

These results have important consequences for the conduct of economic policy. For a long time it seemed that by virtue of a flexible exchange rate regime different countries could pursue independent monetary policies. However one implication of currency substitution models is that this freedom no longer exists. According to McKinnon (1982), the world demand for all existing money is stable, but the demand for individual currencies is unstable because of the substitution phenomena. This viewpoint accords with the work of Brittain (1981) who demonstrated that the velocity of circulation in the U.S., Germany and the U.K. could be explained with the aid of a model of portfolio choice. A similar approach was pursued by Brillembourg and Schadler (1979) whose analysis explicitly incorporated the risks associated with different foreign currencies. Using monthly data for the period March 1973 to June 1978, for the French franc, Swiss franc, Deutschmark, pound sterling, the yen, the Canadian dollar and the U.S. dollar, they found that there existed a strong complementarity between currencies which were all substitutes for the U.S. dollar.

3.8   Recent developments and concluding remarks

The preceding sections described some competing theories of exchange rate determination. This section describes some more recent studies which have attempted to integrate many theoretical aspects which previously remained disassociated. Articles, such as Kouri (1983), Dornbusch and Fisher (1980), Stockman (1980) and Helpman and Razin (1982), have opened promising avenues of research for the future.

Kouri (1983) developed a model to explain the dynamic interaction between the components of current-account flows and capital account stocks of foreign exchange. He assumed a small country where foreign residents do not hold domestic assets, and a world where prices and interest rates are stable. At any given moment domestic residents hold the quantity F^0 of foreign assets. Suppose that they desire to hold the quantity F^d such that its value in domestic money is a function f of their non-human wealth w. Thus f is the desired function of wealth to be held in foreign assets and is a function of the yields of domestic assets i and foreign assets $(i^* + d^e)$, where i^* is the foreign interest rate and d^e the expected appreciation of foreign exchange. Then the short-run equilibrium condition in the foreign exchange market is given by

$$F^d S \equiv f(i, i^* + d^e)w = F^0 S$$

and in long-run equilibrium d^e must be zero. It should be noted that demand F^d expressed in foreign currency, is a decreasing function of the spot price of foreign exchange S.

In the absence of intervention on the foreign exchange markets, a current-account surplus (or deficit) $S^p(D)$ is necessarily equal to the change in the stock of foreign assets F so that

$$\dot{F} = S^p(D)$$

In this framework a country in current account surplus must experience a currency appreciation to induce domestic residents to acquire additional foreign assets and a deficit country must experience currency depreciation in order to induce sales of foreign denominated assets. Such a phenomenon, termed the acceleration hypothesis by Kouri conforms to what generally has been observed. However, if investors expectations are rational, the progressive evolution of the exchange rate predicted by the model, must be forecast without any systematic error. Furthermore, the exchange rate should adjust whenever there is a change in expectations. Kouri's model has the advantage of explaining the transition from the short to the long run and of integrating the current and the capital accounts in analysing the foreign exchange market. However, it still neglects a number of important phenomena since it is a partial equilibrium model and can be further generalised.

Dornbusch and Fisher (1980) extend Kouri's model in a general-equilibrium context, relating the current account balance to savings behaviour as a function of desired wealth. Unlike the earlier studies, the authors assume that the traded goods produced in the two countries differ. They also consider the effect of anticipated future disturbances on the behaviour of the exchange rate and enrich the analytical framework by introducing the terms of trade as a supplementary endogenous variable. Their model enables a distinction to be drawn between the variation in the exchange rate due to monetary disturbances without real effects and the variations induced by a change in the relative prices of imported goods as a ratio of exported goods. It also extends Kouri's approach in emphasising the importance of wealth effects. Wealth accumulation together with agent's expectations play the most important role in determining the dynamic behaviour of exchange risk. In this set up, it is the agents, who are supposed to increase or decrease their savings in order to progressively return to their optimal wealth position. Hence, a deficit in the current account does not reveal a weakness in competitiveness but a deliberate desire to reduce the wealth of a country by accrued consumption.

Dornbusch and Fisher showed that the acceleration hypothesis no longer holds in cases where there is an anticipated future disturbance. Suppose that it was announced that money supply would increase at some future date. The exchange rate would initially jump and then be followed by further gradual depreciation. However, given rational expectations the anticipated depreciation would lower desired real balances, wealth, and spending and thus result in a current-account surplus. Thus if a current account surplus and currency appreciation were observed, one could conclude that agents were reacting to unanticipated news about contemporaneous events. Conversely, if a current account surplus and currency depreciation were observed, then agents were supposedly reacting to the expectations of a future disturbance.

The above models do not provide a justification for the form of the demand for money functions. Stockman (1980) addressed this problem and showed how the supply and demand for money functions were related to the demand and supply for foreign goods. He assumed a two-country–two-goods world, and two liquidity constraints faced by agents. The first liquidity constraint requires the payment for domestic goods to be made with domestic money balances; the second requires that the purchase of imported goods should be regulated with foreign currencies. These two constraints influence the intertemporal behaviour of agents and imply that monetary balances are determined by the usual transactions motives and also by precautionary motives in the event of uncertainty regarding future income.

Stockman's model described the equilibrium exchange rate, the factors which influenced the terms of trade and the different components of the balance of payments. The model assumed very general behaviour for agents and produced tangible results amenable to empirical testing.

Motivated by Stockman's (1980) approach, Helpman and Razin (1982) developed a more complete model which described the determination of the equilibrium exchange rate, the domestic interest rate and the prices of non-traded goods in each country. Focusing on 'real' variables different from those in the Stockman model, they modelled the behaviour of the real exchange rate over time as a function of differences in the rate of time preference among countries. It assumed that agents hold domestic and foreign money balances due to the liquidity constraints with which they are confronted. It also assumed that each agent maximises the expected value of a utility function of an additive type and that all markets adjusted instantaneously. However, the authors enriched the basic model by analysing the general case where savings behaviour differed in each country.

To have a better understanding of the original contribution of Helpman and Razin, consider the extremely simplified case where two countries A and B are identical except that the residents of A have a greater propensity to consume than the residents in B, who initially lend to the residents of A to finance an excess of consumption on the market for traded goods; A then accumulates a deficit in its trade balance leading to negative national saving. Conversely, because the residents in A have a higher propensity to consume than those in B, it must lead to a stronger demand in A on the market for non-traded goods than in B; consequently the relative prices of these goods and the cost of living must initially be higher in A than in B. (i.e. the real exchange rate of A must depreciate).

Following this, the residents of A must honour the contractual debt owed to residents of B, since this necessarily implies a progressive reduction in the commercial deficit and its eventual transformation into a surplus. During the transitional phase of convergence to long-run equilibrium, the wealth of the residents of A diminishes and that of the residents of B must increase; these will thus see their demand for non-traded goods increased, which then implies a progressive reduction in the disparities of purchasing power parity. It follows that during the transitional period the rate of appreciation of money in A must remain less than the inflation differential, for the reason that there is a progressive increase in the prices of non-traded goods in B as a ratio to their prices in A. This increase in prices in B will then lead to a depreciation in its real exchange rate.

Helpman and Razin perceived the current account balance as the outcome of the differences in the time preferences between countries. Consequently, the real exchange rate adjusts in response to this time preference. They also view the real exchange rate, which they define as the price of tradeable goods relative to non-tradeable goods, as being affected only by unanticipated changes in money supply. The effects of unanticipated changes in money supply, however, arise because they affect the value of real external indebtedness, which accompanies the evolution of current account surpluses and deficits over time.

The model of Helpman and Razin provides an alternative explanation of the reasons why the evolution of the exchange rate does not conform to the hypothesis of PPP; an explanation which does not depend on the traditional arguments of the differences in productivity or the inflexibility of prices. Hence, the exchange rate changes in response to desired differences in spending relative to income in the context of intertemporal utility maximisation and leads to movement of resources between the traded and non-traded sectors of the economy.

Appendix

It will already have become apparent that a considerable number of models concerning the foreign exchange market involve the expectations of certain variables. In keeping with the recent developments in the new classical macroeconomics the assumption of rationality of expectations is now commonplace, and as in other areas of macroeconomics, is generally invoked in foreign exchange market literature. The purpose of this appendix is to provide an introduction to the relationship between adaptive, extrapolative and rational expectations and to consider the solutions and econometric testing of some models involving rational expectations. It should be noted that the material presented in this section is extremely selective and just concerns some of the models encountered in the rest of this book. No attempt is made at giving anything like a general treatment. Readers who are interested in the general application of rational expectations in macroeconomics, should see Begg (1982), Attfield *et al.* (1985), or Minford and Peel (1983).

Chapter 2 introduced the idea of a fair game sequence, and the rational expectation of a random variable y_t was defined as the expectation of y conditional on all relevant and available information at time $t - h$, say. Then

$$E_{t-h} y_t = E(y_t | \Omega_{t-h}) \tag{3.A.1}$$

where Ω_{t-h} is the set of all relevant and available information at time $t - h$. Thus agents when forming the expectation are considered to have perfect information about the structure of the economy (or model), the relevant parameters and knowledge of the current and past values of all the variables within the model. For the moment at least, nothing is being said about learning processes made by agents, nor the problems of groups of agents having heterogeneous sets of information.

Since y_t is included in Ω_t, it follows that

$$E_t y_t = y_t$$

91

Rational expectations made one period ahead will have the property that

$$y_t - E_{t-1}y_t = \varepsilon_t \tag{3.A.2}$$

where ε_t is an uncorrelated process. Generally ε_t will be considered to be white noise, or a sequence of uncorrelated random variables with mean zero and constant variance σ^2. The rational expectation $E_{t-1}y_t$ is then optimal in the sense that it is the expectation of y_t which is unbiased and minimises the one step ahead prediction mean squared error. Equations (3.A.1) and (3.A.2) define two of the general properties of rational expectations. Before considering some explicit aspects of rational expectations it is convenient to consider two suboptimal expectations schemes. Since Keynes (1936), the notion of expectations of economic variables has always been considered important by economists, but since expectations are generally unobservable they have to be artificially generated from available data. A well-known and intuitively reasonable method is the so-called *Adaptive Expectations* mechanism, which is defined as

$$E_{t-1}y_t - E_{t-2}y_{t-1} = \theta(y_{t-1} - E_{t-2}y_{t-1}) \quad 0 < \theta < 1 \tag{3.A.3}$$

This method was originally proposed by Cagan (1956) in a demand for money in a hyperinflations study, and also used by Friedman (1957) in formulating a permanent income stream. The model simply states that the markets or individuals expectation is adjusted proportionately to the amount the previous periods expectation departed from the actual.

By use of the lag operator, (3.A.3) can be expressed as

$$[1 - (1 - \theta)L]E_{t-1}y_t = \theta y_{t-1}$$

and hence

$$E_{t-1}y_t = \theta \sum_{j=0}^{\infty} (1 - \theta)^j y_{t-1-j} \tag{3.A.4}$$

so that the expectations scheme places geometrically declining weight on past observations $y_{t-1}, y_{t-2} \cdots$.

In the first of two famous papers, Muth (1960) showed that (3.A.4) is optimal in the sense of providing minimum mean squared error forecasts, if the process y_t is generated by the ARIMA $(0, 1, 1)$ process

$$y_t - y_{t-1} = \varepsilon_t - (1 - \theta)\varepsilon_{t-1} \tag{3.A.5}$$

where ε_t is a white noise process with zero mean, constant variance σ^2 and is serially uncorrelated. This can be simply seen by expressing (3.A.5) as

$$\varepsilon_t = [1 - (1 - \theta)L]^{-1}(1 - L)y_t$$
$$= [1 + (1 - \theta)L + (1 - \theta)^2L^2 + \cdots](y_t - y_{t-1})$$

so that

$$\varepsilon_t = y_t - \theta[y_{t-1} + (1-\theta)y_{t-2} + (1-\theta)^2 y_{t-3} + \cdots]$$

and hence

$$y_t = \theta \sum_{j=0}^{\infty} (1-\theta)^j y_{t-1-j} + \varepsilon_t \qquad (3.A.6)$$

Then

$$E[y_t - E_{t-1} y_t]^2 = E(\varepsilon_t^2) = \sigma^2$$

and (3.A.4) is trivially seen to be the minimum mean squared error predictor of y_t, conditional on its past history of observations available at time $t - 1$.

Box and Jenkins (1970) and many subsequent time series studies have concluded that the ARIMA $(0, 1, 1)$ model, (3.A.5) is perhaps the most commonly occurring non-seasonal linear time series model, so that (3.A.4) may well be a reasonable method to form expectations. However, there is no general reason why (3.A.5) should always be a good representation of an empirical time series and it is natural to seek a method of generating expectations which is an optimal predictor of a particular time series. However any time series which is covariance stationary, or stationary in its second moment will possess a Wold decomposition which allows it to be expressed as an infinite autoregressive representation or infinite moving average representation. The former autoregressive representation can be written as

$$y_t = \sum_{j=1}^{\infty} \pi_j y_{t-j} + \varepsilon_t \qquad (3.A.7)$$

and the minimum mean squared error predictor, or expectation of y_t contingent on knowledge of the past history of the process at time $t - 1$ is given by

$$E_{t-1} y_t = \sum_{j=1}^{\infty} \pi_j y_{t-j} \qquad (3.A.8)$$

In this instance (3.A.8) is known as the *Extrapolative Expectation* since it possesses minimum mean squared error within the class of linear predictors. The process (3.A.7) which can be written as

$$\pi(L) y_t = \varepsilon_t$$

where

$$\pi(L) = 1 - \pi_1 L - \pi_2 L^2 - \cdots$$

may possibly be non-stationary, with either unit roots or explosive roots in its autoregressive representation. As long as these roots are known and the appropriate predictor (3.A.8) used, the theory will go through as before.

The above schemes of Adaptive and Extrapolative expectations are obviously sub-optimal in the sense they only condition on the past history of y_t. To see the relationship of these two methods with that of rational expectations which conditions on the complete model, consider the following example, which is based on the bivariate autoregressive model

$$\begin{bmatrix} \alpha_{11}(L) & \alpha_{12}(L) \\ \alpha_{21}(L) & \alpha_{22}(L) \end{bmatrix} \begin{bmatrix} y_t \\ x_t \end{bmatrix} = \begin{bmatrix} \varepsilon_{1t} \\ \varepsilon_{2t} \end{bmatrix} \tag{3.A.9}$$

$$A(L)Y_t = \varepsilon_t$$

where $\alpha_{ij}(L)$ is a pth order polynomial in the lag operator,

$$E(\varepsilon_t \varepsilon_s') = \begin{cases} \Omega & s = t \\ 0 & s \neq t \end{cases}$$

$$\Omega = \begin{bmatrix} \sigma_1^2 & \sigma_{12}^2 \\ \sigma_{12}^2 & \sigma_2^2 \end{bmatrix}$$

and all the roots of $A(L)$ are assumed to lie outside the unit circle, so that the process y_t is stationary.

On solving out (3.A.9):

$$Y_t = A(L)^{-1} \varepsilon_t$$

Hence

$$|A(L)| Y_t = \text{adjoint } A(L) \varepsilon_t$$

which in the bivariate case is

$$[\alpha_{11}(L)\alpha_{22}(L) - \alpha_{12}(L)\alpha_{21}(L)] \begin{bmatrix} y_t \\ x_t \end{bmatrix} = \begin{bmatrix} \alpha_{22}(L) & -\alpha_{12}(L) \\ -\alpha_{21}(L) & \alpha_{11}(L) \end{bmatrix} \begin{bmatrix} \varepsilon_{1t} \\ \varepsilon_{2t} \end{bmatrix}$$

This type of formulation is sometimes known as an autoregressive final form, although in this case no exogenous variables are included in the model. The above equation shows that both variables, y_t, and x_t will have an ARMA time series representation. Applying the results on aggregation of time series developed by Granger and Morris (1976) and Tiao and Guttman (1980), it can be shown that the *invertible* univariate ARMA representations will have disturbance variance which generally exceed σ_1^2 and σ_2^2 in the original model (3.A.9). As a simple example, consider

$$\begin{bmatrix} 1 & -\beta L \\ 0 & 1 - \gamma L \end{bmatrix} \begin{bmatrix} y_t \\ x_t \end{bmatrix} = \begin{bmatrix} \varepsilon_{1t} \\ \varepsilon_{2t} \end{bmatrix}$$

which can be written as

$$y_t = \beta x_{t-1} + \varepsilon_{1t} \tag{3.A.10}$$

$$x_t = \gamma x_{t-1} + \varepsilon_{2t} \tag{3.A.11}$$

Solving out for x_t gives

$$y_t = \beta \frac{\varepsilon_{2t-1}}{(1-\gamma L)} + \varepsilon_{1t}$$

and hence

$$y_t = \gamma y_{t-1} + \beta \varepsilon_{2t-1} + \varepsilon_{1t} - \gamma \varepsilon_{1t-1} \tag{3.A.12}$$

The above composite disturbance is MA(1) and the univariate model for y_t is ARMA (1, 1) of the form

$$y_t = \gamma y_{t-1} + v_t - \theta v_{t-1} \tag{3.A.13}$$

where v_t is a zero mean white noise process with variance σ_v^2. On equating the autocovariances of (3.A.12) and (3.A.13)

$$(1 - 2\theta\gamma + \theta^2)\sigma_v^2 = \sigma_1^2(1 + \gamma^2) + \beta^2 \sigma_2^2$$

and

$$(1 - \gamma\theta)(\gamma - \theta)\sigma_v^2 = \beta\gamma\sigma_2^2$$

Solving the above equations will lead to two solutions for θ, one invertible and one non-invertible and hence two solutions for σ_v^2.

The rational expectation $E_{t-1} y_t$ will be based on the entire current and past history of x and y at time $t - 1$, so that

$$E_{t-1} y_t = E(y_t \mid y_{t-1}, y_{t-2} \cdots x_{t-1}, x_{t-2} \cdots)$$

From (3.A.10) the rational expectation can be trivially seen to be

$$E_{t-1} y_t = \beta x_{t-1}$$

with mean squared error σ_1^2. Now consider the optimal extrapolative expectation y_t^e, which is *only* based on the past history of y_t. Then

$$y_t^e = E(y_t \mid y_{t-1} y_{t-2} \cdots)$$

and from (3.A.13)

$$y_t^e = \gamma y_{t-1} - \theta v_{t-1}$$

Given numerical values of $\gamma = 0.50$, $\beta = 1$, $\sigma_1^2 = 1$ and $\sigma_2^2 = 2$ the invertible form of (3.A.12) will be

$$y_t = 0.50 y_{t-1} + v_t - 0.10 v_{t-1}$$

$$\sigma_v^2 = 1.32$$

Hence $\mathrm{mse}(E_{t-1}\,y_t) = E(y_t - E_{t-1}\,y_t)^2 = \sigma_1^2 = 1$

and $\quad y_t^e = 0.50 y_{t-1} - 0.10 v_{t-1}$

with

$$\mathrm{mse}\ y_t^e = E(y_t - y_t^e) = \sigma_v^2 = 1.32$$

so that with these parameter values the extrapolative expectation is 32 per cent inefficient relative to the rational expectation.

In order to see the mechanical manipulations required to find a rational expectations solution in a model, a convenient starting point is the other famous article by Muth (1961), who considered the following three equation model with market clearing

$$d_t = -\beta p_t \tag{3.A.14}$$

$$s_t = \gamma E_{t-1} p_t + x_t \tag{3.A.15}$$

$$s_t = d_t$$

where d is demand, s is supply, p is price and x is an exogenous variable responsible for other supply shocks, and all variables are measured as deviations from their equilibrium values. Solving the model gives

$$\beta p_t = -\gamma E_{t-1} p_t - x_t \tag{3.A.16}$$

On taking the expectations operator at time $t-1$ through the above gives

$$(\beta + \gamma) E_{t-1} p_t = -E_{t-1} x_t \tag{3.A.17}$$

so that the rational expectation of price is dependent on the expectation of the exogenous variable x_t. For example if

$$x_t = \rho x_{t-1} + \varepsilon_{1t}$$

where ε_{1t} is a white noise process with zero mean and variance σ^2 then $E_{t-1} x_t = \rho x_{t-1}$ and

$$E_{t-1} p_t = -\frac{\rho}{(\beta + \gamma)} x_{t-1}$$

Suppose x_t has the interpretation in (3.A.15) of being a white noise process itself, so that in (3.A.17) it follows that unless $\beta + \gamma = 0$ then $E_{t-1} p_t = 0$ and from (3.A.16)

$$p_t = -\frac{1}{\beta} x_t$$

and from (3.A.14) and (3.A.15)

$$d_t = s_t = u_t$$

so that the rational expectations solution implies that the only difference between the variables and their equilibrium values is due to unanticipated random shocks.

In his article, Muth (1961) assumed x_t in the supply equation (3.A.15) to follow the random walk process

$$x_t = x_{t-1} + \varepsilon_t$$

Then from (3.A.17)

$$(\beta + \gamma)E_{t-1}p_t = -x_{t-1}$$

and on substituting for x_t from the above into (3.A.16) gives

$$\beta p_t = -\gamma E_{t-1}p_t + (\beta + \gamma)E_t p_{t+1}$$

hence price is now generated by the Adaptive Expectations Mechanism

$$E_t p_{t+1} = \left(\frac{\gamma}{\beta+\gamma}\right)E_{t-1}p_t + \left(\frac{\beta}{\beta+\gamma}\right)p_t \tag{3.A.18}$$

In this rather pathological case, the rational expectations solution for prices (3.A.18) is then identical to the adaptive expectations formation. To an extent this result is pathological since it results from the assumption of x following a random walk process; however it may have misled the economics profession into thinking that rational expectations were not significantly different to adaptive expectations. Hence almost a decade elapsed, following Muth (1961) before the reemergence of rational expectations.

When dealing with econometric models a large literature has developed on the identification and estimation of models containing the rational expectation of random variables conditioned on current or past information. For example, Hoffman and Schmidt (1981) consider the model

$$y_t = \beta'x_t + \alpha E_{t-1}y_t + \varepsilon_t, \tag{3.A.19}$$

where x_t is a k dimensional vector of exogenous variables, β is the corresponding vector of parameters and ε_t is a white noise disturbance. Hoffman and Schmidt (1981) consider the identification of (3.A.19) under a variety of assumptions concerning the data generating process for the exogenous variables x_t. For example in the simple case of one exogenous variable generated by an AR(2) process the two equation model is

$$y_t = \beta x_t + \alpha E_{t-1}y_t + \varepsilon_{1t}$$
$$x_t = \varphi_1 x_{t-1} + \varphi_2 x_{t-2} + \varepsilon_{2t} \tag{3.A.20}$$

which can be expressed as

$$y_t = \beta x_t + \alpha\beta\varphi_1(1-\alpha)^{-1}x_{t-1} + \alpha\beta\varphi_2(1-\alpha)^{-1}x_{t-2} + \varepsilon_{1t}$$
$$x_t = \varphi_1 x_{t-1} + \varphi_2 x_{t-2} + \varepsilon_{2t}$$

(3.A.21)

When contrasted with the unrestricted distributed lag model (3.A.22)

$$y_t = \gamma_0 x_t + \gamma_1 x_{t-1} + \gamma_2 x_{t-2} + \varepsilon_{1t}$$
$$x_t = \varphi_1 x_{t-1} + \varphi_2 x_{t-2} + \varepsilon_{2t}$$

(3.A.22)

it can be seen that the 4 parameter rational expectations model (3.A.21) imposes one restriction on the 5 parameter model (3.A.22). The restriction is seen to be given by

$$\varphi_1\gamma_2 - \varphi_2\gamma_1 = 0$$

Estimation and testing of models with such non-linear restrictions are discussed by Hoffman and Schmidt (1981) and Gregory and Veall (1985).

Wallis (1980) and Revankar (1980) have considered inference in simultaneous equation models of the form

$$By_t + A_1 E_{t-1}y_{1t} + Cx_t = \varepsilon_t$$

(3.A.23)

where y_t is a vector of g endogenous variables, y_{1t} is a vector of the first $h < g$ endogenous variables, x_t is a k dimensional vector of exogenous variables, ε_t is a vector white noise process and B, A_1 and C are appropriately dimensioned coefficient matrices. As long as the extra identification requirement $h \leqslant k$ is satisfied, and given some data generation process for x_t, such as a vector autoregression, then (3.A.23) can be written in terms of observables with coefficients which are non-linear functions of the parameters of the original model. Inference is again possible due to the uniqueness of the solution for $E_{t-1}y_{1t}$.

In particular (3.A.23) can be written as

$$By_t + AE_{t-1}y_t + Cx_t = \varepsilon_t,$$

where $A = (A_1 \vdots 0)$. The Reduced Form of the model is

$$y_t = (-B^{-1}A)E_{t-1}y_t - B^{-1}Cx_t + B^{-1}\varepsilon_t$$

(3.A.24)

On taking expectations conditional on information at time $t-1$ through (3.A.24) we obtain

$$E_{t-1}y_t = -(I + B^{-1}A)^{-1}B^{-1}CE_{t-1}x_t$$

(3.A.25)

Suppose x_t is generated by the first order vector autoregression

$$x_t = Fx_{t-1} + \varepsilon_{2t}$$

then

$$E_{t-1}x_t = Fx_{t-1} \tag{3.A.26}$$

and substitution of (3.A.25) and (3.A.26) into the original model gives a model in terms of observables which can be represented as

$$y_t = B^{-1}A(I + B^{-1}A)B^{-1}CFx_{t-1} - B^{-1}Cx_t + B^{-1}\varepsilon_t \tag{3.A.27}$$

However many models of exchange rate determination are similar to asset pricing models which involve the rational expectations of future variables. The simplest example of this is the scalar model

$$E_t y_{t+1} = \alpha y_t + x_t \tag{3.A.28}$$

Assuming x_t is stationary and has the infinite moving average representation

$$x_t = \sum_{j=0}^{\infty} a_j \varepsilon_{t-j}$$

and assuming a solution for y_t of the form

$$y_t = \sum_{j=0}^{\infty} c_j \varepsilon_{t-j}$$

it follows that

$$E_t y_{t+1} = \sum_{j=0}^{\infty} c_{j+1} \varepsilon_{t-j}$$

which on substitution in (3.A.28) realises

$$\sum_{j=0}^{\infty} c_{j+1} \varepsilon_{t-j} = \alpha \sum_{j=0}^{\infty} c_j \varepsilon_{t-j} + \sum_{j=0}^{\infty} a_j \varepsilon_{t-j}$$

and on equating coefficients of $\varepsilon_t, \varepsilon_{t-1}, \varepsilon_{t-2} \dots$ we obtain:

$$c_1 = \alpha c_0 + a_0$$

$$c_2 = \alpha c_1 + a_1$$

$$\vdots$$

$$c_{j+1} = \alpha c_j + a_j \tag{3.A.28}$$

which gives multiple solutions since c_0 is a free parameter. A general solution of (3.A.28) is of the form

$$c_j = \alpha^j c_0 + \sum_{k=0}^{j-1} \alpha^k a_{j-1-k} \tag{3.A.29}$$

Hence an infinite number of possible stochastic processes will satisfy (3.A.29) depending on the initial condition c_0. If x_t is the AR(1) process

$$x_t = \lambda x_{t-1} + \varepsilon_t \quad |\lambda| < 1$$

then $a_{j-1-k} = \lambda^{j-1-k}$ in (3.A.29) and

$$y_t = \sum_{j=0}^{\infty} \{\alpha^j c_0 + (\lambda^j + \alpha^j)/(\lambda - \alpha)\}\varepsilon_{t-j}$$

and it is straightforward to show that y_t follows the ARMA (2, 1) process

$$y_t = (\alpha + \lambda)y_{t-1} - \alpha\lambda y_{t-2} + \varepsilon_t - \theta\varepsilon_{t-1}$$

where the moving average parameter θ is a complicated function of all the original parameters including c_0.

Evans and Honkapohja (1986) have extended this result by showing that

$$y_t = \sum_{j=0}^{k} \alpha_j E_{t-1} y_{t+j} + \sum_{j=1}^{l} \gamma_j y_{t-j} + \varepsilon_t \tag{3.A.30}$$

$$\varepsilon_t \text{ iid } (0, \sigma^2)$$

is consistent with the process $y_t \sim \text{ARMA } (k+l, l)$.

In general two solutions of the equation

$$y_t = \alpha E_t y_{t+1} + x_t \tag{3.A.31}$$

are considered particularly useful. One the backward solution is

$$y_t = -\sum_{j=0}^{\infty} \alpha^{-j} x_{t-j} \tag{3.A.32}$$

requires $|\alpha| < 1$ and x_t to be stationary. The other, known as the forward solution is of the form

$$y_t = \sum_{j=0}^{\infty} \alpha^j E_t x_{t+j} \tag{3.A.33}$$

The form of the solution (3.A.33) assumes the existence of the transversality condition that $\lim_{j\to\infty} \alpha^j E_t x_{t+j} = 0$. There are many possible ways this could be violated in which case bubble solutions exist: in particular see Flood and Garber (1980), Blanchard (1979) and Meese (1986). Many of these ideas appear to have interesting applications for the behaviour of asset prices in general.

A further solution to (3.A.31) derived by Gourieroux, Laffont and Monfort (1982) is to assume that x_t follows the ARMA (p, q) process $\phi(L)x_t = \theta(L)\varepsilon_t$ in which case (3.A.31) can be reduced to

$$\theta(L)y_t = C(L)x_t$$

which is basically a rational distributed lag model. In particular

$$C(L) = \sum_{j=0}^{p-1} C_j L^j, \qquad C_0 = \theta(\alpha)/\phi(\alpha)$$

and

$$C(L) = (L-\alpha)^{-1}[L\theta(L) - C_0\phi(L)].$$

CHAPTER 4

Statistical analysis of exchange rates and tests of efficiency

4.1 Introduction

This chapter considers the statistical time series properties of nominal exchange rates and attempts to give empirical content to the theory concerning efficient markets developed in Chapter 2. A full understanding of the methodology used in this chapter requires a reasonable working knowledge of time series analysis and dynamic econometric models as found in Harvey (1981a and b). However, the techniques are used for particular problems in such a way that it should be possible for readers with a limited background in these areas to still obtain some understanding of the approach. The general strategy is to state the technique or model which is used and to refer the reader to other texts for proofs or further information.

4.2 Time series analysis of exchange rates

The appendix to Chapter 1 contained the graphs of monthly nominal exchange rates plotted between March 1973 and June 1985. An initial exploratory technique, which usefully takes precedent over more complex model building, is to consider the univariate time series properties of the exchange rate series. Apart from giving understanding of the internal characteristics and mechanisms generating the series, this analysis is also important for testing forms of the efficient market hypothesis and for measuring volatility and risk.

We begin by giving an outline of some basic statistical techniques, models and tests that will be used. The treatment is in no way self-contained and merely states the method and references for more detailed reading. The intention is to alert readers to the type of method being used and give them the opportunity to follow up the more detailed descriptions provided in the references.

In the following we consider a realisation of a single time series y_t, measured at discrete intervals of time, t. The series may, for example, be a simple transformation of a spot exchange rate. The theoretical autocovariance function of lag j for y_t is given by

$$\gamma_j = E(y_t y_{t+j}) - E(y_t)E(y_{t+j}) \tag{4.2.1}$$

the theoretical autocorrelation function is given by

$$\rho_j = \gamma_j/\gamma_0$$

with spectrum

$$f(\omega) = \frac{1}{2\pi} \sum_{j=-\infty}^{\infty} e^{-i\omega j} \gamma_j, \tag{4.2.2}$$

where i is the complex number. Given a sample of n observations of y_t the autocovariance function (4.2.1) is estimated by the sample autocovariance function

$$r_j = \frac{1}{n} \sum_{t=1}^{n-j} (y_t - \bar{y})(y_{t+j} - \bar{y}) \tag{4.2.3}$$

where $\bar{y} = \frac{1}{n} \sum_{t=1}^{n} y_t$. The estimated autocorrelation function is then

$$c_j = r_j/r_0$$

Under the null hypothesis that y_t is a realization from an uncorrelated or 'white noise' process, then

$$\sqrt{n}(r_j) \sim N(0, 1)$$

so that

$$\operatorname{var} r_j \approx \frac{1}{n}$$

which allows approximate significance levels to be calculated for estimated autocorrelation coefficients.

A weakly or covariance stationary process will possess a constant mean and variance and autocorrelation function which is just a function of lag j and is independent of time; then Wold's decomposition states that any stationary process y_t can be uniquely represented as the sum of two mutually uncorrelated processes ζ_t and η_t. These processes are respectively a purely indeterministic one-sided infinite moving average process of a stationary uncorrelated sequence (i.e. 'white noise') and the other, a deterministic process. Thus

$$y_t = \zeta_t + \eta_t \tag{4.2.4}$$

where

$$\zeta_t = \sum_{j=0}^{\infty} \psi_j \varepsilon_{t-j} \tag{4.2.5}$$

In all that follows ε_t will denote such a white noise process with $E(\varepsilon_t) = 0$, $E(\varepsilon_t^2) = \sigma^2$ and $E(\varepsilon_t \varepsilon_r) = 0, r \neq t$. The validity of Wold's decomposition also requires that

$$\sum_{j=0}^{\infty} \psi_j^2 < \infty .$$

Furthermore, the spectral distribution function of y_t can be split into the sum of three components

$$F(\omega) = F_1(\omega) + F_2(\omega) + F_3(\omega),$$

where $F_1(\omega)$ is discontinuous and is due to the presence of η_t, $F_2(\omega)$ is absolutely continuous and corresponds to ζ_t, while $F_3(\omega)$ is singular, continuous and has a derivative of ∞ or 0 and is not considered to naturally occur in time series processes. (See Whittle 1963, p. 25 for further details.) Since economic time series are not generally considered to possess pure harmonics or deterministic components, it follows that processes we will consider will be expressed in terms of ζ_t alone as in (4.2.5) which is known as an infinite order moving average process. A natural subset of (4.2.5) are finite parameter models with rational spectra and are of the form:

Autoregressive process of order p; AR(p):

$$y_t = \sum_{j=1}^{p} \phi_j y_{t-j} + \varepsilon_t \tag{4.2.6}$$

Moving average process of order q, MA(q):

$$y_t = \varepsilon_t - \sum_{j=1}^{q} \theta_j \varepsilon_{t-j}, \tag{4.2.7}$$

and the mixed autoregressive moving average process, ARMA (p, q):

$$y_t - \sum_{j=1}^{p} \phi_j y_{t-j} = \varepsilon_t - \sum_{j=1}^{q} \theta_j \varepsilon_{t-j} \tag{4.2.8a}$$

which can be conveniently written in lag operator notation as

$$\phi(L) y_t = \theta(L) \varepsilon_t \tag{4.2.8b}$$

where $\phi(L) = 1 - \phi_1 L - \cdots - \phi_p L^p$, $\theta(L) = 1 - \theta_1 L - \cdots - \theta_q L^q$ and $L^j y_t = y_{t-j}$ for integer values of j.

For y_t to be stationary it is necessary that all the roots of $\phi(L)$ lie outside the unit circle. To avoid model multiplicity it is required that all the roots of $\theta(L)$ also lie outside the unit circle; this is known as the requirement for invertibility.

Box and Jenkins (1970), among others, have greatly popularised the use of these models and have developed a so called identification procedure whereby estimated autocorrelation and partial autocorrelation patterns are compared with the theoretical equivalents generated from known theoretical models and the most appropriate ARMA (p, q) selected for estimation. More formal, less subjective model selection procedures also exist for the choice of p and q. On making the additional assumption that ε_t is normally distributed, maximum likelihood estimates (MLE) can be obtained of the unknown parameters, see Box and Jenkins (1970, pp. 208–84) and Harvey (1981a, pp. 120–32).

Given a model estimated by MLE; Score Tests or Lagrange Multiplier (LM) tests exist for model specification.

Box and Pierce (1970) showed that, under the null hypothesis of no serial correlation, the portmanteau statistic

$$Q_m = n \sum_{j=1}^{m} r_j^2 \tag{4.2.9}$$

will have an asymptotic chi squared distribution with m degrees of freedom. Ljung and Box (1978) showed that a statistic with better small sample properties was provided by the modified portmanteau statistic

$$Q_m^* = n(n+2) \sum_{j=1}^{m} (n-j)^{-1} r_j^2$$

where r_j denotes the estimated autocorrelation coefficient of lag j (4.2.3) from the residuals $\hat{\varepsilon}_t$ from (4.2.8). These portmanteau statistics are asymptotically the same as Lagrange Multiplier (LM) or Score Tests obtained by computing nR^2 of the regression of $\hat{\varepsilon}_t$ on its last m lags, where R^2 is the multiple correlation coefficient and n is the sample size. Such a statistic is asymptotically equivalent to doing a likelihood ratio test that the disturbances are generated by an AR(m) or MA (m) process (see Godfrey 1978 and Harvey 1981a, pp. 167–78, pp. 209–12).

One major problem concerns the fact that the above mentioned methodology is predicated on the assumption of y_t being covariance stationary. Box and Jenkins (1970) recommended differencing series to achieve stationarity. There has subsequently been concern over problems arising from the possible over differencing of time series (see Plosser and Schwert 1977 and Harvey 1981a, pp. 181–6, 1981b, pp. 247–9). In order to determine the presence of a unit root in the autoregressive polynomial operator $\phi(L)$ in (4.2.8b), which is a particular and presumably common form of non-stationarity, many types of tests have been suggested. One test employed in this study is the Augmented Dickey Fuller statistic and is discussed by Fuller (1976, pp. 366–82), while variations of it appear in Dickey and Fuller (1979, 1981). The hypothesis of a unit root in an autoregression is tested by means of estimating the model

$$\Delta y_t = \beta y_{t-1} + \sum_{j=1}^{p} \gamma_j \Delta y_{t-j} + \varepsilon_t \qquad (4.2.10)$$

and testing

$$H_0: \quad \beta = 0$$

versus

$$H_1: \quad \beta < 0$$

so that the null hypothesis implies a unit root. It should be noted that the critical values of the above one sided test statistic, based upon the standard t statistic is denoted by Fuller (1976) as $\hat{\tau}$ and $\hat{\tau}_\mu$ respectively depending on whether or not an intercept is included in (4.2.10). For a sample size of $n = 100$ at the 1 per cent, 5 per cent and 10 per cent significance levels, the critical values of $\hat{\tau}$ are -2.60, -1.95 and -1.61 respectively (see Fuller 1976, p. 373). When a constant is included in (4.2.10) the test statistic at the same significance levels and sample size is -3.51, -2.89 and -2.58 respectively. The value of p is chosen on the basis of being sufficiently large that ε_t is a close approximation to white noise. An unnecessarily large value of p would reduce the power of the test. The null hypothesis of a unit root can be rejected against the explosive alternative, i.e. $\beta > 0$ for values of the test statistics that lie in the right hand tails of the Dickey Fuller distributions. For $n = 100$ the 1 per cent and 5 per cent critical values of $\hat{\tau}$ are 2.03 and 1·64 and for $\hat{\tau}_\mu$ are -0.05 and 0.63 respectively.

Some alternative tests for the presence of unit roots have recently been proposed by Phillips (1987), Phillips and Perron (1986) and Perron (1986). The tests involve computing the OLS regressions

$$y_t = \tilde{\mu} + \tilde{\beta}(t - n/2) + \tilde{\alpha} y_{t-1} + \tilde{u}_t \qquad (4.2.11)$$

and

$$y_t^* = \mu^* + \alpha^* y_{t-1} + u_t^* \qquad (4.2.12)$$

where n is the sample size and $\tilde{u}_t$ and u_t^* are allowed to follow a wide variety of stochastic behaviour. Two null hypotheses on (4.2.11) are given by

$$H_0^{(1)}: \quad \tilde{\alpha} = 1$$
$$H_0^{(2)}: \quad \tilde{\beta} = 0, \quad \tilde{\alpha} = 1$$

and are tested by means of the statistics $Z(t_{\tilde{\alpha}})$ and $Z(\Phi_3)$ respectively.

The null hypothesis $H_0^{(3)}: \alpha^* = 1$ on (4.2.12) is tested by the statistic $Z(t_{\alpha^*})$. These test statistics all involve long algebraic expressions and are given in the Appendix to this chapter. Under their null hypotheses $Z(t_{\tilde{\alpha}})$ and $Z(t_{\alpha^*})$ have the Dickey Fuller $\hat{\tau}_\tau$ and $\hat{\tau}_\mu$ distributions respectively.

If $(1-L)^d y_t$ is stationary and has an invertible ARMA representation, then following Engle and Granger (1987) y_t is said to be *integrated of order* d, i.e. $y_t \sim I(d)$. This also assumes that y_t contains no purely deterministic or purely harmonic component.

There are many important differences in the behaviour of an $I(0)$ and $I(1)$ variable. The mean of an $I(0)$ series will exist and the series will tend to oscillate around its mean with few extensive departures from its mean. The autocorrelation function of such a series will decline fairly quickly as the lag increases and so the process has a finite memory.

The simplest example of an $I(1)$ variable is the random walk model without drift

$$y_t = y_{t-1} + \varepsilon_t \tag{4.2.13}$$

The initial starting date of the process is now important since the process has a long memory. Suppose $y_{-1} = 0$ and the process started at time $t = 0$; then

$$y_t = \sum_{j=0}^{t} \varepsilon_{t-j} \tag{4.2.13a}$$

and the variance of y_t is $t\sigma^2$ i.e. it is explosive. If the random walk model has a drift term included, then

$$y_t = y_{t-1} + m + \varepsilon_t \tag{4.2.14}$$

which can now be written as

$$y_t = mt + \sum_{j=0}^{t} \varepsilon_{t-j} \tag{4.2.14a}$$

so that a linear trend and a drift free $I(1)$ process or random walk now constitute the joint process.

A related and important concept to be used later, is that of *Cointegration*, also described in detail by Engle and Granger (1987). Suppose two variables x_t and y_t are both I(d), then it will generally be true that a linear combination

$$z_t = x_t - ay_t \qquad (4.2.15)$$

will also be I(d) where a is a constant. However, it may happen that $z_t \sim I(d-b)$ where $b > 0$ and x_t and y_t are then said to be cointegrated of order (d,b). A particularly important case is where x_t and y_t are both I(1) but (4.2.15) is I(0). Hence although the two individual series are non-stationary, there exists a linear combination of them that is I(0) and can be regarded as an equilibrium error. This idea can be extended to the multivariate case where y_t represents a g dimensional vector of random variables and all the components are I(d). If there exists a vector $\alpha \neq 0$ such that

$$z_t = \alpha' y_t \sim I(d-b). \qquad (4.2.16)$$

then α is known as a cointegrating vector. In the case where $z_t \sim I(0)$ the implication is that z_t will rarely drift from zero and equilibrium will occasionally occur. Engle and Granger (1987) show that the cointegrating factor a in (4.2.15) can be estimated by OLS and the possible endogeneity of a right hand side variable is irrelevant. Essentially the OLS estimates of a will be consistent and will have a variance of $0(n^{-2})$, where n is the sample size (see Stock 1988). If there are only two variables in y_t which are I(1), the existence of $z_t \sim I(0)$ can be checked by applying a test for a unit root to the OLS residuals of (4.2.16). When $g > 2$ there may be more than one cointegrating vector and Baillie (1989) and Baillie and Bollerslev (1989a) describe how a new test due to Johansen can be applied to this situation.

Given the above brief introductory comments on time series analysis techniques we now consider the characteristics of nominal exchange rate series. The perceived conventional wisdom, e.g. Mussa (1979) is that the nominal exchange rate is more or less a random walk. Analysis by means of testing for unit roots, Meese and Singleton (1982) and Diebold and Nerlove (1986), broadly confirms this view, although in some cases the first differences of the logarithm of the exchange rate does exhibit weak autocorrelation which can be explained by low order ARMA processes.

Table 4.1 presents some results on applying Dickey Fuller tests to weekly nominal exchange rate series which are opening bid prices from the New York foreign exchange market. The data are recorded each Thursday between June 1973 and April 1980. It can be seen that the unit root cannot be rejected for any of the four currencies.

Table 4.2, contains some of the results presented in Baillie and Bollerslev (1989a) from applying the Phillips and Perron tests to daily data from the

Table 4.1 *Dickey/Fuller tests for unit roots in the autoregressive representatives of the logarithms of weekly spot exchange rates*

Country	$\hat{\tau}$	$\hat{\tau}_\mu$
U.K.	$-.82$	-1.11
France	0.32	-0.24
West Germany	-0.98	-1.12
Italy	-1.12	-1.41

June 1973 to April 1980.

Table 4.2 *Phillips/Perron tests for unit roots in the autoregressive representations of the logarithms of daily spot and forward exchange rates (1245 Observations)*

Country	y_t	$z(t_{\alpha*})$	$z(t_{\hat{a}})$	$z(\Phi_3)$
U.K.	$\ln s_t$	0.727	-2.495	4.023
	$\ln f_t$	0.807	-2.427	3.951
West Germany	$\ln s_t$	-0.908	-2.398	2.885
	$\ln f_t$	-0.910	-2.399	2.887
France	$\ln s_t$	-0.674	-2.573	3.334
	$\ln f_t$	-0.711	-2.426	2.976
Italy	$\ln s_t$	-0.969	-2.127	2.404
	$\ln f_t$	-1.024	-2.131	2.439
Switzerland	$\ln s_t$	-0.490	-2.271	2.791
	$\ln f_t$	-0.569	-2.272	2.272
Japan	$\ln s_t$	-1.796	-2.582	3.871
	$\ln f_t$	-1.741	-2.535	3.773
Canada	$\ln s_t$	-1.145	-2.793	3.912
	$\ln f_t$	-1.196	-2.773	3.852

New York foreign exchange market between March 1, 1980 and January 28, 1985; which realised a total of 1,245 observations. It should be noted that the test statistics derived from (4.2.11) and (4.2.12) require consistent estimates of the variances of sums of the disturbances $\tilde{u}_t$ and u_t^*. The results in the table are based on a maximum lag of 40 on the autocovariances of the residuals. Full details are given in Baillie and Bollerslev (1989a) and Perron (1986). The analysis for six currencies spot and thirty day forward rate series shows that in no instance can the unit root hypothesis be rejected.

For the 1973 to 1980 period there is some evidence of small but significant autocorrelation existing in the differenced logarithm of the

Table 4.3 *Estimation of autoregressive models on weekly spot exchange rate data, 1973 to 1980*

Country	Var(Δs_t)	$\hat{\phi}_1$	$\hat{\phi}_2$	$\hat{\sigma}^2$	LR
U.K.	$0.1227(10)^{-3}$	0.039 (0.053)	0.165 (0.053)	$0.1198(10)^{-3}$	10.39 (0.01)
West Germany	$0.1334(10)^{-3}$	0.129 (0.053)	0.143 (0.052)	$0.1283(10)^{-3}$	15.65 (0.00)
France	$0.1139(10)^{-3}$	0.118 (0.053)	0.143 (0.052)	$0.1099(10)^{-3}$	14.52 (0.00)
Italy	$0.1243(10)^{-3}$	0.083 (0.053)	0.131 (0.053)	$0.1217(10)^{-3}$	9.41 (0.01)

For each country an AR(2) model $\Delta s_t = \phi_1 \Delta s_{t-1} + \phi_2 \Delta s_{t-2} + \varepsilon_t$, $\mathrm{var}(\varepsilon_t) = \sigma^2$ was estimated. Estimates of ϕ_1 and ϕ_2 have standard errors in parentheses below them and LR is the likelihood ratio test that Δs_t is white noise against the alternative that it is AR(2). Significance levels are in parentheses beside each LR statistic.

weekly spot exchange rate series. Table 4.3 shows the results obtained from estimating the AR(2) model of the form

$$\Delta s_t = \phi_1 \Delta s_{t-1} + \phi_2 \Delta s_{t-2} + \varepsilon_t$$

It is interesting that extremely similar results for weekly data over a slightly different sampling period were obtained by Diebold and Nerlove (1986).

Most of the exchange rate series considered in the 1980s period are closely approximated by a random walk with drift model where the drift parameter varies seasonally, i.e. with the day of the week.

The disturbance of the model is assumed to have a normal distribution, conditional on all relevant and available information at time $t-1$, which is included in the information set Ω_{t-1}. Hence the model is

$$100\Delta s_t = b_0 + \varepsilon_t$$
$$\varepsilon_t \mid \Omega_{t-1} \sim N(0, \omega_0)$$

$$(4.2.17)$$

and the estimation of the above model on daily data from the New York Foreign Exchange market are presented in Table 4.4. Apart from Japan the $Q(\hat{\varepsilon}_t)$ statistic is not significant for any of the series, indicating the absence of serial correlation in Δs_t. However, there is substantial autocorrelation in the squared residuals of each model, which suggests misspecification of the distribution of the disturbances, or at least in their higher moments. This property undoubtedly reduces the power of the basic Ljung Box statistic $Q(\hat{\varepsilon}_t)$, where daily seasonality is apparent. One possible model to account for the significant autocorrelation for Japan is a higher order MA process.

Estimation of an ARIMA $(0, 1, 5)$ realised:

$$\Delta s_t = 0.0173(10)^{-3} + \hat{\varepsilon}_t - 0.0679\hat{\varepsilon}_{t-1} + 0.0010\hat{\varepsilon}_{t-2}$$
$$[0.2102(10)^{-3}] \qquad (0.0194) \qquad (0.0256)$$

$$+ 0.0248\hat{\varepsilon}_{t-3} + 0.0583\hat{\varepsilon}_{t-4} + 0.0415\hat{\varepsilon}_{t-5}$$
$$(0.0247) \qquad (0.0243) \qquad (0.0241)$$

$$\hat{\sigma}_2 = 0.4530(10)^{-4}$$
$$[0.0118(10)^{-4}]$$

$$Q_{15}(\hat{\varepsilon}) = 12.83$$

and

$$Q_{15}(\hat{\varepsilon}^2) = 127.88$$
$$m_3 = 0.6104$$
$$m_4 = 7.55$$

Table 4.4 *Estimation of a random walk with drift model: daily data, March 1980 to January 1985*

$100 . \Delta \log s_t = b_0 + \varepsilon_t \qquad t = 1 \cdots 1244$

$\varepsilon_t | \Omega_{t-1} \sim N(0, \omega_0)$

	France	Italy	Japan	Switzerland	U.K.	West Germany
b_0	-0.067	-0.069	-0.002	-0.035	-0.056	-0.045
	(0.021)	(0.17)	(0.006)	(0.021)	(0.019)	(0.020)
ω_0	0.563	0.407	0.450	0.581	0.430	0.495
	(0.010)	(0.012)	(0.010)	(0.019)	(0.013)	(0.016)
$\text{Log } L$	-1410.135	-1206.888	-1279.872	-1426.069	-1240.379	-1324.871
Q (15)	19.319	22.406	24.987	19.025	18.021	13.483
Q^2 (15)	25.864	118.161	127.574	252.640	102.707	156.834
m_3	-0.269	0.256	0.652	0.349	-0.274	0.345
m_4	11.292	4.915	8.178	4.208	4.814	4.205

Asymptotic standard errors in parentheses.

Although the model has successfully accounted for serial correlation, strong temporal dependence in the residuals remain and the sample skewness and kurtosis statistics reveal significant departures from normality. Recall that under normality the asymptotic distributions of m_3 and m_4 are $m_3 \sim N(0, 6/n)$ and $m_4 \sim N(0, 24/n)$ respectively. The time dependent heteroskedasticity and non-normal residual distribution will be discussed later in 4.6 and 4.7.

As previously indicated the unit root testing framework can be applied to testing for cointegration between spot and forward exchange rates. With daily data twenty two working days should intervene between a thirty day forward rate and its associated spot rate. Hence u_t in the equation

$$s_{t+1} - a - bf_t = u_{t+1} \qquad (4.2.18)$$

should be an MA(21) process in the case of the forward rate being an efficient expectation of the future spot rate. Since both s and f are I(1), u_t must be I(0) for spot and forward rates to be cointegrated. The OLS estimates of a and b in (4.2.18) are given by the second and third columns of Table 4.5. Two alternative specifications for u_t in (4.2.18) which generate unit root tests are:

$$u_t = \mu + \beta(t - n/2) + \alpha u_{t-1} + \varepsilon_t \qquad (4.2.19)$$

and

$$u_t = \mu + \alpha u_{t-1} + \varepsilon_t \qquad (4.2.20)$$

where ε_t is I(0) and may follow some stationary ARMA representation. A test for cointegration then amounts to testing $H_0 : \alpha = 1$ versus $H_1 : |\alpha| < 1$ in both (4.2.19) and (4.2.20). Again the Phillips Perron statistics $Z(t_{\hat{a}})$ and $Z(t_{a^*})$ can be used and show that the unit root hypothesis can be clearly rejected, thus providing strong evidence that the spot and forward exchange rate series are indeed cointegrated.

It should also be noted that the estimated slope and intercept coefficients are close to one and zero for all the currencies except Japan. The final two columns of Table 4.5 give the results of applying the unit root tests when $a = 0$, $b = 1$ is imposed. The 1 per cent and 5 per cent critical values for the test statistic are -2.59 and -1.95 with u_t observable (i.e. $a = 0$, $b = 1$ constrained) and -4.00 and -3.37 respectively when based on OLS residuals. The unit root hypothesis can be rejected in all cases implying that the expectational error $s_{t+1} - f_t$ is stationary, i.e. I(0).

As noted by Granger (1986) if x_t and y_t are cointegrated with cointegrating relationship (4.2.15) then $w_t = x_t - by_{t-k}$ for any k with $w_t \sim I(0)$ will also be a cointegrating relationship with a possible change in b the cointegrating parameter compared to a in (4.2.15). Hence the forward premium, or discount $(s_t - f_t)$ will also be I(0).

Table 4.5 Tests for cointegration between the logarithms of spot and forward rates: daily data 1980 to 1985

Country	$\hat{a}$	$\hat{b}$	$\hat{a}, \hat{b}$			$a = 0, b = 1$	
			$z(t_{\hat{a}})$	$z(t_{a^*})$	$z(t_{\hat{a}})$	$z(t_{a^*})$	
U.K.	−0.0187	1.0135	−5.164	−5.106	−5.175	−5.009
West Germany	−0.0301	0.9802	−5.778	−5.701	−5.784	−5.778
France	−0.0379	0.9852	−5.634	−5.593	−5.625	−5.637
Italy	−0.0892	0.9886	−5.726	−5.688	−5.725	−5.740
Switzerland	−0.0298	0.9756	−5.710	−5.579	−5.717	−5.668
Japan	−0.8347	0.8476	−5.209	−4.952	−5.165	−5.106
Canada	−0.0095	0.9599	−6.133	−5.948	−6.135	−6.087

4.3   Statistical tests of weak form efficiency

Chapter 2 considered the various definitions of market efficiency and the purpose of this section is to test weak form efficiency, defined in 2.2 where a price is hypothesised to incorporate all the information in past prices. In order to simplify subsequent notation we will continue with the convention developed in the last chapter of representing $E(. \,|\, \Omega_t)$ by E_t. In the following E_t implies a truly rational expectation which is conditioned on the set of all available and relevant information. Since much of the work in this area has been concerned with asset prices rather than exchange rates the variable to be considered will be denoted by p_t and, as in (2.3.2), the random walk model is

$$p_t = p_{t-1} + \varepsilon_t$$

$E(\varepsilon_t) = 0$, $E(\varepsilon_t) = \sigma^2$ and $E(\varepsilon_t \varepsilon_r) = 0$, $r \neq t$. For weak form market efficiency it is necessary that
(i) $\Delta p_t = \varepsilon_t$ can be an independent sequence and
(ii)   that it should be identically distributed.

One implication of these requirements is that the distribution of price changes, conditional on the set of available information Ω_t, should be identical to its marginal distribution, so that

$$f(\varepsilon_{t+1} \,|\, \Omega_t) = f(\varepsilon_t) \qquad\qquad (4.3.1)$$

and hence the entire distribution is independent of Ω_t. This is a strong requirement and one that is difficult to empirically test. In practice only the mean of ε_{t+1} is hypothesised to be independent of Ω_t since analysis of its statistical distribution is generally complicated. Thus initial empirical research concentrated on the question of autocorrelation, so that tests are really performed on the martingale property, rather than the random walk property. It is also frequently assumed that ε_t is normally distributed, which can be partly justified by appealing to the central limit theorem.

The history of empirical work in this area starts with Bachelier (1900) who examined stock price movements and noted that 'expected profits should be zero'. Subsequently a number of other researchers claimed to find empirical support for the random walk or martingale behaviour of stock prices, commodity prices and exchange rates. Most of this work was almost purely statistical in nature until Mandelbrot (1966), Samuelson (1965) and Fama (1965, 1970) provided the economic theory described in Chapter 2.

Overall, there has been widespread agreement among financial economists and others that weak form efficiency and the random walk model provide reasonable descriptions of the movement of asset prices. A typical statement to this effect is provided by Jensen (1978): 'I believe there is no other proposition in economics which has a more solid empirical evidence supporting it than the efficient market hypothesis; it has been tested and, with very few exceptions, found consistent with the data in a wide variety of markets.'

Following the work of Bachelier (1900) several researchers examined the hypothesis in the context of stock prices. The area attracted several statisticians since it has the desirable quality of being one of the few sources of economic data that is observed with extreme regularity and contains few measurement errors or subsequent data revisions. Kendall (1953) and Working (1958) both attempted to test the lack of serial correlation assumption implied by the random walk hypothesis. Kendall (1953) analysed nineteen indices of weekly security prices on data between 1928 and 1938. After extensive examination of the autocorrelation structure of the series, Kendall concluded that: 'Such serial correlation as is present in these series is so weak as to dispose at once of any possibility of being able to use them for prediction.' In many ways, not the least the formidable amount of computations performed on hand calculating machines, the work of Kendall (1953) was significantly ahead of its time. Interestingly enough Kendall (1953) was also aware of the possibility of non-linear effects in Δp_t and suggested that a model of Brownian motion might explain the movements of asset prices.

A similar statistical analysis was performed by Moore (1964) on weekly Friday closing prices of the Standard and Poor Industrial Index of common stock prices on the New York exchange for the period 1942 to 1958. On the basis of examining the significance of estimated autocorrelations, Moore was unable to reject the random walk hypothesis.

Moore (1964) also used a non-parametric Runs Test which is performed by comparing the number of runs of positive and negative values of a zero mean variable, Δp_t, with the number expected by chance from a random process. Moore divided the observations into three groups containing positive, negative and zero changes in share prices respectively. The test statistic is the total number of runs μ, in the elements of the groups of the observed series of share price changes. The distribution of μ is approximately normal, with the following mean and variance.

$$E(\mu) = \frac{n(n+1) - \sum_{i=1}^{n} n_i^2}{n}$$

and

$$\mathrm{Var}(\mu) = \frac{\sum_{i=1}^{3} n_i^2 \sum_{i=1}^{3} n_i^2 + n(n+1) - 2n \sum_{i=1}^{3} n_i^3 - n^3}{(n-1)}$$

where n_i is the number of elements in the ith group and $\sum n_i = n$. On the basis of these results Moore (1964) was again unable to reject the random walk hypothesis.

Some further work based on a non-parametric approach is provided in the work of Cowles (1960) who considered the number of 'sequences' and 'reversals' in a series of share price changes. A 'sequence' is defined as a series with values of the same sign and a 'reversal' refers to the situation where a positive value is followed by a negative value, or vice versa. The outcomes of sequences and reversals can be regarded as Bernoulli trials and, assuming the probability of occurrence of both results is $\frac{1}{2}$, then for $n - 2$ observations (one being lost due to differencing) the number of sequences q, will for sufficiently large n have the distribution

$$q \sim N \left[\frac{n-2}{2}, \frac{n-2}{4} \right]$$

Cowles (1960) examined an extremely detailed set of share prices for the U.S.A. between 1835 and 1935, with observations recorded every twenty minutes, one hour, one day, one, two and three weeks and one, two to eleven months, and one up to ten years. For series with sampling frequency of less than six months there was evidence of autocorrelation. For series recorded at units of time greater than six months the random walk hypothesis could not be rejected.

The spectrum defined in (4.2.2) can also be useful in testing (2.3.2) since for a white noise or uncorrelated process it is expected to be flat with every frequency equally unimportant. Granger and Morgenstern (1963) used this technique as well as cross spectral analysis to examine the relationship between price changes in different asset markets. They concluded that there was almost no relationship between changes in the Financial Times Indicator and the New York Standard and Poor Industrial Index.

An alternative technique to assessing the market efficiency hypothesis is to analyse the 'trading rules' or 'filter rules' used by market analysts. Suppose for example that a large increase in the price of an asset or an exchange rate is invariably followed by further increases rather than decreases. Then purchasing the appreciating currency after the first increase will, on average, yield abnormal returns. The existence of this profitable trading rule critically depends on the positive dependency, or autocorrelation, that exists in the price series since the market has not reacted instantaneously to the random arrival of new information. In a weak form efficient market the filter technique would not be expected to outperform a naive buy and hold strategy.

A typical k per cent filter rule can be illustrated by the following example. Suppose that if an exchange rate increases by at least k per cent then the agent should buy and hold the currency until the exchange rate decreases by at least k per cent from the highest level following the purchase. At this time the agent should simultaneously sell the holding and go short (i.e. sell forward), and maintain the short position until the currency price rises by at least k per cent above a subsequent low. At this point the agent should cover the short position and go long (i.e. buy forward). Exchange rate changes of less than k per cent in either direction should be ignored. Filter rules of this type have been used on stock markets, although little is known about the long-term profitability of such methods.

Some analysis of the success of similar trading rules has been carried out on gold and silver prices by Solt and Swanson (1981), by Alexander (1964) and Fama and Blume (1966). Fama and Blume examined a rule of 'if the price increases (decreases) by k per cent, buy (sell) the stock and hold money or bonds until the price of the stock falls (rises) by k per cent'. Once trading costs were included in the calculations Fama and Blume (1966) did not find this type of trading rule to be profitable and for thirty U.S. companies stock prices they could not refute the random walk hypothesis.

Another attempt at outperforming the simple buy and hold strategy has been by Girmes and Damant (1975) who tried to identify 'head and shoulder' formations from charts of 484 stocks using relative prices over the period 1969 to 1973. A head and shoulder formation is defined as a share whose price increases strongly, to be followed by investors selling to make profits and so causing the price to decline again. This is followed by the head represented by a stronger increase in the price and a subsequent fall followed by a much weaker rise, i.e. the shoulder. When the shoulder appears the investors know that it is not a sustained share price rise and that the share should therefore be sold before it turns down sharply. Girmes and Damant claimed that such head and shoulder trading rules more than covered transactions costs. In a further study, Girmes and Benjamin (1975) examined the prices of 543 stocks and shares listed on the London Stock Exchange to find that in 70 per cent of the cases, there was a clear sign of non-randomness.

Both these studies have had their critics; in the former test it was pointed out that the profits gained by using this head and shoulder technique were not risk-adjusted and that the rule was based not on *ex-ante* projections but *ex-post* data. In the latter test there was no investigation as to whether this dependency could have been used to gain profits in excess of those of a buy and hold policy, but also it was mainly price changes of smaller companies securities which were examined, and these tend not to be so closely scrutinised in the stock market.

Further attempts at testing weak form efficiency have considered alternative formulations of the alternative hypothesis and have sometimes used the notion of continuous time models to specify behavioural relationships. For example, Taylor (1980) suggests that 'price changes have appeared random because the alternative hypothesis of trends has been described vaguely'. Taylor suggests the alternative specification of

$$\Delta p_t = \mu_t + \varepsilon_t \tag{4.3.2}$$

where the trend value μ_t is determined by current information and changes on a proportion of p days when new information arrives. Otherwise it remains constant at $\bar{\mu}$ with probability $1 - p$. On specifying ε_t and η_t to be independent white noise processes Taylor suggests the following model for μ_t.

$$\mu_t = \begin{bmatrix} \mu_{t-1} & \text{with probability } p \\ \bar{\mu} + \eta_t & \text{with probability } 1 - p \end{bmatrix}$$

An alternative to the above specification, is the first order autoregressive trend model:

$$\mu_t = \begin{bmatrix} \bar{\mu} + k(\mu_{t-1} - \bar{\mu}) & \text{with probability } p \\ \bar{\mu} + \phi(\mu_{t-1} - \bar{\mu}) + \eta_t & \text{with probability } 1 - p \end{bmatrix}$$

These models can in fact be shown to be special cases of the first order autoregressive model with stochastic parameter α_t

$$(\mu_t - \bar{\mu}) = \alpha_t(\mu_{t-1} - \bar{\mu}) + \eta_t$$

where α_t are a set of independent, identically distributed random variables and is similar to models used in different contexts by Cooley and Prescott (1976) and to the Kalman filter; e.g. Harvey (1981, pp. 101–19). The autocovariance and autocorrelation functions for this type of process are similar to that of the constant coefficient type of first order autoregression and can be described as

$$\gamma_j = [E(\alpha_j)]^j \, \text{var}(\mu_t)$$

and

$$\rho_j = A p^j \quad \text{where } A > 0$$

Taylor also allows for the possibility of the variance of μ_t changing slowly over time and suggests an exponentially weighted moving average type model to pick up these effects. Taylor then examined ten commodity price series between 1961 and 1978 on a daily basis and also the pound sterling/U.S. dollar exchange rate. The conclusions reached by Taylor were that the random walk hypothesis could be overwhelmingly rejected in favour of the price trending model (4.3.2) for each series. Although in a sense quite detailed, Taylor's alternative model is essentially very simple.

No attempt is made to find the most appropriate model specification, the parameter values are merely guessed, and, as Taylor acknowledges, it would be more satisfactory to estimate μ_t from an econometric model. Despite these problems, Taylor's work does provide additional evidence against the random walk model.

To conclude this section we consider approaches to the problem that are based on a model formulated in continuous time. Firstly, Osborne (1959) suggested that stock prices might be subject to the law of Brownian motion. A botanist Robert Brown gave his name in 1827 to the time series behaviour of a particle that is suspended in a fluid and is subjected to successive random collisions with a set of neighbouring particles. Intuitively, the idea is that the particle follows a random walk in each small time interval. Osborne postulated that observed stock prices were the outcome of an ensemble of decisions in statistical equilibrium, with similar properties to the ensemble of particles in statistical mechanics. A justification for this approach is provided by the Weber–Fechner law which states that equal ratios of physical stimuli (or information), give rise to equal intervals of some output.

On defining

$$y = \ln(p_{t+j}/p_t)$$

where p_{t+j} and p_t are the spot price of a stock at times $t+j$ and t respectively, then y will have the steady state distribution

$$g(y) = (2\pi\sigma^2 j)^{-1/2} \exp(-y^2/2\sigma^2 j)$$

which is the probability distribution of a particle in Brownian motion with σ representing the dispersion developed at the end of unit time. The expected value of price is then

$$E(p) = \int_0^\infty pg(y)\frac{dy}{dp}\,dp$$

and increases as j, the interval, increases.

The validity of the Weber–Fechner law depends on there being only one feature for evaluation by market participants, in this case it is price. Osborne assumes all market participants behave rationally and that they select a negotiating strategy with the greatest expected profit. It is assumed that market participants can form opinions about the outcome of all alternatives and their probability distributions. It is also assumed that both buyers and sellers behave rationally during every transaction, then their information determines the conditions under which transactions occur. Osborne argues that in every transaction both buyer and seller have to agree, which makes the most probable condition for the outcome

$$E(\Delta \ln p_t) = 0$$

for the market as a whole, once buyers and sellers expectations have been equated as

$$E(\Delta \ln p_t)_{\text{buyers}} = E(\Delta \ln p_t)_{\text{sellers}}$$

The assumption of a rational method of behaviour guarantees that before accepting a transaction both seller and buyer do not know of any possible alternative transaction with a higher expected profit. Of course it does not follow from this that over any interval j both would estimate an expected stock price change of the same amount with different signs. For example, suppose the seller of a stock can only sell it today at a price of a 100, and after today a price of 97 is expected. It is possible that the buyer of this stock expects a price of 107 after the next day. According to the condition of the equation both parties must agree on a price of 102 which can only occur after negotiation. For these negotiations there must also be additional assumptions made to those already mentioned, that both parties simultaneously wish to accept the expected profit in equal parts. For this condition, the assumptions made by Osborne are not enough.

Within the interval $(t, t+j)$ there are k transactions and there is an interval of ∂ between each individual transaction. The ith transaction will be fulfilled since the value of the random variable y_i is defined as

$$y_i = \left[\ln s_{t+i\partial} - \ln s_{t+(i-1)\partial} \right]$$

It is assumed that each y_i has the same dispersion σ_i; then after k trades, at time $j = k\partial$ periods later

$$y_j = y_{k\partial} = \sum_{i=1}^{k} y_i = \ln s_{t+j} - \ln s_t = \Delta_j \ln s_t$$

The dispersion of y_j is then given by

$$\sum \sigma_i^2 = k\sigma_i = \partial/\partial \sigma_i$$

so that the variance of y directly depends upon the interval length, a typical result of a variable generated by Brownian motion. It also follows from the central limit theorem that y will approach a normally distributed random variable, assuming the y_i's have a stable distribution function.

Osborne's empirical results were based upon looking at distribution functions and he found that the random walk approximation was sufficiently good for intervals of a month or a year. Osborne also presented the changes in σy_j as a function of j and concluded that there was evidence in favour of the random walk and Brownian motion hypotheses.

The random walk model and Brownian motion are related to the more general Wiener process, which can be derived from the notion of a particle starting at the origin and, in each small time interval of length τ, either taking a small step Δ with probability p, or step $-\Delta$ with probability $1 - p$. It can be shown that at time t the position of the particle p_t will have the distribution

$$p_t \sim N(\mu t, \sigma^2 t)$$

where $(2p - 1)\Delta/\tau \to \mu$ and $4p(1 - p)\Delta^2/\tau \to \sigma^2$.

Shiller (1981) has suggested a 'Fads Model' based on the above notion of a Wiener process. Basically stock prices are considered to move because of fads on the part of investors. The model is specified by the stochastic differential equations

$$H_0 : dp_t = \sigma_0 dw_t \qquad\qquad\qquad t > 0$$
$$H_1 : dp_t = -\tau(p_t - \mu)dt + \sigma_1 dw_t \quad -\infty < t < \infty, \quad \tau > 0$$

where w_t is a unit Wiener process. Thus the null hypothesis specifies a random walk process in continuous time and the alternative represents price movements due to successive investor fads $\sigma_1 dw_t$. As noted by Shiller and Peron (1985) 'forgetting takes place with an exponential decay pattern as commonly modelled by mathematical psychologists' and the τ parameter represents human memory retention. If the process is observed at discrete time intervals of length h, the processes (4.3.2) are

$$H_0 : p_{ht} = p_{h(t-1)} + \varepsilon_{ht}$$

$$H_1 : p_{ht} = \mu + \beta_h(p_{h(t-1)} - \mu) + \xi_{ht}$$

where $\varepsilon_{ht} \sim N(0, h\sigma_0^2)$, $\xi_{ht} \sim N\{0, \sigma_1^2[1 - \exp(-2h\tau)]/(2\tau)\}$ and $\beta_h = \exp(-\tau h)$ is the discrete time autoregressive coefficient.

4.4   Tests of weak form efficiency of exchange rates

Much of the work in the previous section and in fact many of the empirical studies referred to are of course directly relevant to the possible weak form efficiency of nominal exchange rates. Firstly, it is worth considering if the foreign exchange market possesses any substantially different features from other financial markets and whether this might affect subsequent weak form efficiency tests. There are a variety of mechanisms by which individuals acquire information about market prices which are likely to prevail for financial assets, exchange rates, commodities or goods. However, detailed forward and occasionally futures markets exist for exchange rates and these markets make expectations about the future certain and identical for all market participants. Hence the forward foreign exchange market performs the function of aggregating and disseminating information and gives agents the opportunity to adjust their own expectations as they become aware of the expectations of other agents. It may be that the existence of such markets aids the efficient use of information and pushes the market towards efficiency. However, uncertainty in some form or another may still persist since information is frequently costly to collect, process and transmit. Also market imperfections due to political risk, default risk and limitations on borrowing and lending may prevent the production and the distribution of the optimum amount of information.

It is also likely that the existence of the forward market encourages the activities of private speculators which may make the overall structure of the markets quite different from other financial markets. Also, while there is no direct official intervention in equity markets, the foreign exchange rates have rarely been determined entirely by market forces for any significant length of time and are frequently the subject of official intervention. Weak form tests for efficient market behaviour cannot discriminate between exchange rate movements caused by speculators or those caused by intervention on the part of the government or monetary authorities. Since data on the timing and volume of central bank intervention are generally unknown or cannot be isolated it is thus impossible to tell whether the inefficiency in any particular market arises from destabilising speculation or from the actions of official intervention by the monetary authorities.

Before considering the empirical work on testing weak form efficiency for exchange rates it is convenient to examine a simple model due to König and Gaab (1982) which suggests how central bank intervention affects exchange rate dynamics and properties of efficiency. It is assumed that in the absence of central bank intervention the market is efficient so that the equilibrium exchange rate is a martingale difference.

The model is given by

$$s_t^* = s_{t-1}^* + \varepsilon_t \qquad\qquad\qquad (4.4.1)$$

$$x_t^E = \frac{1}{\alpha}(s_t^* - s_t), \quad \alpha > 0 \qquad\qquad (4.4.2)$$

so that (4.4.1) expresses the martingale property and (4.4.2) defines x_t^E which is the excess demand for foreign exchange; s_t is the actual spot exchange rate and s_t^* is the equilibrium exchange rate. In equilibrium $x_t^E = 0$ and hence

$$s_t = s_{t-1} + \varepsilon_t$$

so that the actual exchange rate is also a martingale.

It is now assumed that the central bank operates according to IMF guidelines and its activities are composed of two components. Specifically it is assumed that the central bank has some concept of a normal or permanent level of the exchange rate which is achieved in the long run. To avoid large deviations from this normal level the central bank purchases, (sells) foreign exchange when the actual spot exchange rate is smaller, (greater) than the normal rate. In addition, the central bank attempts to smoothen daily exchange rate fluctuations by a policy of 'leaning against the wind', i.e. by supplying (demanding) foreign exchange when the spot exchange rate increases (falls). Both approaches represent a regressive attitude of the central bank, in its attempt to stabilise exchange rate movements. The excess demand function of the central bank for foreign exchange can be written as

$$x_t^Z = \lambda_1(\bar{s}_t - s_t) - \lambda_2(s_t - s_{t-1}), \quad \lambda_1, \lambda_2 \geq 0, \tag{4.4.3}$$

where $\bar{s}_t$ denotes the 'normal' or 'permanent' level of the spot exchange rate.

It is assumed that banks generate the permanent exchange rate by the two period adaptive expectations or error learning model

$$\bar{s}_t - \bar{s}_{t-1} = (1-c)(s_t - \bar{s}_{t-1}) + b(\bar{s}_{t-1} - \bar{s}_{t-2}) \tag{4.4.4}$$

with $b \geq 0$ and $0 \leq c \leq 1$, which, on using the lag operator can be written as

$$\bar{s}_t = \frac{(1-c)}{[1 - (c+b)L + bL^2]} s_t$$

Equilibrium on the foreign exchange market occurs when

$$x_t^E + x_t^Z = 0 \tag{4.4.5}$$

Substitution of (4.4.2), (4.4.3) into (4.4.5) gives

$$\Delta s_t = \frac{c_1 + c_2 L + c_3 L^2}{1 - b_1 L - b_2 L^2 - b_3 L^3} \varepsilon_t \tag{4.4.6}$$

where

$$b_1 = [(c+b)(1+\alpha\lambda) + (1+c+b)(\alpha\lambda_2)]/N$$

$$b_2 = [-\lambda_2\alpha(c+2b) - b(1+\alpha\lambda_1)]/N$$

$$b_3 = \alpha b\lambda_2/N$$

$$c_1 = 1/N$$

$$c_2 = -(b+c)/N$$

$$c_3 = b/N$$

and $N = 1 + \alpha(\lambda_2 + c\lambda_1)$

According to the assumptions of the model the spot exchange rate will then follow the ARIMA $(3, 1, 2)$ process given by equation (4.4.6) and the model takes on the particular parameterisation

$$\Delta s_t = \frac{(c+b)\left[1 + \alpha\lambda_1 + (1 + c + b)\alpha\lambda_2\right]}{1 + \alpha(c\lambda_1 + \lambda_2)}\, \Delta s_{t-1}$$

$$-\frac{b(1 + \alpha\lambda_1) + \alpha(c + 2b)\lambda_2}{1 + \alpha(c\lambda_1 + \lambda_2)}\, \Delta s_{t-2}$$

$$+\frac{\alpha b\lambda_2}{1 + \alpha(c\lambda_1 + \lambda_2)}\, \Delta s_{t-3} + \frac{1}{1 + \alpha(c\lambda_1 + \lambda_2)}\, \varepsilon_t$$

$$-\frac{c+b}{1 + \alpha(c\lambda_1 + \lambda_2)}\, \varepsilon_{t-1} + \frac{1}{1 + \alpha(c\lambda_1 + \lambda_2)}\, \varepsilon_{t-2}$$

A number of interesting special cases can also be distinguished:

(a) When no intervention is undertaken by the central bank then

$$\lambda_1 = \lambda_2 = c = b = 0$$

and (4.4.6) reduces to the random walk/martingale model

$$\Delta s_t = \varepsilon_t$$

(b) The central bank pursues a policy of leaning against the wind and attempts to smoothen daily exchange rate movements. This results in the parameter values of $\lambda_1 = c = b = 0$ and (4.4.6) becomes the ARIMA $(1, 1, 0)$ process:

$$\Delta s_t = \frac{\alpha\lambda_2}{1 + \alpha\lambda_2}\, \Delta s_{t-1} + \frac{1}{1 + \alpha\lambda_2}\, \varepsilon_t$$

Since $0 < \alpha\lambda_2/(1 + \alpha\lambda_2) < 1$ the process will be stationary in first differences, i.e. I(1).

(c) The central bank attempts to smoothen exchange rate movements around the expected normal level. In the simplest case, this gives $\lambda_2 = b = 0$ and implies the ARIMA $(1, 1, 1)$ process:

$$\Delta s_t = d_1 \Delta s_{t-1} + d_2 \varepsilon_2 - d_3 \varepsilon_{t-1}$$

and

$$\mathrm{var}(\Delta s_t) = \left[d_2^2 + \frac{(d_1 d_2 - d_3)^2}{1 - d_1^2} \right] \sigma_\varepsilon^2$$

where

$$d_1 = \frac{c(1 + \alpha\lambda_1)}{1 + \alpha c\lambda_1}; \quad d_2 = \frac{1}{1 + \alpha c\lambda_1}; \quad d_3 = \frac{c}{1 + \alpha c\lambda_1}$$

An examination of the limiting values of the parameters α, λ_1 and c demonstrate that this policy of leaning against the wind does not in every case lead to a reduction in the variance of exchange rate changes. The above hypothetical model thus provides some evidence of how the activities of speculators and the central bank can induce autocorrelation in spot exchange rate series which will thus lead to a breakdown of weak form efficiency.

Section 4.3 discussed the methodology and results obtained by previous authors on testing weak form efficiency on stock and commodity prices; some of these studies also examined one or two foreign exchange rates. We now turn to some specific studies of the foreign exchange market.

One of the first such studies was by Poole (1967a and b) who examined the history of several currencies during the 1920s float and also the Canadian dollar between 1950 and 1962. By using tests of autocorrelation and examining various filter rules, Poole detected significant serial dependence, which he attributed to inventory carrying and transaction costs. This did not imply that market participants were irrational but that market information was inefficiently disseminated. Dooley and Schafer (1975) also found similar results leading to a rejection of the random walk hypothesis on daily data for several currencies between 1973 and 1975.

One of the most detailed studies in this area was provided by Giddy and Dufey (1975). They examined the forecasting accuracy of five methods:
(i)   the martingale–random walk model,
(ii)   the sub-martingale model incorporating the relevant interest rate differential;
(iii)   the forward exchange rate,
(iv)   Box–Jenkins ARMA models and
(v)   exponential smoothing.

Giddy and Dufey found the random walk was an adequate description of the exchange rate series and could not be substantially improved upon by other models. The best predictor of future exchange rates was found to be current spot rates adjusted for the interest rate differential. The forward rate was found to have a poor predictive performance. A similar study was undertaken by Cornell (1977) on monthly data between 1974 and 1977 for the pound sterling, Canadian dollar, Deutschmark, Swiss franc, Dutch guilder and Japanese yen. Cornell compared the random walk model with the forward rate and a second order autoregressive model. The differences between the methods were slight with the autoregression generally proving superior, but unfortunately no formal hypothesis test was given to compare one method with another.

The above time series approaches to testing weak form efficiency are the natural ones for statisticians to apply, although more market orientated workers sometimes prefer to think in terms of filter rules. Logue and Sweeney (1977) claim that these methods are more likely to detect non-linear relationships and find unexploited profit opportunities between the French franc and U.S. dollar. However, in a subsequent study of seven currencies, Logue, Sweeney and Willett (1978) concluded that: 'foreign exchange markets seem to be efficient at least in the weak form sense'. Their results only provided very weak evidence for exchange rate overshooting or bandwagon effects.

Cummins *et al.* (1979) examined the Canadian–U.S. dollar spot exchange rate on about 800 successive daily observations and managed to construct a filter rule which was profitable compared with the profit that would have been made without entering the market. However, all the filter rules considered were very sensitive to the data period chosen and did not perform consistently well over the entire sample.

Finally, we turn to our own results and the time series analysis of monthly, weekly and daily data discussed at the end of Section 4.2. It can be seen that apart from Japan the first difference of the logarithms of the daily data between 1980 and 1985 are close to being uncorrelated and consequently supportive of weak form efficiency. Analysis of weekly data in the 1970s suggest mild departure from the random walk model. This could of course be due to some form of market intervention rather than the breakdown of market efficiency.

The models in Table 4.4 show a significant value for $Q(\hat{\varepsilon}_t^2)$ the portmanteau statistic (4.2.9) for autocorrelations based on squared residuals. The hugely significant value of $Q(\hat{\varepsilon}_t^2)$ indicates a predictable pattern in the second moments of the disturbances that clearly violates (4.3.1) the condition necessary for random walk behaviour. In Section 4.6 we shall discuss the precise model suggested by this pattern in the squared residuals.

4.5 Tests of strong form efficiency of exchange rates

This section considers tests of strong form efficiency that have been undertaken to see whether or not certain forms of information (other than just own past prices) are incorporated into the markets expectation. As before E_t denotes a Muthian rational expectation based on all relevant and available information at time t; and, since we are examining the spot exchange rate, $E_{t-1}(s_t)$, will be compared with the markets expectation s_t^e

which is formed at time $t-1$. When these expectations are fully rational, then

$$E_{t-1}s_t = s_t^e, \qquad (4.5.1)$$

and $s_t = s_t^e + \varepsilon_t$, where ε_t is white noise, and this will be the subject of empirical testing. A slightly weaker test which is designed to test (4.5.1) is given by

$$E_{t-1}(s_t - s_t^e) = 0 \qquad (4.5.2)$$

The different approaches to testing the above have been discussed in detail by Mishkin (1981, 1983) and implemented on a wide variety of macroeconomic issues. It should be noted that any test of (4.5.2) will implicitly be a joint test of market efficiency/rational expectations and a test of the validity of the model in calculating $\varepsilon_t = s_t - s_t^e$.

One procedure is to test whether all the information contained in the h dimensional row vector z_{t-1}, which itself is a subset of the total information set, has been incorporated into the markets expectation s_t^e. Then a natural procedure is to test the hypothesis that $\alpha = 0$ in the regression model

$$\varepsilon_t = z_{t-1}\alpha + \eta_t \qquad (4.5.3)$$

where $E_{t-1}\eta_t = 0$. An inability to reject the F test statistic, that the h dimensional vector $\alpha = 0$, will lead to the conclusion that the markets expectation has utilised all the information in z_{t-1}.

Suppose also that the market agents have used rational expectations on the information in y_{t-1} which is a subset of z_{t-1}, then a corollary of this is that only 'news', i.e. the unanticipated component of the forecast of y_t made at time $t-1$, will be correlated with ε_t, the markets forecast error. This concept of 'news' will be seen later to be of particular importance in generating shocks to the exchange rate in the monetary approach to exchange rate determination. To see this, note that

$$E_{t-1}(y_t - y_t^e) = 0 \qquad (4.5.4)$$

where $y_t^e = E_{t-1}y_t$. On assuming

$$s_t = y_t\beta + e_t \qquad (4.5.5)$$

where y_t' and β are $k \times 1$ vectors and $E_{t-1}e_t = 0$. Then

$$s_t^e = y_t^e\beta \qquad (4.5.6)$$

and from (4.5.5) and (4.5.6) it follows that

$$\varepsilon_t = (y_t - y_t^e)\beta + e_t \qquad (4.5.7)$$

so that β indicates the importance of each of the relative 'news' items on the unanticipated change in the spot exchange rate.

Abel and Mishkin (1983) have formalised some of the alternative approaches to testing market efficiency/rational expectations. Suppose

$$y_t = z_{t-1}\gamma + u_t \tag{4.5.8}$$

where z is again an h dimensional row vector, γ is on $h \times k$ matrix of coefficients and u_t is a k dimensional row vector of disturbances.

Assuming that

$$E_{t-1}u_t = 0$$

then

$$E_{t-1}y_t = z_{t-1}\gamma$$

and provided that

$$E_{t-1}(y_t - y_t^e) = 0$$

then (4.5.7) becomes

$$\varepsilon_t = (y_t - z_{t-1}\gamma)\beta + e_t \tag{4.5.9}$$

One approach is to jointly estimate the system of equations given by unrestricted versions of (4.5.8) and (4.5.9), that is

$$\left.\begin{aligned} y_t &= z_{t-1} + u_t \\[2mm] \varepsilon_t &= (y_t - z_{t-1}\omega)\beta + e_t \end{aligned}\right\} \tag{4.5.10}$$

and

where $\begin{pmatrix} u_t \\ \varepsilon_t \end{pmatrix} \sim \text{NID}(0, \Omega)$.

Under the efficient market/rational expectations hypothesis there is a cross equation restriction on the structural parameters of the above model, namely $\gamma = \omega$. Thus the unrestricted model (4.5.10) will contain $k(2h + 1)$ structural parameters and the constrained model (4.5.8) and (4.5.9) contains $k(h + 1)$ so that hk restrictions are generated. Abel and Mishkin formally prove the intuitively obvious result that the F test on α in (4.5.3) is asymptotically equivalent to testing the hypothesis $\omega = \gamma$ in (4.5.10). From a computational point of view the F test in (4.5.3) is probably the simplest procedure.

The concept of a variable including information contained in its own past history and/or the history of some other group of variables is closely related to the so called 'tests of causality' that have been widely used in economics in recent years (see Zellner 1979 for an excellent survey, plus comments on the philosophy behind these kinds of tests).

In order to discuss the tests and how they have been applied it is convenient to first introduce some multivariate time series theory. Consider two jointly covariance stationary time series x_t and y_t, which do not contain any purely deterministic harmonic components, so that they possess bounded spectral densities. From a multivariate analogue of Wold's decomposition theory introduced in Section 4.2 it follows that $Y_{t'} = (y_t x_t)$ possesses the unique infinite moving average representation.

$$\begin{bmatrix} y_t \\ x_t \end{bmatrix} = \begin{bmatrix} \psi_{11}(L) & \psi_{12}(L) \\ \psi_{21}(L) & \psi_{22}(L) \end{bmatrix} \begin{bmatrix} \varepsilon_{1t} \\ \varepsilon_{2t} \end{bmatrix} \tag{4.5.11}$$

Or,

$$Y_t = \psi(L)\varepsilon_t = \sum_{j=0}^{\infty} \psi_j \varepsilon_{t-j}$$

where $\varepsilon_{t'} = (\varepsilon_{1t}\varepsilon_{2t})$ and

$$E(\varepsilon_t) = 0 \begin{cases} \Omega & s = t \\ E(\varepsilon_t \varepsilon_s') = \end{cases} \begin{cases} 0 & s \neq t \end{cases}$$

$\psi_0 = I$ and $\psi(L)$ is a 2×2 coefficient matrix whose elements are functions of the lag operator L. As shown by Whittle (1963, section 2.8) the process (4.5.11) will generally possess the vector autoregressive representation

$$\begin{bmatrix} \beta_{11}(L) & \beta_{12}(L) \\ \beta_{21}(L) & \beta_{22}(L) \end{bmatrix} \begin{bmatrix} y_t \\ x_t \end{bmatrix} = \begin{bmatrix} \varepsilon_{1t} \\ \varepsilon_{2t} \end{bmatrix} \tag{4.5.12}$$

which can be expressed as

$$B(L)Y_t = \varepsilon_t$$

That is

$$Y_t = \sum_{j=1}^{\infty} B_j Y_{t-j} + \varepsilon_t \tag{4.5.13}$$

Granger (1969) proposed a definition of causality based on an estimation of a multivariate time series model. According to Granger's definition: 'a variable x causes another variable y, if the one step ahead predictor of y based on all present and past information *including* x has a lower mean squared error than the predictor of y based on all present and past information *excluding* x'.

With regard to the infinite moving average representation (4.5.11) this definition implies that x does not cause y if and only if $\psi_{12}(L) = 0$ or either $\psi_{11}(L) = 0$ or $\psi_{11}(L)$ is proportional to $\psi_{12}(L)$. Within the vector autoregression (4.5.12) Granger (1969) showed that x does not cause y if and only if $\beta_{12}(L) = 0$; while x and y are independent if $\beta_{12}(L) = \beta_{21}(L) = \omega_{12} = 0$, where ω_{12} is the off diagonal element of the error covariance matrix Ω and represents the degree of contemporaneous relationship between x and y. It should be noted that a more convenient parameterisation of contemporaneous causality requires multiplying through (4.5.13) by a lower triangular matrix R, which is defined as

$$R'R = \Omega^{-1} \tag{4.5.14}$$

so that $R\Omega R' = I$. Then the system

$$RY_t = \sum_{j=1}^{\infty} RB_j Y_{t-j} + \eta_t \tag{4.5.15}$$

where

$$E(\eta_t \eta_s) = \begin{cases} I & s = t \\ 0 & s \neq t \end{cases}$$

will have the contemporaneous value y_t appearing in the second equation. This coefficient will then allow a direct test for 'contemporaneous causality'. It should be noted that the null hypothesis that x does not cause y in the bivariate model (4.5.13), can be tested easily by running the two regressions

$$y_t = c + \sum_{j=1}^{p} \beta_{11j} y_{t-j} + \sum_{j=1}^{p} \beta_{12j} x_{t-j} + \varepsilon_{1t} \tag{4.5.16}$$

and

$$y_t = c + \sum_{j=1}^{p} \beta_{11j} y_{t-j} + \varepsilon_{t'} \tag{4.5.17}$$

and comparing the residual sums of squares, RSS_1 and RSS_0 from the models (4.5.16) and (4.5.17) respectively, by means of a likelihood ratio statistic or through the statistic

$$\frac{(RSS_0 - RSS_1)/p}{RSS_1/(n - 2p - 1)} \tag{4.5.18}$$

which would have an $F_{p,n-2_p-1}$ distribution under the null hypothesis and with no lagged endogenous variables present. Despite the presence of lagged endogenous variables the F distribution may still be a reasonable small sample approximation to (4.5.18).

It should be noted that tests of causality crucially depend on the information set they are conditioned upon and little meaning may be attached to simple bivariate tests where several variables linking x to y may have been omitted. In particular see Jacobs, Leamer and Ward (1979), Zellner (1979) and Engle, Hendry and Richard (1983) for a review of the limitations of this type of approach.

Many of the tests of strong form efficiency have originally been done on the stock market and we will briefly look at these before turning to the foreign exchange market. As in the weak form test most interest has focused on what extent various pieces of publicly known information can generate abnormal risk adjusted returns. Several studies have examined whether capitalisation issues affect share prices. In particular Fama, Fisher, Jensen and Roll (1969) demonstrated that the market had already incorporated information contained in a stock split announcement at the time it occurred, thus making it impossible for any profitable trading strategy to be applied on the basis of this information. Finn (1974) and Firth (1977) found similar evidence for Canada and U.K. respectively. Firth found that the announcement that 10 per cent investment holdings had accumulated in a firm was quickly reflected in share price and ruled out opportunities for profitable trading. In these strong form tests Firth compared the actual share price against the 'expected' share performance, where the 'expected' price is based on the market model of the form proposed by Sharpe (1964) and Lintner (1965) and used basic regression analysis of regressing the change in share price against the announcement.

Other types of 'news' that have been examined is earnings announcements and dividends. Ball and Brown (1968) found that for the U.S. most of the material in annual reports had been previously predicted, while Charest (1978) showed that trading based on dividend news could have earned significant abnormal returns, presumably because the stock market seemed to be slow in processing this information. This assertion was based on a study of selected changes in cash dividends of stocks and shares on the New York Stock Exchange for the period 1947 to 1967. Similarly Niederhoffer and Osborne (1966) and Lorie and Niederhoffer (1968), showed that inside information can be used profitably, but only on a very small scale.

A large amount of research, however, has centred on the performance of Unit Trusts and mutual funds since not only are they 'informed' professional investors but a long record of their performance is also available. Tests in this area try to determine whether a professionally selected portfolio performs better than a randomly generated portfolio of the same risk class (or better than the average market performance). Jensen (1968) examined 115 U.S. mutual funds from 1955 to 1964, and found that none consistently performed better than the average, with fifty eight performing poorer than the general market index. Other studies for the U.S., by Friend (1972), Sharpe (1966), and Williamson (1972) have upheld the theory of strong form efficiency in the matter of portfolio performance. Contrary evidence has been obtained by Richards (1978) concerning the managed Becker Securities Fund Performance who found that in several cases U.K. pension funds outperformed the market.

Overall, the evidence on strong form efficiency on the stock market is rather mixed. One paper by Lloyd-Davies and Canes (1978) provided evidence that individual investment recommendations by professional analysts contained inside information. Their evidence was based on the fact that after a secondary dissemination of information in the Wall Street Journal column 'Heard on the Street', stock market prices were significantly affected for a relatively long subsequent trading period. However, as with other studies, no account was taken of transactions costs which led to the general conclusion that it is very difficult to 'beat the market' in a consistent manner. This has been taken logically as a criticism of the competence of the 'professional' and of the value of market analysis. To quote from Lorie and Hamilton (1973), 'the most general implication of the efficient market hypothesis is that most security analysis is logically incomplete and valueless'.

Those who believe in efficient markets argue that the model can still accommodate analysts who, through extraordinary talents, can earn consistently above average profits. Grubel (1979) has suggested that, in the securities industry, successful managers are very quickly promoted, making it difficult for empirical studies to identify them.

However, the reality of the situation for most stock market participants is that if they observed the gains and losses that actually resulted from their researched trades then their expectations of gain would be negatively correlated with the level of market efficiency. As the market becomes more efficient, so that prices incorporate more information, then exploitable opportunities decline. Sooner or later investors realise that they can no longer hope to achieve or 'win' the personal gains of an inefficient market and so curtail their security analysis efforts. When market efficiency once more declines then investors are once more willing to pay for the chance of above average performance, and more research takes place.

A considerably fewer number of studies have been concerned with testing strong form efficiency on the foreign exchange market. Since central banks may freely intervene and use insider information, it is likely that participants in the foreign exchange market have a much greater variability of expectations and diversity of beliefs than stock exchange agents. Thus there is *a priori* reasoning to believe that strong form efficiency is less likely to hold in the foreign exchange markets. Also the strong form is obviously difficult to rigorously test and the scope for research into the profit earning potential from 'insider' trading is severely limited, especially in the U.K., where trading on such information is a criminal offence. However of the studies that have been done, Henfrey, Allbrecht and Richards (1977) have conducted a survey on a largely non-technical basis; while Goodman (1979) has examined the exchange rate forecasting performance of several information agencies that used economic models, judgemental forecasts and filter rules. Goodman found that technically orientated agencies performed the best and concluded (1979, p. 426) that 'speculative runs do occur in the exchange market and that the foreign exchange market is not efficient'.

Two further studies of note are by Rogalski and Vinso (1977), and Caves and Feige (1980). In the former study, Rogalski and Vinso used six exchange rate series between 1920 and 1924 and for Canada between 1953 to 1957, and found that the spot rate was efficient with respect to prices and rates of inflation. Hence the information conveyed to market participants in the nature of price level changes is immediately incorporated into current exchange rates.

The study of Caves and Feige (1980) is the most technically sophisticated and is based on the causality tests discussed earlier. Since the asset market approach to exchange rate determination allows the spot rate to be determined by innovations in the relative supplies of national monies, a natural approach is to see if last periods unanticipated money supply $(m_{t-1} - \hat{m}_{t-1})$, where $\hat{m}_{t-1} = E_{t-2}(m_{t-1})$ can improve in terms of reducing MSE of a model with spot rates depending on past spot rates. From (4.5.12) we have

$$\begin{bmatrix} \beta_{11}(L) & \beta_{12}(L) \\ \beta_{21}(L) & \beta_{22}(L) \end{bmatrix} \begin{bmatrix} \Delta m_t \\ \Delta s_t \end{bmatrix} = \begin{bmatrix} \varepsilon_{1t} \\ \varepsilon_{2t} \end{bmatrix}$$

then strong form efficiency implies $\beta_{21}(L) = 0$ and $\beta_{22}(L) = 1$. This is indeed the type of test undertaken by Caves and Feige (1980) who took monthly Canadian data between January 1953 and April 1963 when the Canadian dollar was freely floating against the U.S. dollar. The authors concluded in favour of semi-strong efficiency, since lagged changes in money supply and spot rates could not reduce the one step ahead forecast mse of s_t.

4.6   The distribution of changes in the exchange rate

The original work on price changes in speculative markets generally assumed normally distributed errors, so that the basic model was one of a Gaussian Random Walk (see Bachelier 1900, Kendall 1953 and Osborne 1959). However, consequent analysis of stock market prices by Fama

(1965), Mandelbrot (1963, 1969) and Granger and Morgenstern (1970); and on foreign exchange rates by Upson (1972), Giddy and Dufey (1975), Westerfield (1977), Cornell and Dietrich (1978) and McFarland, Pettit and Sung (1982) have cast doubt on this assumption.

In general there appears to have been a concensus on the following facts:

(i)   speculative market price changes have peaked, long tailed distributions with a possibly infinite variance,

(ii)   the price changes are not necessarily independent, identically distributed (iid),

(iii)   extending the observation period from daily to weekly to monthly levels etc., generally tends to reduce the non-normality within the data.

As can be seen from the results presented in Tables 4.4, there is indeed evidence of leptokurtosis (i.e. fat tails) with the daily data examined earlier in Section 4.2. Analysis of weekly data between 1973 and 1985 reveals that about 3 per cent of the observations for the exchange rate series examined lie in excess of three standard deviations, while normality would predict only 0.3 per cent. Previous studies in the literature have suggested a variety of tests for departures from normality. In particular, the non-parametric Kolmogorov-Smirnov test given by

$$D = \frac{\max |F_B - F_E|}{n}$$

where F_E denotes the cumulated frequencies expected under the null hypothesis of normality and F_B the cumulated frequencies of the observed distribution, has had its exact bounds tabulated by Lilliefors (1967). Fama and Roll (1971) have alternatively used the studentised range test statistic given by

$$SR = \frac{\max x_i - \min x_i}{S(x)} = \frac{x_n - x_1}{\left[\dfrac{1}{n-1} \displaystyle\sum_{j=1}^{n} (x_j - \bar{x})^2 \right]^{1/2}}$$

where x_i $(i = 1, 1 \ldots n)$ denote the observations in ascending order of magnitude and $S(x)$ their standard deviation. Exact fractiles for SR have been given for the normal distribution for different sample sizes by David, Hartley and Pearson (1954, p. 491).

The fairly widespread agreement on leptokurtosis in speculative price changes led Mandelbrot (1963) to suggest a non-normal stable Paretian distribution. The basic idea is that whatever the shape of the distribution of a price change, the process by which price changes are formed over a time period should follow the Generalised Central Limit Theorem of Gnedenko and Kolmogorov (1954) where a sum of independent drawings tends to a stable Pareto–Levy distribution. The stable Pareto distribution has characteristic function $f(\phi)$ given by

$$\ln f(\phi) = i\partial\phi - \gamma|\phi|^{\alpha}[1 + i\beta(\phi/i\sigma)w(\phi, \alpha)] \tag{4.6.1}$$

where

$$w(\phi, \alpha) = \begin{cases} \tan(\gamma\alpha/2) & \alpha \neq 1 \\ \dfrac{2}{\pi}\ln|\phi| & \alpha = 1 \end{cases}$$

$i^2 = -1$; the mean of the distribution is ∂.

The symbol γ denotes a scale parameter, β determines skewness, so that $\beta = 0$ gives the symmetric density with characteristic function

$$\ln f(\phi) = i\partial\phi - \gamma|\phi|^{\alpha} \tag{4.6.2}$$

There are only two cases where the density can be represented in closed form. Firstly when $\alpha = 1$, $\beta = 0$ the distribution tends to a Cauchy and when $\alpha = 2$ the distribution becomes the normal. Another important property of the distribution is that all moments of order $r < \alpha$ are finite, so that only in the case of the normal does the mean and variance exist. For $1 < \alpha < 2$, only the mean exists and for $0 < \alpha < 1$, neither the mean nor variance exists. There have been many attempts following Fama (1965) at estimating stable Paretian densities; a useful survey of available methods is by Arnold and Press (1983). Most studies on the change in exchange rates have estimated α between 1.3 and 1.8. Westerfield (1977) analysed weekly data between 1972 and 1975 for the U.K., Canada and West Germany; McFarland, Pettit and Sung (1982) examined daily data for the U.K., West Germany and Japan between 1975 and 1979, while Friedman and Vandersteel (1982) looked at daily, weekly and monthly data between 1973 and 1979. The vast majority of cases lead to an estimate of α between 1.25 and 1.80 implying the non-existence of the variance for the change in the exchange rate. The study by Friedman and Vandersteel (1982) found the hypothesis that Δs_t is iid from a stable Paretian distribution could be rejected in favour of a hypothesis that it comes from a normal distribution with time varying mean and variance.

A slightly more tractable distribution for estimation purposes is that of the Power Exponential given by

$$f(y) = w(\alpha)\tau^{-1}\exp\left[-c(\alpha)\left|\frac{y_1}{\sigma}\right|^{2/(1+\alpha)}\right] \quad -\infty \leqslant y \leqslant \infty \tag{4.6.3}$$

$$w(\alpha) = \frac{[\Gamma(3(1+\alpha)/2]^{1/2}}{(1+\alpha)[\Gamma((1+\alpha)/2)]^{3/2}}$$

$$c(\alpha) = \left[\frac{\Gamma(3(1+\alpha)/2)}{\Gamma((1+\alpha)/2)} \right]^{1/2}$$

when $\alpha = 0$ the distribution reduces to the normal density, $\alpha < 0$ implies leptokurtosis and $\alpha < 0$ gives a platykurtic distribution.

The implication of the existence of an infinite variance in the unconditional distribution of exchange rate changes are interesting in terms of understanding the underlying mechanism generating changes in the exchange rate. However it is unclear how much this matters in terms of estimating models of exchange rate determination since the important quantity is then the conditional distribution of residuals given the estimated model. We will see in the next section that conditional distributions with finite moments can explain the reported phenomena in unconditional distributions.

4.7   Volatility and conditional variance models of changes in the log of the exchange rate

It has long been recognised that asset price and foreign exchange markets have the characteristic of time varying volatility. For example Mandelbrot (1963) noted that 'large changes [in speculative asset prices] tend to be followed by large changes . . . of either sign . . . and small changes tend to be followed by small changes . . .'. Mussa (1979) described this time varying volatility as an empirical regularity of exchange rate behaviour and Engle (1982) has discussed the presence of similar phenomenon in other forms of economic data. We have previously noted the significant values of $Q(\hat{\varepsilon}^2)$ for daily exchange rates reported in Table 4.4; before analysing this in more detail we consider some definitions and models of volatility.

Some results on applying standard definitions of volatility to weekly nominal exchange rates for each year are given in Tables 4.6 along with the various definitions used. The data is transferred according to

$$S_t^* = 100 S_t / S_1, \quad t = 1, 2 \ldots \eta$$

so that the first observation in each series is equal to 100. To complete the picture the minimum and maximum values as well as the greatest positive and negative changes in spot exchange rates over the previous period are presented. Broadly it appears that Italy has had the most unstable exchange rate against the U.S. dollar, while France has experienced relatively low variability. The U.K. pound was highly volatile in 1972 and 1973 and this dampened down until 1976 when it increased in variability, reaching a peak in 1978.

Table 4.6A *Volatility in weekly spot exchange rates*
West Germany

Year	0	1973	1974	1975	1976	1977	1978	1979
Number of observations	362	30	52	52	52	52	52	52
Mean	118.494	106.806	102.691	107.861	105.448	114.251	132.228	144.809
Minimum	92.817	98.516	92.817	99.417	101.484	109.170	122.794	138.378
Maximum	155.606	115.213	109.647	116.168	112.457	125.550	150.093	154.280
Maximum positive step	6.28147	5.67188	3.04797	2.14683	1.80228	2.51789	6.28147	3.49854
Maximum negative step	-8.69335	-4.45269	-3.23350	-2.75643	-1.24569	-1.69626	-8.69335	-2.46488
Range	62.788	16.698	16.830	16.751	10.973	16.380	27.299	15.902
Mean absolute change	1.05326	1.70175	1.05303	0.86060	0.53996	0.66624	1.47280	0.96142
Adjusted range	0.52988	0.15634	0.16389	0.15530	0.10406	0.14336	0.20646	0.10982
Relative mean deviation	0.12409	0.04002845	0.03304090	0.04814222	0.02449533	0.02526331	0.03876072	0.02390280
Variance	284.952	23.980	17.387	29.165	9.27269	13.667	38.871	18.085
Coefficient of variation	0.14246	0.04584863	0.04060496	0.05006833	0.02887794	0.03235803	0.04715055	0.02936700
Kolmogorov-Smirnov D	0.19135	0.13865	0.11624	0.22080	0.21953	0.12925	0.12878	0.09588580

Year	1980
Number of observations	19
Mean	147.843
Minimum	134.959
Maximum	155.606
Maximum positive step	5.19481
Maximum negative step	-4.24066
Range	20.647
Mean absolute change	1.87590
Adjusted range	0.13965
Relative mean deviation	0.03345887
Variance	34.673
Coefficient of variation	0.03982883
Kolmogorov-Smirnov D	0.16536

Table 4.6B *Volatility in spot exchange rates*
United Kingdom

Year	0	1973	1974	1975	1976	1977	1978	1979
Number of observations	362	30	53	52	52	52	52	52
Mean	80.637	95.222	91.027	86.252	70.159	67.967	74.643	82.685
Minimum	60.864	89.659	84.783	78.731	60.864	66.324	70.422	77.167
Maximum	100.545	100.545	94.594	94.602	79.191	74.256	80.171	90.757
Maximum positive step	2.84102	1.33878	2.19887	1.10917	2.33119	1.85250	2.76318	2.84102
Maximum negative step	-3.54155	-2.29617	-2.29617	-1.87585	-3.54155	-0.47091	-2.95777	-2.57638
Range	39.681	10.885	9.81125	15.871	18.327	7.93150	9.74898	13.590
Mean absolute change	0.61082	0.65584	0.59694	0.52333	0.73113	0.19016	0.62811	0.86001
Adjusted range	0.49209	0.11432	0.10778	0.18401	0.26121	0.11670	0.13061	0.16435
Relative mean deviation	0.10716	0.02736017	0.01836347	0.06149776	0.05693879	0.01986209	0.02667255	0.03824702
Variance	98.006	10.413	4.71912	32.303	25.264	3.19166	5.55472	12.571
Coefficient of variation	0.12277	0.03388811	0.02386490	0.06589485	0.07164119	0.02628504	0.03157498	0.04287994
Kolmogorov–Smirnov D	0.09237853	0.09658135	0.12779	0.17174	0.12923	0.27259	0.16145	0.12219

Year	1980
Number of observations	19
Mean	87.403
Minimum	83.207
Maximum	89.815
Maximum positive step	1.96536
Maximum negative step	-2.33508
Range	6.60829
Mean absolute change	0.88322
Adjusted range	0.07560709
Relative mean deviation	0.01672667
Variance	3.09928
Coefficient of variation	0.02014206
Kolmogorov–Smirnov D	0.19880

Table 4.6C *Volatility in spot exchange rates*

France

Year	0	1973	1974	1975	1976	1977	1978	1979
Number of observations	362	30	53	52	52	52	52	52
Mean	96.135	101.416	90.651	101.641	91.093	88.592	96.646	102.388
Minimum	83.246	92.559	83.246	95.561	86.945	87.163	88.773	98.042
Maximum	108.964	107.180	97.607	108.964	97.998	92.298	106.440	108.225
Maximum positive step	3.69887	2.34987	2.56745	2.61097	0.73977	1.47955	3.69887	2.04526
Maximum negative step	−5.35248	−4.91732	−4.00348	−3.00261	−3.26371	−0.78329	−5.35248	−1.52306
Range	25.718	14.621	14.360	13.403	11.053	5.13490	17.668	10.183
Mean absolute change	0.74086	1.09991	0.83266	0.80547	0.43175	0.30205	1.05633	0.63056
Adjusted range	0.26752	0.14417	0.15841	0.13187	0.12134	0.05796116	0.18281	0.09945239
Relative mean deviation	0.06010277	0.03050708	0.02205337	0.03208290	0.03510624	0.01092694	0.03749307	0.01701487
Variance	42.125	14.407	7.63075	14.174	13.201	1.31124	17.007	5.51123
Coefficient of variation	0.06751316	0.03742635	0.03047257	0.03704090	0.03988628	0.01292544	0.04267078	0.02292839
Kolmogorov–Smirnov D	0.10827	0.10865	0.11340	0.17116	0.21237	0.15291	0.11601	0.12148

Year	1980
Number of observations	19
Mean	103.960
Minimum	96.171
Maximum	108.790
Maximum positive step	2.95909
Maximum negative step	−2.30635
Range	12.620
Mean absolute change	1.11691
Adjusted range	0.12139
Relative mean deviation	0.03000595
Variance	13.274
Coefficient of variation	0.03504557
Kolmogorov–Smirnov D	0.16054

Table 4.6D *Volatility in spot exchange rates*

Italy

Year	0	1973	1974	1975	1976	1977	1978	1979
Number of observations	362	30	53	52	52	52	52	52
Mean	78.798	101.822	91.239	80.895	71.316	67.223	69.529	71.483
Minimum	65.579	94.659	87.893	86.231	66.053	66.825	67.656	69.377
Maximum	105.579	105.579	95.549	95.193	87.122	67.953	74.421	73.828
Maximum positive step	4.33234	4.33234	2.31454	1.30564	2.90801	0.35608	1.66172	1.12760
Maximum negative step	-6.29080	-5.34125	-3.62018	-1.48368	-6.25080	-0.47478	-2.96736	-0.94955
Range	40.000	10.920	7.65579	8.96142	21.068	1.12760	6.76558	4.45104
Mean absolute change	0.53758	1.10099	0.74070	0.45500	0.84017	0.07563856	0.39681	0.30023
Adjusted range	0.50763	0.10724	0.08390913	0.09859120	0.29542	0.01677391	0.09674892	0.06226749
Relative mean deviation	0.14011	0.02440598	0.01774508	0.03216509	0.04289754	0.00325252	0.01613235	0.01494358
Variance	143.504	8.87358	3.79445	9.69744	20.167	0.07577048	2.07187	1.50806
Coefficient of variation	0.15203	0.02925554	0.02134980	0.03426018	0.06297034	0.00409478	0.02058367	0.01717946
Kolmogorov–Smirnov D	0.25192	0.12291	0.10664	0.17057	0.33208	0.14162	0.10707	0.10947

Year	1980
Number of observations	19
Mean	71.085
Minimum	65.579
Maximum	74.243
Maximum positive step	2.01780
Maximum negative step	-2.19585
Range	8.66469
Mean absolute change	0.77151
Adjusted range	0.12189
Relative mean deviation	0.03410715
Variance	7.46111
Coefficient of variation	0.03842564
Kolmogorov–Smirnov D	0.21152

In order to motivate the class of conditional heteroskedasticity models originally proposed by Engle (1982) it is convenient to emphasise the effect of conditioning on the moments of a process. For example the common AR(1) model (4.2.6):

$$y_t = \phi y_{t-1} + \varepsilon_t \tag{4.7.1}$$

$$E(\varepsilon_t^2) = \sigma^2, \quad E(\varepsilon_t \varepsilon_r) = 0 \quad r \neq t$$

has an unconditional mean and variance of 0 and $\sigma^2/(1 - \phi^2)$ respectively. At time t the conditional mean will be

$$E_t y_{t+1} = \phi y_t$$

and the conditional variance

$$\text{var}_t \, y_{t+1} = E_t(y_{t+1} - E_t \, y_{t+1})^2$$
$$= E_t \varepsilon_{t+1}^2 = \sigma^2$$

As noted by Engle and Bollerslev (1986) 'one might claim that the success of time series models is attributable to the use of the conditional mean for forecasting rather than the unconditional mean. Presumably similar gains are available for variances from using more sophisticated models of the conditional variances.'

This idea can be illustrated by allowing the AR(1) model (4.7.1) to have a time dependent conditional variance in the following way

$$y_t = \phi y_{t-1} + \varepsilon_t$$

$$E_t \varepsilon_{t+1} = 0 \quad \text{and} \quad \text{var}_t \, \varepsilon_{t+1} = h_{t+1} = \omega + \alpha \varepsilon_t^2 \tag{4.7.2}$$

where $|\phi| < 1, \omega > 0$ and $\alpha \geqslant 0$. Now the disturbance term ε_t is still serially uncorrelated but is not independent, since its second moment is related through time.

If $\alpha < 1$ the unconditional variance of ε_t is given by

$$\text{var}(\varepsilon_t) = \omega/(1 - \alpha) = \sigma^2$$

and is thus still a constant. However the conditional variance (4.7.2) will vary over time and will be usable for prediction. In his seminal paper Engle (1982) considered the so-called Autoregressive Conditional Heteroskedasticity (ARCH) regression model of the form

$$y_t \,|\, \Omega_{t-1} \sim N(x_t' \beta, h_t) \tag{4.7.3}$$

$$h_t = f(\varepsilon_{t-1}, \varepsilon_{t-2}, \ldots \varepsilon_{t-q}, \alpha) \tag{4.7.4}$$

$$\varepsilon_t = y_t - x_t' \beta$$

where (4.7.3) states that the conditional distribution of y_t given an information set Ω_{t-1} will be normal, with mean $x_t'\beta$ which is a linear combination of k explanatory variables x_t and variance h_t which is a function of the q past innovations plus other exogenous variables. A specific parameterisation of (4.7.4) is the ARCH (q) model

$$h_t = \alpha_0 + \sum_{j=1}^{q} \alpha_j \varepsilon_{t-j}^2 \tag{4.7.5}$$

Engle (1982) also developed the necessary theory to obtain MLE of the parameters in (4.7.3) and (4.7.4) and showed that a Lagrange Multiplier (LM) test for ARCH (q) errors in a regression can be obtained by regressing the squared residual on its last q lags and taking n times the multiple correlation coefficient. An asymptotically equivalent formulation of the LM test for ARCH errors is to take $Q(\hat{\varepsilon}_t^2)$ as in Table 4.4. It is also necessary to impose conditions on the parameters in (4.7.5) to ensure existence of higher moments and maintenance of a positive conditional variance.

The minimum requirement is one of non-negativity for all the α parameters in (4.7.5). A convenient model that avoids the necessity of imposing such constraints and uses relatively few parameters is the Generalized Autoregressive Conditional Heteroskedasticity (GARCH) model introduced by Bollerslev (1986). The GARCH (p, q) model is then

$$h_t = \alpha_0 + \sum_{j=1}^{q} \alpha_j \varepsilon_{t-j}^2 + \sum_{j=1}^{p} \beta_j h_{t-j} \tag{4.7.6}$$

Pantulla (1986) has shown the above model can be rewritten as

$$\varepsilon_t^2 = \omega + \sum_{j=1}^{m} (\alpha_j + \beta_j)\varepsilon_{t-j}^2 - \sum_{j=1}^{p} \beta_j v_{t-j} + v_t \tag{4.7.7}$$

where $m = \max(p, q)$ and v_t is a serially uncorrelated but heteroskedastic process. From (4.7.7) it can be shown that ε_t^2 will approximately have the properties of an ARMA (m, p) process as defined in (4.2.8). The implications of this, is, that the same techniques of model identification introduced by Box and Jenkins (1970) for ARMA processes can be used to identify the orders of a GARCH process from analysis of the autocorrelations and partial autocorrelations of the squares of a realisation or set of residuals. Hence the GARCH $(1, 1)$ process

$$h_t = \alpha_0 + \alpha_1 \varepsilon_{t-1}^2 + \beta_1 h_{t-1} \tag{4.7.8}$$

will induce autocorrelation in ε_t^2 similar to that of an ARMA $(1, 1)$ process.

Models of this type have been applied to exchange rate data by a variety of authors (in particular see McCurdy and Morgan 1987, Engle and

Bollerslev 1986, Milhoj 1987, Hsieh 1985, etc.). The results presented are discussed in more detail in Baillie and Bollerslev (1989b) who used the same daily data between 1980 and 1985 as discussed earlier.

The basic model can be summarised by the equations

$$100\Delta s_t = b_0 + \sum_{j=1}^{6} b_j D_{jt} + \varepsilon_t \tag{4.7.9}$$

$$\varepsilon_t | \Omega_{t-1} \sim t(0, h_t, v) \tag{4.7.10}$$

$$h_t = \omega_0 + \alpha_1 \varepsilon_{t-1}^2 + \beta_1 h_{t-1} + \sum_{j=1}^{6} \omega_j D_{jt} \tag{4.7.11}$$

where $D_{1t} \ldots D_{5t}$ are a set of dummy variables for Monday through Friday respectively, D_6 is a vacation dummy which takes the value unity following the market being closed for any reason other than a weekend. The model then allows daily seasonal variation to effect the conditional mean (4.7.9) and the conditional variance equation (4.7.11), which is otherwise a GARCH $(1, 1)$ process. The conditional distribution in (4.7.10) is the t distribution where the arguments in parenthesis represent the mean variance and degrees of freedom respectively. Following Bollerslev (1987) the likelihood of the model is given by

$$\log L = \sum_{t=1}^{n} \left\{ \log \Gamma\left(\frac{v+1}{2}\right) - \log \Gamma\left(\frac{v}{2}\right) - \frac{1}{2}\log(v-2)h_t \right.$$
$$\left. - \frac{1}{2}(v+1)\log[1 + \varepsilon_t^2 h_t^{-1}(v-2)^{-1}] \right\}$$

where $\Gamma(\cdot)$ denotes the usual gamma function. Maximum likelihood estimates of the parameters and their asymptotic standard errors were obtained by numerical methods from using the Berndt, Hall, Hall and Hausman (1974) algorithm. The results are given in Table 4.7 and reveal some striking regularities across currencies. The coefficient estimates of the dummy variables generally have the same sign across currencies in both the conditional mean and the conditional variance parts of the model. It is particularly interesting to note that $\hat{b}_3$ and $\hat{b}_4$ indicate that Tuesday to Wednesday price changes tend to be positive and Wednesday to Thursday changes tend to be negative. Similar effects have been noted by Levi (1978) and McFarland, Pettit and Sung (1982). Prior to October 1981 Wednesday transactions of foreign currencies cleared on the Friday, while dollar transactions did not clear until the following Monday (see Levi 1983). The potential loss of two days interest reduces the demand for dollars relative to other currencies and hence depreciates the value of the dollar on Wednesdays.

Differing rates of flow of information probably account for the fact Monday's price reflects the accumulation of news that occurs since the market closed on the Friday, while Thursdays are conventionally the day when money supply figures are announced.

In the conditional variance equation (4.7.11), Mondays and the vacation dummy are associated with increased volatility and Thursdays, a reduction in variance.

Another interesting aspect of the estimated models is the closeness of the estimate of $\alpha_1 + \beta_1$ to unity, indicating the probable existence of the so called integrated GARCH or IGARCH process (see Engle and Bollerslev 1986). For the GARCH(p, q) model the unconditional variance is given by $\omega_0/(1 - \alpha_1 - \beta_1)$. In the GARCH$(1, 1)$ model a value of $\alpha_1 + \beta_1$ equal to unity implies an infinite variance in the unconditional distribution for Δs_t. The degrees of freedom parameter v is generally estimated between about 6 and 16, suggesting a quite fat tailed conditional distribution.

Overall, the combined effect of the conditional t distribution and the time dependent heteroskedasticity is generally successful in explaining the kurtosis present in the unconditional distribution of Δs_t. Use of the conditional normal distribution gave similar parameter estimates but was unable to explain the leptokurtic unconditional distribution. Baillie and Bollerslev (1989b) also report estimates on the same data set sampled on a weekly, biweekly and four weekly frequency. ARCH type effects remain very strong in weekly data, less so in biweekly data and are undetectable in the four weekly data. The assumption of normality appears to be a reasonable approximation to four weekly and biweekly data, very marginal on weekly data and quite inappropriate on daily data.

In conclusion we should note that there is a surprising regularity of the statistical models to explain exchange rate changes. The need for an economically based model to explain the nature of the excess kurtosis and time dependent heteroskedasticity seems more crucial.

Table 4.7 Daily GARCH models

$$100 \cdot \Delta \log s_t = b_0 + \sum_{j=1}^{6} b_j D_{jt} + \varepsilon_t$$

$$\varepsilon_t | \Omega_{t-1} \sim t(0, h_t, v) \qquad t = 1 \cdots 1244$$

$$h_t = \omega_0 + \sum_{j=1}^{6} \omega_j D_{jt} + \alpha_1 \varepsilon_{t-1}^2 + \beta_1 h_{t-1}$$

	France	Italy	Japan	Switzerland	U.K.	West Germany
b_0	−0.063	−0.074	−0.028	−0.048	−0.043	−0.058
	(—)	(—)	(—)	(—)	(—)	(—)
b_1	−0.028	−0.037	−0.042	−0.048	−0.017	−0.079
	(0.046)	(0.038)	(0.038)	(0.040)	(0.041)	(0.041)
b_2	−0.003	0.016	0.063	0.019	−0.011	0.020
	(0.036)	(0.035)	(0.038)	(0.046)	(0.040)	(0.040)
b_3	0.114	0.100	0.063	0.093	0.069	0.094
	(0.036)	(0.032)	(0.033)	(0.040)	(0.033)	(0.04)
b_4	−0.051	−0.053	−0.021	−0.046	−0.025	−0.016
	(0.032)	(0.031)	(0.030)	(0.041)	(0.034)	(0.036)
b_5	−0.030	−0.025	−0.062	−0.019	−0.017	−0.019
	(0.035)	(0.033)	(0.035)	(0.043)	(0.037)	(0.038)
b_6	−0.202	−0.224	−0.217	−0.315	−0.176	−0.239
	(0.142)	(0.127)	(0.118)	(0.130)	(0.117)	(0.139)
ω_0	0.030	0.016	0.008	0.008	0.012	0.015
	(—)	(—)	(—)	(—)	(—)	(—)

ω_1	0.199	0.091	0.072	0.052	0.049	0.109
	(0.069)	(0.043)	(0.042)	(0.051)	(0.045)	(0.047)
ω_2	-0.165	-0.085	-0.005	-0.007	0.019	-0.080
	(0.067)	(0.043)	(0.049)	(0.063)	(0.052)	(0.054)
ω_3	-0.003	-0.016	-0.063	-0.042	-0.096	-0.020
	(0.053)	(0.035)	(0.044)	(0.059)	(0.048)	(0.047)
ω_4	-0.075	-0.025	-0.058	-0.021	-0.018	-0.049
	(0.042)	(0.029)	(0.034)	(0.048)	(0.040)	(0.038)
ω_5	0.043	0.035	0.055	0.021	0.045	0.041
	(0.045)	(0.032)	(0.031)	(0.047)	(0.039)	(0.040)
ω_6	0.383	0.158	0.080	0.085	0.124	0.234
	(0.121)	(0.070)	(0.054)	(0.068)	(0.065)	(0.082)
α_1	0.146	0.132	0.083	0.075	0.066	0.108
	(0.031)	(0.027)	(0.018)	(0.017)	(0.018)	(0.023)
β_1	0.793	0.827	0.901	0.908	0.902	0.855
	(0.038)	(0.034)	(0.022)	(0.021)	(0.026)	(0.029)
$1/\nu$	0.153	0.103	0.169	0.068	0.112	0.067
	(0.006)	(0.024)	(0.005)	(0.006)	(0.038)	(0.022)
Log L	-1251.758	-1106.722	-1155.047	-1342.007	-1171.106	-1240.828
Q (15)	11.418	9.881	14.052	9.263	9.818	9.352
Q^2 (15)	6.861	17.267	24.093	22.472	9.002	19.098
m_3	-0.109	0.097	0.296	0.169	-0.297	0.202
m_4	7.417	4.031	5.282	3.549	4.607	3.668
$3(\hat{\nu}-2)(\hat{\nu}-4)^{-1}$	5.366	4.051	6.130	3.560	4.217	3.549
$\mathrm{LR}_{1/\nu=0}$	75.874	24.630	60.842	9.238	35.826	11.160

Key: $3(\hat{\nu}-2)(\hat{\nu}-4)^{-1}$ is the theoretical Kurtosis of the conditional t density and should be compared with m_4 the sample Kurtosis coefficient.

Appendix

The Phillips Perron test statistics used in Section 4.2 are defined as follows. For equation (4.2.12):

$$Z(t_{\alpha^*}) = (S_u/S_{nl})t_{\alpha^*} - (1/2S_{nl})(S_{nl}^2 - S_u^2)$$
$$\times \left[n^{-2}\sum(y_{t-1} - \bar{Y}_{-1})^2\right]^{-1/2} \qquad (4.A.1)$$

$$Z(\Phi_1) = (S_u^2/S_{nl}^2)\Phi_1 - (1/2S_{nl}^2)(S_{nl}^2 - S_u^2)$$
$$\times \left\{n(\alpha^* - 1) - (1/4)(S_{nl}^2 - S_u^2)\left[n^{-2}\sum(y_{t-1} - \bar{Y}_{-1})^2\right]^{-1}\right\} \qquad (4.A.2)$$

where

$$t_{\alpha^*} = (\alpha^* - \alpha_0)\left[\sum_{t=1}^{n}(y_{t-1} - \bar{Y}_{-1})^2\right]^{1/2}\bigg/ S^*,$$

$$\Phi_1 = (2S^{*2})^{-1}(nS_0^2 - nS^{*2})$$

$$\alpha^* = \sum_{t=1}^{n}(y_t - \bar{Y}_0)y_{t-1}\bigg/ \sum_{t=1}^{n}(y_{t-1} - \bar{Y}_{-1})^2,$$

$$\mu^* = \bar{Y}_0 - \alpha^*\bar{Y}_{-1},$$

$$S^{*2} = n^{-1}\sum_{t=1}^{n}(y_t - \mu^* - \alpha^*y_{t-1})^2,$$

$$\bar{Y}_{-i} = n^{-1}\sum_{t=1}^{n}y_{t-i} \quad (i = 0, 1)$$

For equation (4.2.11):

$$Z(t_{\tilde{\alpha}}) = (S_u/S_{nl})t_{\tilde{\alpha}} - (n^3/4\sqrt{3}D_x^{1/2}S_{nl})(S_{nl}^2 - S_u^2) \qquad (4.A.3)$$

$$Z(\Phi_3) = (S_u^2/S_{nl}^2)\Phi_3 - (1/2S_{nl}^2)(S_{nl}^2 - S_u^2)$$
$$\times \left[n(\tilde{\alpha} - 1) - (n^6/48D_x)(S_{n_e}^2 - S_u^2)\right] \qquad (4.A.4)$$

$$Z(\Phi_2) = (S_u^2/S_{nl}^2)\Phi_2 - (1/3S_{nl}^2)(S_{nl}^2 - S_u^2)$$
$$\times \, [n(\tilde{\alpha} - 1) - (n^6/48D_x)(S_{nl}^2 - S_u^2)] \qquad (4.A.5)$$

where

$$t_{\tilde{\alpha}} = (\tilde{\alpha} - \alpha)/(\tilde{S}^2 C_3)^{1/2},$$

$$\Phi_2 = (3\tilde{S}^2)^{-1}(nS_0^2 - n\tilde{S}^2),$$

$$\Phi_3 = (2\tilde{S}^2)^{-1}[nS_0^2 - n(\bar{Y} - \bar{Y}_{-1})^2 - n\tilde{S}^2],$$

$$\tilde{S}^2 = n^{-1} \sum_{t=1}^{n} [y_t - \tilde{\mu} - \tilde{\beta}(t - n/2) - \tilde{\alpha}y_{t-1}]^2,$$

$$S_0^2 = n^{-1} \sum_{t=1}^{n} (y_t - y_{t-1})^2$$

and C_i is the (i,i) element of the matrix $(X'X)^{-1}$. D_x denotes the determinant of $(X'X)$ and is given by

$$D_x = [n^2(n^2 - 1)/12] \sum y_{t-1}^2 - n \sum (y_{t-1})^2 + n(n + 1)$$
$$\times \sum ty_{t-1} \sum y_{t-1} - [n(n + 1)(2n + 1)/6](\sum y_{t-1})^2.$$

S_u^2 is a consistent estimator of $\sigma_u^2 = \lim n^{-1} \sum E(u_t^2)$ given by the sample analogue under the appropriate null hypothesis. S_{nl}^2 is a consistent estimator of $\sigma^2 = \lim n^{-1} E(S_n^2)$ under the appropriate null hypothesis, where $S_n = \sum_{t=1}^{n} u_t$.

In Section 4.2 the version of S_{nl}^2 used is

$$\tilde{S}_{nl}^2 = n^{-1} \sum_{t=1}^{n} \tilde{u}_t^2 + 2n^{-1} \sum_{t=1}^{n} \sum_{t=\tau+1}^{n} \tilde{u}_t \tilde{u}_{t-\tau} \omega_{\tau l} \qquad (4.A.6)$$

When $\omega_{\tau l} = 1$ for all τ, l. Phillips (1987) has shown that (4.A.6) is a consistent estimator of σ^2 under a wide variety of behaviour of $\tilde{u}_t$. In particular if $\tilde{u}_t$ follows a moving average process of order l, with possible time varying conditional heteroskedasticity but finite unconditional second moment then $\tilde{S}_{nl}^2$ provides a consistent estimator of σ^2. Following a suggestion of Perron and Phillips (1987), the method of Newey and West (1987) was implemented in choosing $\omega_{\tau l} = 1 - \tau/(l + 1)$.

Interest rate parity, transactions costs and the modern theory

5.1 Introduction

The last chapter dealt with certain aspects of spot and forward foreign exchange rate behaviour. One aspect of this was that the random walk and martingale models were seen to be based on the assumption that the equilibrium rate of return on the international financial and foreign exchange markets is either zero or constant. This assumption is generally unrealistic since profit opportunities will clearly depend on the relative interest rates confronting speculators. The interest rate parity theory (IRPT) provides more economic structure to the problem and is an alternative model of exchange rate determination. It is in fact one of the key relationships to be found in recent asset equilibrium models of the dynamics of exchange rate behaviour, since it provides a link between interest rate differentials, the spot and forward exchange markets and the expectations of speculators. In the next section we discuss the key ingredients of the IRPT both in terms of covered and uncovered interest rate parity and the general role played by domestic and foreign interest rates. The following section deals with certain modifications that have to be made to handle transactions costs and the next section then deals with some empirical results of testing the theory. The final section considers the so-called Modern Theory of forward exchange which emphasises the role of speculators' expectations and allows for agents to be risk averse.

5.2 The interest rate parity theory (IRPT)

One of the attractive features of IRPT is that it provides a definite theoretic link between domestic and foreign interest rates and the spot and forward exchange rate markets. The basic notion of speculators switching portfolios depending on the relative rates of interest available is a fairly obvious one and has been around historically for some time. Einzig (1967) attributes its origin to an article by Walther Lotz in 1884 which was concerned with the Vienna forward market. Keynes (1927) also noted that forward premiums were influenced by relative interest differentials.

Before setting out the IRPT in detail it is necessary to make the following assumptions. Domestic and foreign securities are considered to be identical in terms of maturity time and risk; it is assumed that there are no capital controls or transactions costs, nor any other market imperfections. Then the IRPT states that forward exchange rates are determined by the activities of pure interest arbitrageurs possessing an infinitely elastic excess demand for short-term capital and hence of foreign exchange. The activities of hedging traders and speculators will thus have no influence on the determination of forward exchange rates. In turn this means that covered interest differentials are zero because any existing profit opportunity will be eliminated instantaneously by the process of interest arbitrage.

In equilibrium the activities of pure interest arbitrageurs will ensure that the interest rate parity condition will hold so that in the notation introduced earlier

$$\frac{F_t}{S_t} = \frac{1 + r_t^d}{1 + r_t^f} \tag{5.2.1}$$

We can slightly rewrite the above to give

$$F_t^* = \frac{1 + r_t^d}{1 + r_t^f} S_t, \tag{5.2.2}$$

where F_t^* denotes the theoretical parity forward rate determined in equilibrium and is on the average, equal to the forward rate determined by the market. A profitable arbitrage opportunity will only exist if $F_t^* \neq F_t$, and such a disequilibrium situation would be eliminated immediately by the activities of pure interest arbitrageurs in an efficient market. These arbitrageurs will act in such a way to ensure that $F_t^* = F_t$ always holds providing there are no transaction and information costs and no risk premium.

Equation (5.2.1) is known as the covered interest parity (CIP) condition and explicitly assumes the absence of default risk. By a slight rearrangement the CIP condition is also sometimes expressed as

$$\frac{F_t - S_t}{S_t} = \frac{r_t^d - r_t^f}{1 + r_t^f} \tag{5.2.3}$$

Since $1 + r_t^f \approx 1$ the CIP is also approximately

$$\frac{(F_t - S_t)}{S_t} = r_t^d - r_t^f$$

A much stronger IRPT theory is provided by the uncovered interest parity (UIP) condition that

$$\frac{E_t(S_{t+1}) - S_t}{S_t} = \frac{r_t^d - r_t^f}{1 + r_t^f},$$ (5.2.4)

which implicitly assumes foreign exchange market efficiency so that the forward rate is an unbiased predictor of the future spot exchange rate.

5.3   Transactions costs and modifications to IRPT

Some of the empirical testing of the IRPT will be discussed in Section 5.5. In the meantime we now consider some possible reasons to account for the fact that several empirical studies have found periods of time when there have been substantial deviations of forward exchange rates from their interest rate parity rates. A large body of literature has developed on the causes of these deviations which are thoroughly discussed in a survey article by Officer and Willet (1970), and by Stoll (1972). Two of the major reasons for departure from IRPT are considered to be the occurrence of significant transactions costs and the existence of risk aversion on the part of market participants. Officer and Willett (1970) emphasise a third reason as being a composite of non monetary returns, default risk, non-unitary correlation of returns and premature repatriation'. While the above provides sufficient conditions for an exploited profit opportunity, a necessary condition is that an agent pays a higher price for foreign exchange on the forward market than on the spot market. Aliber (1973) has pointed out that speculators generally prefer forward contracts, mainly because they can obtain 'greater leverage' than on spot markets since forward contracts generally do not specify explicit margin requirements. Thus there is a market imperfection in the supply of foreign exchange which can be exploited by speculators.

There are several further possible explanations to explain the breakdown of IRPT. In particular, Agmon and Bronfeld (1975), Holmes and Schott (1965), Minot (1974) and Prachowny (1970) highlight the existence of capital controls, the differing taxation systems in various countries, and the quality of data used to examine IRPT. With regard to the last point it should be noted that the practice of averaging bid and ask prices is undesirable and that in some cases different interest rates exist for borrowers and lenders. In many instances short-term interest rates cannot be specified unambiguously for each country since different rates prevail on bank deposits, bank loans, Treasury bills, commercial bills, etc. The interest rate finally chosen to represent each country's short-term interest rate will generally not be the definitive rate and may be a reason why discrepancies appear between the actual and the theoretical forward premium. Investors face rising interest rates as they increase their borrowing of funds and hence the marginal interest rate relevant to actual lenders and borrowers will differ from the average interest rate parity recorded in official statistical sources. Tests conducted with the Eurodollar and Eurocurrency markets show that the interest rate parity theory holds with much greater accuracy than with other sets of interest rate data. One reason for this is that Eurocurrency markets have been free from capital controls and other restrictions throughout their existence. Also all Eurocurrency markets are equally exposed to the risk of future capital controls and hence expectations of future controls do not inhibit interest arbitrage between Eurocurrencies. It is generally assumed to be unlikely for capital controls to be applied to assets denominated in Eurocurrencies.

As it stands the IRPT identity (5.2.3) states an equilibrium condition between the forward premium and the interest rate differential and clearly ignores any transactions costs in the security and foreign exchange markets. It is well known that the existence of transactions costs implies a neutral band around the interest parity line, within which no additional arbitrage is profitable. Points within this neutral band still correspond to interest rate parity equilibrium since they are not attributed to a less than perfectly elastic covered arbitrage schedule. When costs are present and are proportional to the value of transactions it is possible to derive a lower limit on the forward premium for which covered capital outflow is profitable, and also an upper limit for which covered inflow is profitable.

Firstly, consider an outflow of covered arbitrage funds from the domestic to the foreign market and let t, t^*, t_s and t_f, denote the percentage cost of transactions in domestic and foreign securities and in spot and forward exchange rates, respectively. The cost C, of a capital outflow of amount K, is the foregone earnings on the holdings of domestic securities and is

$$C = K(1 + r_t^d) \tag{5.3.1}$$

The revenue R derived from a covered investment of these funds in comparable securities is then given by

$$R = K\Omega(1 + r_t^f)F_t/S_t \tag{5.3.2}$$

where

$$\Omega = (1 - t)(1 - t_s)(1 - t^*)(1 - t_f) \tag{5.3.3}$$

and Ω denotes transactions costs in the case where potential arbitrageurs always hold securities and consequently the initial transaction has to be a sale of securities. Covered outflow then requires the execution of four successive transactions in a 'round trip', namely (a) the sale of domestic securities with transactions costs of t per cent, (b) spot purchase of foreign currency with transactions costs of t_s per cent, (c) purchase of foreign security with transactions costs of t^* per cent and (d) forward sale of foreign currency with transactions costs of t_f per cent. However, at each period, some arbitrageurs may hold cash as securities mature and may wish to purchase another currency without completing the round trip. In this case some of the costly transactions could be avoided and the resulting band will be narrower than that derived below. From (5.3.1) the marginal cost of a capital outflow is given by

$$\frac{\partial c}{\partial K} = 1 + r_t^d \tag{5.3.4}$$

and from (5.3.2) the marginal revenue of covered investment abroad is denoted by

$$\frac{\partial R}{\partial K} = \Omega(1 + r_t^f)F_t/S_t \tag{5.3.5}$$

In equilibrium marginal cost will equal marginal revenue and equating (5.3.4) and (5.3.5) yields the lower limit on the premium $p = \dfrac{F_t - S_t}{S_t}$ for which the marginal outflow of funds is profitable.

Thus

$$1 + r_t^d = \Omega(1 + r_t^f)F_t/S_t$$

Or,

$$F_t/S_t = 1 + r_t^d/\Omega(1 + r_t^f)$$

Hence

$$p_t = \frac{F_t - S_t}{S_t} = \frac{(1 + r_t^d) - \Omega(1 + r_t^f)}{\Omega(1 + r_t^f)} \tag{5.3.6}$$

By similar reasoning it can be shown that the upper limit on the forward premium for which covered inflow is profitable is

$$p_t = \frac{\Omega(1 + r_t^d) - (1 + r_t^f)}{1 + r_t^f}, \tag{5.3.7}$$

which is smaller than the value indicated by equation (5.3.1). Equations (5.3.6) and (5.3.7) set the limits for a neutral band within which covered interest arbitrage is not profitable. Whenever the forward premium falls within the neutral band such that

$$\frac{\Omega(1 - r_t^d) - (1 + r_t^f)}{1 + r_t^f} \leqslant p_t \leqslant \frac{(1 + r_t^d) - \Omega(1 + r_t^f)}{\Omega(1 + r_t^f)}$$

there will be no incentive for covered interest arbitrage. Thus points which are bounded within the neutral band may be viewed as equilibrium points even though the conditions of equation (5.3.1) are not satisfied. The width of the neutral band increases with the cost of transactions.

The above neutral band can also be reformulated in terms of the so-called parity forward rate F_t^* given from equation (5.3.1) by

$$F_t^* = \frac{1 + r_t^d}{1 + r_t^f} S_t$$

In equilibrium $F_t^* = F_t$ and interest arbitrageurs will determine the forward rate, while both speculators and commercial hedgers determine the quantity of forward commitments and the current capital flow. Profitable arbitrage opportunities will only exist when $F_t^* \neq F_t$.

The incorporation of transactions costs modifies the equilibrium condition of interest parity without altering the fundamental point that only the activities of pure interest arbitrageurs determine the forward rate.

The types of transactions costs and their relative importance or level can vary considerably. Transactions costs can include brokerage fees, margin requirements leading to foregone interest earnings, and bid-ask spreads on forward price quotations. Differences in the estimated level of transactions costs can thus be partly attributed to the different methods used to calculate them. Also, transactions costs have varied substantially over time, particularly since 1973 when floating was introduced. McKinnon (1976), Frenkel and Levich (1975, 1977) have considered this to be partly due to the increased difference between money and security rates.

The influence of uncertainty on transactions costs has also been discussed by Fieleke (1975) who, with Levich (1979, p. 32), has shown that transactions costs are lower on spot than forward foreign exchange.

One of the first studies on the level of transaction costs was by Keynes (1924), who assumed that a value of about 0.5 per cent per annum transaction costs above the interest differential was necessary to induce capital flows. Other estimates of 0.6 per cent have been provided by Einzig (1967), 0.25 per cent by Holmes and Schott (1965), 0.18 per cent by Branson (1969), 0.15 per cent by Frenkel and Levich (1975), and 1.1 per cent by Frenkel and Levich (1977). Since there is no direct measure of transactions costs in the foreign exchange market they must be estimated indirectly, and the approach suggested by Frenkel and Levich (1975) is to study the behaviour of triangular arbitrage. The essence of triangular arbitrage is to assume consistent cross exchange rates. In the absence of transactions costs, consistency of equilibrium requires that

$$(\$/£)_\tau = (\$/DM)_\tau (DM/£)_\tau \qquad (5.3.8)$$

for the three exchange rates of the U.S. dollar, the pound sterling and the Deutschmark. The subscript τ indicates that the prices are for foreign exchange delivered at the same maturity. Deviations from the above triangular arbitrage condition in the spot and forward markets have been interpreted by Frenkel and Levich as being due to transaction costs and various estimates have been presented by them for different periods and intermediate currencies. When the exchange rates are quoted at the same instant of time the above method may well provide an approximate estimate of the level of transactions costs. Unfortunately, however, in the study by Frenkel and Levich (1975) a time span of several hours separated the quotations on the U.S. market from the European markets and deviations from interest parity cannot necessarily be interpreted as transactions costs, particularly as a speculative attack occurred against a currency in this period. Overall it seems likely that the level of transactions costs computed by Frenkel and Levich was too high.

In equation (5.3.8) arbitrage between the pound sterling and U.S. dollar was assumed by Frenkel and Levich to take place through the Deutschmark although some other currency might be used as the intermediate vehicle. However, at the margin it is presumed that competition will assure that the cost of transactions will tend to be equalised among the various major currencies. This was examined by replacing the Canadian dollar by the Deutschmark as the intermediate vehicle.

Transactions costs in the securities market have been estimated on the basis of two elements, the ask-bid spread and the brokerage fee. The ask-bid spread measures the price of immediacy in both buying and selling securities, and under competitive conditions corresponds to the cost of an immediate round trip (Demsetz, 1968). The total cost of transacting in securities is obtained by following Demsetz's suggestion of taking about 2.5 times the bid-ask spread. Transactions costs in the foreign exchange market are estimated from equation (5.3.8). If these transactions are costly the two sides of the equation could differ and the maximum discrepancy would correspond to the differential costs involved in executing the two types of exchange. If the transactions costs are approximately equal across currencies then the maximum discrepancy between both sides of equation (5.3.8) should correspond to the cost of one transaction. This estimate encompasses the total cost associated with a transaction and includes elements like brokerage fees, time cost, subscription cost and all other components that comprise the cost of being informed. This approach to estimating transactions costs is based on the assumption that the structure of the costs remains stable throughout the period under examination. Otherwise we could not interpret smaller deviations from triangular arbitrage as being within a neutral band such that the cost of transaction exceeds arbitrage profits. Adding the cost of transactions in securities to the cost of transacting in foreign exchange yields the total cost of transactions in a covered interest arbitrage.

5.4 The modern theory of forward exchange

Whereas the introduction of transactions costs only slightly modified the interest rate equilibrium condition, the introduction of risk aversion leads to a fairly dramatic reappraisal of the basic model. One stringent assumption of IRP is that arbitrageurs face a perfectly elastic demand curve for forward exchange. The Modern Theory replaces this heroic assumption with that of a downward sloping excess demand curve for arbitrageurs of foreign exchange. This will clearly influence the behaviour of other market participants such as speculators, traders and the central bank in the determination of the forward rate.

Several reasons have been suggested to justify the existence of risk aversion in this context. There is the obvious risk of insolvency through default, and the other main type of risk has been termed 'political risk' by Aliber (1973). This is meant to relate to the probability that controls will be imposed on capital flows resulting in a political risk premium. The concept has nothing to do with any existing capital controls *per se*, but rather with the uncertainty of whether capital controls will be imposed in the future.

These risks may well result from the fact that domestic and foreign securities are imperfect substitutes, which violates an essential assumption of the IRPT. This is the point of departure of the so-called Modern Theory, which postulates that the forward exchange rate is determined not only by interest arbitrage but also by expectations of speculators concerning the expected future spot rate. Since it is assumed that arbitrageurs' excess demand for foreign exchange is not perfectly elastic, it follows that speculative expectations contribute to deviations from IRPT.

We will now give a brief summary of the Modern Theory model. Detailed theoretical treatments are given by Tsiang (1959), Grubel (1963), Stoll (1968), while Officer and Willett (1970) discuss arguments in favour of models with a downward sloping arbitrage schedule.

According to the Modern Theory all activities in the forward exchange market can be reduced to three basic activities: (i) pure interest arbitrage,

(ii) pure speculation and (iii) commercial hedging. Some authors such as Kesselman (1971) and Haas (1974), only consider pure interest arbitrage and speculation and subsume the activities of traders. The implications of these assumptions on the IRPT are discussed by van Belle (1973).

The Modern Theory begins by assuming that the excess demand for forward exchange is an increasing function of the difference between the parity forward rate (F_t^*) and the market forward rate (F_t), so that on taking a linear approximation

$$x_t^A = a_1(F_t^* - F_t), \quad a_1 > 0 \tag{5.4.1}$$

Note that in the above and all subsequent relationships linearity is assumed for simplicity. The parity forward rate is given from the equilibrium condition of the traditional IRPT as

$$F_t^* = S_t \frac{1 + r_t^d}{1 + r_t^f}$$

In contrast to pure interest arbitrageurs who always eliminate the exchange risk by covering in the forward exchange market, speculators hope to profit from fluctuations in the exchange rate by holding open positions in foreign exchange, which depend on their expectations with regard to the future spot exchange rate. For instance, if the spot rate that speculators expect to prevail in three months time is greater than the corresponding three-month forward rate, then speculators will demand forward exchange in order to sell it at maturity with profit in the spot exchange market. Hence speculators excess demand for forward exchange will be an increasing function of the difference between the expected spot rate S_t^e and the corresponding forward rate

$$x_t^S = a_2(S_t^e - F_t) \quad a_2 > 0. \tag{5.4.2}$$

The third component of supply and demand for forward exchange is commercial hedging. Exporters and importers hedge their receipts and payments contracted for a future time by selling or buying forward exchange. Traders who do not hedge are treated as speculators. The excess demand for forward exchange by traders *ceteris paribus* will be a decreasing function of the forward exchange rate

$$x_t^H = a_0 - a_3 F_t, \quad a_0 > 0, a_3 > 0 \tag{5.4.3}$$

In equilibrium, the excess demands of interest arbitrageurs, speculators and commercial hedgers must sum to zero, so that

$$x_t^A + x_t^S + x_t^H = 0$$

From equations (5.2.1), (5.4.1), (5.4.2) and (5.4.3), the Modern Theory solution for the forward rate is found to be

$$F_t = \gamma + \alpha F_t^* + \beta S_t^e \tag{5.4.4}$$

$$\gamma = \frac{a_0}{a_1 + a_2 + a_3},$$

$$\alpha = \frac{a_1}{a_1 + a_2 + a_3},$$

and

$$\beta = \frac{a_2}{a_1 + a_2 + a_3}$$

Since the parameters a_i ($i = 0, 1, 2, 3$) cannot be identified, it follows that only the relative influence of covered interest arbitrage, speculation, and commercial hedging on the forward exchange rate can be estimated from equation (5.4.4). An alternative formulation adopted by Stoll (1968), Kesselman (1971) and Haas (1974) is to subsume commercial hedging, either in pure interest arbitrage or in pure speculation.

In general the Modern Theory assumes the forward rate is determined at $F_t > F_t^*$, showing that not only interest arbitrageurs but also speculators and commercial hedgers play a role in the determination of the forward rate. The relative influence of the different activities of participants in the forward exchange market is an open question in the model and can only be determined from econometric estimation.

Estimation and testing of the modern theory has proved difficult since it depends upon agents expectations of future spot exchange rates, and various studies have made different assumptions about the formation of expectations in this regard, e.g. see Black (1972), Beenstock (1978), Canterbury (1975), Stein (1965, 1980) and Stein and Tower (1967).

5.5   Econometric testing of IRPT

We now turn to some of the econometric evidence concerning the validity or otherwise of IRPT.

Tests of the IRPT have taken a variety of forms. Aliber (1973) has compared the statistical variations of the forward premium and interest rate differentials. He concludes that variations do not appear to be significant and that 'IRPT is consistent with rational investor expectations when the securities used ... are identical in terms of political risk'. Frenkel and Levich (1975, 1977) have also found that deviations from IRP are not significant. Their evidence is also based on statistical analysis and involves estimating models of the form

$$x_t = \alpha + \beta i_t + \varepsilon_t \qquad (5.5.1)$$

where

$$x_t = \ln F_t - \ln S_t$$

and

$$i_t = \ln(1 + r_t^d) - \ln(1 + r_t^f)$$

In a subsequent article Frenkel and Levich (1981) state that 'in most cases transactions costs account for the deviations from IRPT'.

Under the IRPT it follows that $\alpha = 0$, $\beta = 1$ and ε_t should be serially uncorrelated. A departure of any one of these conditions would imply rejection of the IRPT hypothesis. Most authors, such as Frenkel and Levich (1977) assume exogeneity of the interest rate differential so that (5.5.1) can be estimated by OLS. However, IRPT states a continuous relationship between the forward premium and interest rate differential with each variable continually adjusting to changes in the others. It therefore seems quite unsatisfactory to impose the exogeneity assumption. McCallum (1977) has recognised the problem and has applied 2SLS to equations such as (5.5.1) and also a variant involving spot rate expectations, which is an attempt to test the Modern Theory. A completely different route for avoiding the exogeneity assumption was provided by Pippenger (1978) who used cross spectral analysis to estimate a five equation model to test various features of arbitrageurs behaviour and also IRPT. Since Pippenger's technique involves rather specialised statistical techniques, we shall not go into detail describing it, suffice to say that Pippenger generally found support for the IRPT. Browne (1983), on using the same technique, found some deviations from IRPT for the Irish pound against the pound sterling and Deutschmark.

A dynamic version of (5.5.1) which allows IRPT to be a long-run rather than short-run relationship can be given by the model

$$x_t = \beta_0 + \sum_{j=0}^{n} \beta_j i_{t-j} + \varepsilon_t \qquad (5.5.2)$$

Thus short-run IRP corresponds to $\beta_0 = 1$ and $\beta_j = 0$ ($j > 1$); while long-run IRP implies that $\sum_{j=0}^{n} \beta_j = 1$.

It is important to emphasise that some countries have special institutional characteristics which may invalidate formulations such as (5.5.2), or alternatively justify the exogeneity assumption. For example, between 1974 and 1981 the Reserve Bank of Australia continually intervened in the foreign exchange market and set the forward premium. Turnovsky and Ball (1983) have noted this and estimated equations of the form of (5.5.2) on the basis of there being a reaction function of past interest rate differentials. In this situation they generally find support for the IRPT for the Australian dollar against the U.S. dollar. Turnovsky and Ball (1983) also test the unbiasedness of the forward rate as a predictor of the spot rate and include news of the interest rate differential in the models. More will be said about these problems in Chapters 6 and 7 respectively.

More rigorous tests of IRPT could be based on data recorded with very short intervals of time. Taylor (1987) has taken three days of foreign exchange market data recorded every 10 minutes and was unable to determine the existence of any profitable arbitrage opportunity.

CHAPTER 6

The forward rate as a predictor of the future spot rate

6.1 Introduction

This chapter considers in more detail the role of the forward market and its relationship to the spot exchange rate. The next section uses the covered and uncovered interest rate parity conditions for this purpose and shows how the forward rate can be formally regarded as the expected future spot rate. There are various descriptions of this relationship and we prefer to call it the unbiased efficient expectations (UEE) hypothesis. Apart from the Siegel paradox, the UEE condition is generally assumed to be a convenient representation of reality and subsequent sections of this chapter subject the hypothesis to increasing scrutiny using a variety of econometric techniques.

The overall conclusion is that the UEE assumption is probably inappropriate and is consistent with a breakdown of either rational expectations and/or risk neutrality on the part of agents in the market. This leads to the conclusion that the next step is to model time varying risk premia between foreign exchange currencies.

6.2 Interest rate parity and the relationship between spot and forward exchange rates

Chapter 5 described the concepts of covered and uncovered interest rate parity and showed how domestic and foreign bond markets were related to spot and forward exchange rates. Covered interest rate parity was seen to imply

$$\frac{F_t}{S_t} = \frac{1 + r_t^d}{1 + r_t^f} \tag{6.2.1}$$

or alternatively that,

$$\frac{F_t - S_t}{S_t} = \frac{r_t^d - r_t^f}{1 + r_t^f}, \tag{6.2.2}$$

162

where,

r_t^d = interest rate for assets denominated in the currency of the domestic country for the period t to $t + l$,

r_t^f = interest rate for assets denominated in the currency of the foreign country during the period t to $t + l$,

S_t = spot exchange rate of the foreign currency in units of the domestic currency at time t,

and

F_t = forward exchange rate of the foreign currency quoted at time t for delivery at time $t + l$.

Hence under the activity of pure interest arbitrage the forward premium is equated to a type of interest rate differential.

The corresponding uncovered interest rate parity (UIRP) condition is then given by

$$\frac{E_t(S_{t+l}) - S_t}{S_t} = \frac{r_t^d - r_t^f}{1 + r_t^f} \tag{6.2.3}$$

where E_t denotes an expectation conditioned on the set of all relevant and available information at time t. Thus instead of covering against exchange risk in the forward market, the investor can hold an open position in the spot market which will be dependent on his expectations of the future exchange rate. Assuming rational expectations and risk neutrality on the part of agents in the market, the activities of profit maximising investors will bid up or down spot rates and/or interest rates to that point where the market's expected rate of depreciation or appreciation of the spot rate is equal to the interest differential. It is important to reiterate that the above is predicated on the assumption of an *efficient market* which assumes a so called 'perfect' capital market which possesses no transaction costs, capital controls, taxes, default risk, nor constraints with respect to the availability of capital. Furthermore, domestic and foreign assets (and liabilities) are considered to be identical with respect to maturity and risk, the only difference being in the currency of denomination. These assumptions are in practice not as daunting as they appear at first sight and are very closely approximated by assets in the Euro-currency markets. These assets are nearly perfect substitutes since they are issued in the same financial centre by a small group of large banks and do not differ in their degree of political risk.

The UIRP and CIRP conditions imply that

$$E_t(S_{t+l}) = F_t$$

which is the well-known condition that the forward rate is an unbiased and fully efficient prediction of the future spot exchange rate. This condition has existed under a variety of terminology, namely the 'unbiasedness of the forward rate', the 'speculative efficiency hypothesis', Bilson (1981), the efficient market hypothesis, etc. In the following we refer to the forward rate as being the 'unbiased and efficient expectation' (UEE) of the future spot rate. Efficient in this sense is taken to mean that all relevant and available information at time t has been incorporated into the forward rate F_t, so that rational expectations and risk neutrality are necessarily valid. Hence the forward rate is the optimal expectation or prediction of the future spot exchange rate in the sense of minimising mean squared error. It will also be assumed that the UEE condition holds in logarithmic form and this logarithmic relationship will be implicitly taken as being the UEE condition, namely

$$f_t = E_t s_{t+l} \tag{6.2.4}$$

The justification for considering a logarithmic as opposed to levels relationship, is connected to Siegel's paradox and will be dealt with further in the next section.

The realized prediction error associated with the forward rate is then given by

$$u_{t+l} = s_{t+l} - f_t \tag{6.2.5}$$

and will have autocovariances such that

$$E(u_{t+l} u_{t+l-j}) = 0 \quad j \geq l$$

Hence u_{t+l} may be represented by an MA($l-1$) process; although this specification, which depends entirely on second order properties would also be consistent with some non-linear models, such as the bilinear model of Granger and Anderson (1978). However, we will generally take u_{t+l} to be MA($l-1$) as is standard when considering l step ahead prediction. The relationship between spot and forward rates can also be expressed in alternative ways from IRP conditions. On taking natural logarithms in (6.2.1), the IRP condition can be expressed as

$$f_t - s_t = i_t$$

where

$$i_t = \ln(1 + r_t^d) - \ln(1 + r_t^f)$$

From the UIRP condition (6.2.3):

$$E_t s_{t+l} - s_t = i_t$$

and hence

$$E_{t+l}s_{t+2l} - s_{t+l} = i_{t+l} \tag{6.2.6}$$

On taking expectations at time t through the above

$$E_t s_{t+2l} - E_t s_{t+l} = E_t i_{t+l} \tag{6.2.7}$$

and subtracting (6.2.7) from (6.2.6) gives

$$(s_{t+l} - E_t s_{t+l}) = -(i_{t+l} - E_t i_{t+l})$$

$$+ (E_{t+l}s_{t+2l} - E_t s_{t+2l})$$

But since

$$E_{t+l}s_{t+2l} = f_{t+l}$$

and

$$s_{t+2l} = E_{t+l}s_{t+2l} + u_{t+l} = f_{t+l} + u_{t+l}$$

it follows that

$$(s_{t+l} - E_t s_{t+l}) = -(i_{t+l} - E_t i_{t+l}) + u_{t+l}$$

and hence

$$(s_{t+l} - f_t) = u_{t+l} - (i_{t+l} - E_t i_{t+l}) \tag{6.2.8}$$

where the right hand side of the above is also an MA$(l-1)$ process, since it is the sum of two other MA$(l-1)$ processes; u_{t+l} and w_{t+l} where

$$w_{t+l} = i_{t+l} - E_t i_{t+l}$$

In the case of $l = 1$

$$(s_{t+1} - f_t) = u_{t+1} - (i_{t+1} - E_t i_{t+1})$$

so that the right hand side is white noise. In both (6.2.8) and the above the forecast error is seen to depend on the unanticipated part of the interest rate differential and a sequence of random shocks in the forecast period. Rearranging (6.2.8) and subtracting s_t from both sides gives

$$(s_{t+l} - s_t) = (f_t - s_t) + u_{t+l}$$

$$- (i_{t+l} - E_t i_{t+l}) \tag{6.2.9}$$

so that the actual change on the left hand side is expressed in terms of the expected change, plus the unanticipated change in the interest rate differential and random shocks. This formulation has encouraged many authors, e.g. Bilson (1981), to test the UEE hypothesis by estimating models of the form

$$(s_{t+1} - s_t) = \alpha + \beta(f_t - s_t) + u_{t+1}$$

and testing if $\alpha = 0$, $\beta = 1$. Furthermore Frenkel (1981) has estimated so called 'news' models of the form

$$(s_{t+1} - s_t) = \alpha + \beta(f_t - s_t)$$
$$+ \gamma(i_{t+1} - E_t i_{t+1}) + u_{t+1}$$

Analysis of the above news type model will be discussed in detail in Chapter 7.

A further formulation of the relationship between the spot and forward rates is to consider the forward premium, which is similar to (6.2.9) and states that under the UEE hypothesis

$$s_{t+1} - f_t = E_t(s_{t+1} - s_t)$$

so that the expected change in the spot exchange rate is equal to its actual change.

6.3   Possible reasons for breakdown of UEE

Unless explicitly stated to the contrary the UEE condition will always be expressed in terms of the natural logarithms of the spot and forward rates, so that

$$f_t = E_t s_{t+1} \qquad (6.3.1)$$

where $f_t = \ln F_t$ and $s_t = \ln S_t$.

The main reason for this convention is to avoid the so called Siegel paradox. Siegel (1972) noted that in levels the UEE condition that

$$F_t = E_t S_{t+1} \qquad (6.3.2)$$

must hold on both 'sides' of the foreign exchange so that the analogous equation from the perspective of the foreign country is given by

$$E\left[\frac{1}{S_{t+1}}\right] = \left[\frac{1}{F_t}\right] \qquad (6.3.3)$$

However Jensen's inequality states that $E(1/x) > 1/E(x)$ so that (6.3.2) and (6.3.3) cannot simultaneously be true. The problem is avoided by defining the variables in logarithmic form and the UEE condition expressed as (6.3.1). Then

$$E_t(s_{t+1})^{-1} = E_t(\ln S_{t+1})^{-1} = -E_t \ln S_{t+1} = -\ln F_t$$

While the Siegel paradox is conceptually a problem it has been demonstrated by McCulloch (1975), to be irrelevant in empirical work.

Siegel (1975) and Roper (1975) have accepted this viewpoint and general agreement concurs that it is legitimate to express UEE as (6.3.1) in logarithmic form. For an alternative interpretation see McMahon (1988).

Before considering tests of the UEE hypothesis it is important to note that the condition requires the twin assumptions of rational expectations and risk neutrality on the part of agents in the market. As discussed in Chapter 5 the Modern Theory of foreign exchange directly assumed the presence of a time varying risk premium to be incorporated into the forward rate. A similar approach is provided by portfolio theory, as developed by Feldstein (1968), Roll and Solnik (1977) and Stockman (1978). This theory implies that the behaviour of risk averse investors is a function of expected returns, and also of the riskiness associated with individual assets and of the total portfolio. This approach has led to the development of several different models of portfolio consumption behaviour where uncertainty about the future induces risk premia in equilibrium which lead to a breakdown of the UEE hypothesis. There is, however, no general agreement about the sources of uncertainty and risk, nor the most appropriate means of measuring risk. Adler and Dumas (1976) consider uncertainty deriving from default risk, whereas Grauer, Litzenberger and Stehle (1976) posit a risk premium as a purely monetary phenomenon resulting from uncertainty about inflation rates. In their model UEE will only be invalid when there is a positive correlation of unity between domestic and foreign rates of inflation. Other authors, such as Kouri (1976), see risk as arising from a breakdown of purchasing power parity, while in Stockman (1978), risk is a function of uncertainty about the relative money supplies.

One of the most detailed models of risk is due to Solnik (1973, 1974) who developed a model based on differences of national tastes and consumption assuming a free and perfect capital market, homogeneous expectations which could possibly be rational and with no differences in inflation. Solnik is able to show that these assumptions will create uncertain exchange rate movements and therefore real exchange risk.

While many authors have been prepared to acknowledge the presence of risk, the possibility of the failure of rational expectations is less common. In a near perfect market the notion of agents processing all relevant and available information throughout time appears to be a reasonable assumption. However, Frenkel (1980) has attributed a failure of UEE in the pound sterling, Deutschmark data in the 1920s to a failure of market participants to sufficiently adapt to the hyperinflation situation. Unusual periods of history in the foreign exchanges may well be more consistent with some type of learning mechanism in the formation of expectations that gradually converges to rationality in some sense.

6.4   Econometric tests of the unbiased efficient expectations hypothesis

As in many other areas of contemporary macroeconomics the appropriateness of one theory versus another in many cases hinges on empirical evidence. While the new classical macroeconomics provides strong restrictions on the form of models and competing alternative theories, such theories can pose considerable problems in terms of the econometric procedures that are required. The testing of the UEE hypothesis is no exception and developments and sophistications in methodology have frequently produced different conclusions. The null hypothesis of interest is simply that

$$f_t = E_t s_{t+l}$$

and the hypothesis is generally tested by means of taking expectations conditioned on information available at time $t - h$, on both sides of the equation to give

$$E_{t-h}(s_{t+l} - f_t) = 0 \qquad (6.4.1)$$

where $h = 0, 1, 2 \dots$ A major problem apparent in most work in this area is the choice of the most appropriate alternative hypothesis to compete against the UEE model.

A rejection of (6.4.1) against a vaguely specified alternative hypothesis will not generally provide evidence on why UEE has been rejected. Geweke and Feige (1979) have argued in this context that to be powerful, an econometric procedure must throw light on why the hypothesis has been rejected. Ideally a model to compete with UEE should specifically model risk aversion and/or a sub-optimal formation of expectations mechanism.

An obvious approach for testing UEE is to estimate the model

$$(s_{t+l} - f_t) = \psi' x_{t-h} + u_{t+l} \qquad (6.4.2)$$

and to test the hypothesis that

$$H_0 : \psi = 0 \quad \text{versus} \quad H_1 : \psi \neq 0$$

Under the null hypothesis, none of the variables in x_{t-h} help to further explain s_{t+l} given that f_t is already included in the information set. If a set of x_{t-h} can be found which give rise to a rejection of H_0; then there is *prima facie* evidence against the UEE. Non rejection of H_0 may be due to an inappropriate set of x_{t-h} which leads to biased parameter estimates and test statistics. An additional problem concerns the fact the u_{t+l} is MA$(l - 1)$, of which more will be said in the next section.

The general problem of testing the theory is considerably simplified however if the sampling interval of the data is chosen to exactly match the maturity time of the forward contract. Indeed this was the approach taken by Cornell (1977), Frenkel (1977, 1979 and 1980) and Bilson (1981) who were the first authors to exploit the fact that the forward rate is an observable series of expectations and allows a direct test of UEE. Frenkel (1979, 1980) typically considered models of the form

$$s_{t+1} = \alpha + \beta f_t + u_{t+1} \tag{6.4.3}$$

where u_{t+1} is conveniently white noise since $l = 1$. When taking thirty day forward exchange rates, Frenkel and others generally use end of the month data. The UEE hypothesis is given by testing that $\alpha = 0$, $\beta = 1$ and u_{t+1} is not autocorrelated. This is essentially a weak form test since only a constant is included in the information set along with f_t. The above model has been estimated and the UEE tested by a large number of researchers. A summary of just a few of the results are given in Table 6.1. For the period of floating exchange rates beginning in 1972 most studies that have examined (6.4.3) have generally been unable to reject the UEE hypothesis. A variety of estimation methods have been employed on (6.4.3), generally OLS, or IVE, such as Frenkel's (1981) study, where lagged forward rates, time trend and interest rate differentials were used as instruments. Suppose however that there exists a non-constant risk premium w_t, which is a white noise process and that the one period ahead forward rate is thus

$$f_t = E_t s_{t+1} + w_t$$

Then since

$$s_{t+1} = E_t s_{t+1} + \varepsilon_{t+1}$$

it follows that

$$s_{t+1} = f_t + u_{t+1}$$

where

$$u_{t+1} = \varepsilon_{t+1} - w_t$$

Estimation of β by OLS in the regression

$$s_{t+1} = \beta f_t + u_{t+1}$$

will result in

$$\text{plim } \hat{\beta} = \beta + (\text{plim } 1/n \sum f_t u_{t+1})(\text{plim } 1/n \sum f_t^2)^{-1}$$
$$= \beta - \sigma_{fu}^2/\sigma_f^2$$

so that the OLS estimator of β will be downward biased. This type of argument has sometimes been used to justify the use of IV or 2SLS methods

Table 6.1 Estimates of $s_{t+1} = \alpha + \beta f_t + u_{t+1}$ and tests of UEE

Author	Data time period	Frequency	Estimation method	Country	$\hat{\alpha}$	$\hat{\beta}$	F	DW
Frenkel (1981)	June 1973 to July 1979	monthly	OLS	U.K.	0.033 (0.017)	0.956 (0.024)	1.86	1.72
,,	,,	,,	IV	,,	0.030 (0.018)	0.961 (0.025)		1.74
,,	,,	,,	OLS	France	−0.237 (0.078)	0.843 (0.051)	4.83*	2.23
,,	,,	,,	IV	,,	−0.236 (0.080)	0.844 (0.053)		2.24
,,	,,	,,	OLS	West Germany	−0.023 (0.027)	0.971 (0.032)	0.51	2.12
,,	,,	,,	IV	,,	−0.021 (0.027)	0.973 (0.032)		2.10
Bilson (1981)	July 1974 to January 1980	four weekly	OLS	U.K.	1.928 (5.21)	0.628 (0.99)	0.20	1.57
,,	,,	,,	,,	France	0.407 (4.39)	0.849 (0.86)	2.62	2.32

Study	Period	Frequency	Method	Country	α	β	F	DW
,,	,,	,,	,,	West Germany	6.737 (6.29)	0.208 (1.65)	0.37	2.33
Baillie et al. (1983)	June 1973 to April 1980	four weekly	OLS	U.K.	0.033 (0.016)	0.956 (0.022)	2.12	1.33**
,,		,,	,,	France	−0.174 (0.060)	0.884 (0.040)	4.57*	1.85
,,		,,	,,	West Germany	−0.024 (0.020)	0.968 (0.024)	0.97	1.98
Bailey et al. (1984)	January 1975 to April 1980	four weekly	OLS	U.K.	0.032 (0.02)	0.957 (0.031)	1.58	
,,		,,	,,	France	−0.127 (0.067)	0.914 (0.044)	2.67	
,,		,,	,,	West Germany	−0.012 (0.020)	0.918 (0.025)	0.56	
,,		,,	SURE	U.K.	0.024 (0.018)	0.970 (0.027)	1.23	
,,		,,	,,	France	−0.024 (0.043)	0.981 (0.029)	0.97	
,,		,,	,,	West Germany	−0.023 (0.014)	0.968 (0.017)	1.96	

Key: F denotes the conventional calculated F statistic of the hypothesis that $\alpha = 0$ and $\beta = 1$. DW denotes the Durbin Watson test statistic. An asterisk denotes significance at the .05 per cent level.

Table 6.2 Estimates of $s_{t+1} = \alpha + \beta f_t + \gamma f_{t-1} + u_{t+1}$ from 1920s

Author	Data time period	Frequency	Estimation method	Country	$\hat{\alpha}$	$\hat{\beta}$	DW
Frenkel (1980)	February 1921 to August 1923	monthly	OLS	Germany v Britain	−0.45 (0.25)	1.09 (0.03)	1.89
,,	February 1921 to May 1925	,,	,,	France v Britain	0.169 (0.179)	0.962 (0.042)	1.92
,,	,,	,,	,,	U.S. v Britain	0.057 (0.056)	0.964 (0.038)	1.54
,,	,,	,,	,,	France v U.S.	0.203 (0.149)	0.928 (0.054)	1.95

of estimation. Some studies have also been carried out for the floating rates in the 1920s, a summary of a few of the results are given in Table 6.2. In his work on the 1920s, Frenkel (1979, 1980) was generally unable to reject the UEE hypothesis. In one instance Frenkel's conclusions do seem at odds with the available evidence. For the Deutschmark against the pound sterling in the 1920s Frenkel is able to reject the unbiasedness hypothesis but attributes the rejection to individuals lack of experience in forming expectations during a hyperinflation, rather than the existence of risk aversion.

A slightly more stringent test of UEE is to include lagged forward rates in the information set x_{t-h} or one lagged spot rate, as in Longworth (1981). A summary of some of these results is also given in Table 6.3.

A further method of estimating (6.4.2) is to attempt to recognise the dependence between currencies by using Zellners seemingly unrelated regression equations (SURE) estimator. The estimated model is of the form

$$
\begin{bmatrix} s_1 \\ s_2 \\ \vdots \\ s_g \end{bmatrix} = \begin{bmatrix} (jf_1) & & & \\ & (jf_2) & & \\ & & \ddots & \\ & & & (jf_g) \end{bmatrix} \begin{bmatrix} \gamma_1 \\ \gamma_2 \\ \vdots \\ \gamma_g \end{bmatrix} + \begin{bmatrix} u_1 \\ u_2 \\ \vdots \\ u_g \end{bmatrix} \qquad (6.4.4)
$$

$$ Y = X\gamma + u $$

where s_i is a $n \times 1$ vector containing observations on the ith currencies spot rate, j is a $n \times 1$ vector of ones and f_i is a $n \times 1$ vector of observations on the ith currencies forward rate, lagged one period, γ is a $k \times 1$ vector of parameters and $k = 2g$. Also,

$$ E(u_i) = 0 \quad E(u_i u_j') = \sigma_{ij} I $$

and $\quad E(uu') = \Omega \otimes I \quad$ where $\Omega = (\sigma_{ij})$,

which follows the usual SURE formulation (see Zellner 1962). The fact that $\sigma_{ij} \neq 0$ for $i \neq j$ implies contemporaneous correlation of premiums or discounts across currencies, a very reasonable proposition. As is usual with the SURE estimator, an estimate of Ω is obtained by cross correlating the OLS residuals of each equation and the estimated Ω matrix is then used to form the feasible estimator

$$ \hat{\gamma} = (X'\hat{\Omega}^{-1}X)^{-1}X'\hat{\Omega}^{-1}Y \qquad (6.4.5) $$

which is then used to estimate the α_i and β_i parameters in the g equations

$$ s_{it+1} = \alpha_i + \beta_i f_{it} + u_{it} \quad i = 1, 2 \ldots g $$

Table 6.3 *Estimates of* $s_{t+1} = \alpha + \beta f_t + \gamma f_{t-1} + u_{t-1}$ *and tests of UEE from 1970s and 1980s*

Author	Data time period	Frequency	Estimation method	Country	$\hat{\alpha}$	$\hat{\beta}$	$\hat{\gamma}$	F	DW
Frenkel (1981)	June 1973 to July 1979	monthly	OLS	U.K.	0.031 (0.017)	1.047 (0.116)	-0.088 (0.113)	1.94	
,,	,,	,,	,,	France	-0.225 (0.082)	0.706 (0.117)	0.146 (0.117)	1.90	
,,	,,	,,	,,	West Germany	-0.019 (0.028)	0.913 (0.119)	0.063 (0.122)	1.96	
Bailey et al. (1984)	January 1975 to April 1980	four weekly	OLS	U.K.	0.035 (0.021)	1.209 (0.130)	-0.255 (0.128)	2.43	1.79
,,	,,	,,	,,	France	-0.178 (0.068)	0.816 (0.130)	0.104 (0.130)	1.98	1.10
,,	,,	,,	,,	West Germany	-0.009 (0.020)	0.823 (0.133)	0.161 (0.133)	0.87	1.73
,,	,,	,,	SURE	U.K.	0.027 (0.018)	1.183 (0.111)	-0.217 (0.109)		2.16
,,	,,	,,	,,	France	-0.026 (0.045)	1.001 (0.090)	-0.025 (0.082)	0.66	
,,	,,	,,	,,	West Germany	-0.026 (0.014)	0.934 (0.101)	0.037 (0.091)	1.10	

The SURE estimator has been used by Bilson (1981), Edwards (1983) and Bailey et al. (1984) and some of these results are given in Tables 6.1 and 6.3. Bailey et al. (1984) test the UEE hypothesis for the ith currency by considering $H_0 : \alpha_i = 0$ and $\beta_i = 1$ versus $H_1 : H_0$ is incorrect and use the conventional F statistic

$$F = \frac{(R\hat{\gamma} - r)'[R(X'\hat{\Omega}^{-1}X)R']^{-1}(R\hat{\gamma} - r)/m}{(Y - X\hat{\gamma})'\hat{\Omega}^{-1}(Y - X\hat{\gamma})/(ng - k)} \qquad (6.4.6)$$

where R is an $m \times k$ matrix composed entirely of zeros except for ones in the $(1, 2i - 1)$ and $(2, 2i)$ elements; r is an $m \times 1$ null vector except for one in the $2i$ element, and $m = 2$ since there are two restrictions being tested. Under the null hypothesis F will have an $F_{m, ng - k}$ distribution.

Bailey et al. (1984) also test the UEE hypothesis simultaneously across currencies. That is, they consider the hypothesis

$$H_0 : \alpha_i = 0 \quad \text{and} \quad \beta_i = 1, \quad i = 1, 2 \ldots g \qquad (6.4.7)$$

versus

$$H_1 : H_0 \quad \text{is incorrect.}$$

The statistic (6.4.6) is again used; this time with $R = I$, r has zeros in odd numbered elements and ones in even numbered elements, and $m = k = 2g$. Under this null hypothesis F will have an $F_{2g, ng - 2g}$ distribution.

Table 6.1 sets out some of the empirical evidence based on (6.4.3) for the U.K. pound sterling, West German Deutschmark and French franc against the U.S. dollar. Baillie et al. (1983) find the hypothesis can be rejected for France, but not for West Germany, while there are autocorrelated residuals for the U.K. which is also suggestive of rejection of UEE. Baillie et al. (1983) also reject UEE for Canada, but not for Italy or Switzerland. The results of Frenkel (1981) and Bilson (1981) are extremely similar, and the results seem robust to choice of IV or OLS and data set.

Results from using SURE are taken from Bailey et al. (1984) who utilised the same data as Baillie et al. (1983) and they found that the use of the SURE estimator gave quite different results to OLS; the SURE estimator then suggested rejection of UEE for West Germany but not France or Italy. However, between 1971 and September 1974 the German Bundesbank imposed restrictions on capital flows by introducing special minimum reserve requirements on banks liabilities to non-residents and cash deposit requirements on certain types of foreign borrowing by non-German banks. The capital controls caused relatively high inter bank rates in Germany and hence a high covered interest differential which distorted the interest rate parity condition. The results reported by Bailey et al. (1984), Tables 6.1

and 6.3 are for data between January 1975 and April 1980 and give rise to a rejection of the UEE for West Germany. Similar conclusions also hold for Italy but are not reported in Table 6.1.

The statistical validity of using SURE as opposed to OLS for estimating the equations can be formally tested by means of the likelihood ratio statistic

$$\text{LR} = n(\ln|\hat{\Omega}_0| - \ln|\hat{\Omega}_1|)$$

where Ω_1 is the unrestricted SURE error covariance matrix and Ω_0 is the corresponding OLS error covariance matrix. Under the null hypothesis that OLS is adequate, Ω_0 is restricted to being a diagonal matrix and LR has an asymptotic chi squared distribution with $g(g-1)/2$ degrees of freedom. Bailey et al. (1984) found they could reject Ω_0 in favour of the unrestricted positive definite covariance Ω_1 at the 1 per cent level. The use of F statistic (6.4.6) to test the hypothesis (6.4.7) gave rise to fairly weak rejections of the joint efficiency hypothesis.

Table 6.3 presents results based on OLS and SURE estimates that were obtained from extending the information set x_t and including the last periods lagged forward rate f_{t-1}. In general there is nothing to prohibit the inclusion of further explanatory variables in the information set, although most studies have typically only considered past spot and forward rates.

6.5   Single equation tests of the unbiased efficient expectations hypothesis with overlapping data

This section considers further tests of the UEE hypothesis that utilise so called 'overlapping' data; where the maturity time of the forward contract exceeds the sampling interval of the data. Hence $l > 1$ in the UEE equations

$$f_t = E_t s_{t+l} \tag{6.2.4}$$

and

$$E_{t-h}(s_{t+l} - f_t) = 0 \tag{6.4.1}$$

Several authors, notably Hansen and Hodrick (1980), Hayashi and Sims (1983) have noted the potential problems associated with the use of overlapping data and obtained limited information methods to overcome them. Others, such as Hakkio (1981) and Baillie et al. (1983) have used multivariate time series methods and tested UEE by means of examining cross equation restrictions on the models parameters.

The use of overlapping data introduces some additional econometric complications but avoids the severe loss of information involved in discarding enough data to exactly match the maturity time of the contract with the sampling interval. Apart from reducing the econometric efficiency of subsequent estimations and testing, this data discarding process also appears inappropriate since relatively short-lived periods of turbulence and speculative action in markets may well be missed.

From (6.2.4) and (6.2.5)

$$s_{t+l} = f_t + u_{t+l}$$

where $E(u_{t+l}u_{t+l-j}) = 0, j \geqslant l$.

A natural and weak form test of UEE would then be to test the hypothesis $\alpha = 0$ and $\beta = 1$ in the model

$$s_{t+l} = \alpha + \beta f_t + u_{t+l} \tag{6.5.1}$$

where

$$u_{t+l} = \varepsilon_{t+l} + \theta_1 \varepsilon_{t+l-1} + \cdots + \theta_{l-1} \varepsilon_{t+1} \tag{6.5.2}$$

and ε_t is the usual uncorrelated white noise process. Similarly one could test the same hypothesis in the model

$$(s_{t+l} - f_t) = \psi' x_t + u_{t+l} \tag{6.5.3}$$

where x_t' is a k dimensional row vector and includes variables such as lagged forecast errors, i.e. $(s_t - f_{t-l})$. Since (6.5.1) and (6.5.3) are merely regression models with autocorrelated errors, it might be thought that the application of generalised least squares (GLS) would be appropriate. However, Hansen and Hodrick (1980) have noted that many of the explanatory variables it is desirable to include in the x_t vector, say lagged s_t, are such that knowledge of their future values provides valuable information in forecasting s_{t+l}. The implication of this is that some of the x_t variables will not satisfy the strict exogeneity requirement that

$$E(u_{t+l} \mid \ldots x_{t-1}, x_t, x_{t+1} \ldots) = 0$$

Hence the application of GLS will produce inconsistent parameter estimates. However, Hansen and Hodrick (1980) have noted that OLS will produce consistent, albeit inefficient parameter estimates. They show that the limiting distribution of OLS will be

$$\sqrt{n} (\hat{\psi}_{\text{OLS}} - \psi) \to N[0, n(X'X)^{-1} X'\Omega^{-1} X(X'X)^{-1}] \tag{6.5.4}$$

where X is the matrix of observations on the explanatory variables x_t, i.e. $X' = (x_1' \, x_2' \ldots x_n')$ and $\Omega = [E(\xi_t \xi_s)]$, $s, t = 1, 2 \ldots n$.

For practical purposes Hansen and Hodrick (1980) impose the restrictions that u_{t+l} follows on $MA(l-1)$ process and suggest estimating Ω by

$$
\hat{\Omega} = \begin{bmatrix}
c_0 & c_1 & c_2 & \cdots & c_{l-1} & & & \\
c_1 & c_0 & c_1 & & & \cdot & \bigcirc & \\
c_2 & c_1 & c_0 & & \cdot & & \cdot & \\
& & & \cdot & \cdot & & \cdot & c_{l-1} \\
c_{l-1} & & & & \cdot & \cdot & & \vdots \\
& \cdot & & & & \cdot & \cdot & \vdots \\
& & \bigcirc & \cdot & & & \cdot & c_1 \\
& & & & & & & c_0 \\
& \cdot & & \cdot & \cdot & c_{l-1} & & c_1 c_0
\end{bmatrix}
$$

where

$$
c_j = \frac{1}{n} \sum_{t=j+1}^{n^-} \hat{u}_t \hat{u}_{t-j}
$$

are the autocovariances of lag j of the OLS residuals

$$
\hat{u}_{t+l} = (s_{t+l} - f_t) - \hat{\psi}_{OLS} x_t
$$

An alternative possibility would be to leave Ω unrestricted and to estimate it by White's (1980) procedure. The estimate of Ω can then be used in (6.5.4) and the asymptotic covariance matrix of $\hat{\psi}_{OLS}$ used for subsequent hypothesis testing. Hansen and Hodrick (1980) included lagged forecast errors $(s_{t-1} - f_{t-l-1})$ in x_t and computed tests of the hypothesis

$$H_0 : \psi = 0$$

versus   (6.5.5)

$$H_1 : \psi \neq 0$$

Given the estimate $\hat{\psi}_{OLS}$

$$
n\hat{\psi}_{OLS}[(X'X)^{-1}(X'\hat{\Omega}X)(X'X)^{-1}]\hat{\psi}_{OLS} \to \chi_k^2 \tag{6.5.6}
$$

under H_0.

On including the lagged premiums in x_t, Hansen and Hodrick found they could only reject the UEE hypothesis for one out of seven currencies in the 1970s period. On extending the information set in x_t to also include lagged premiums of other currencies, they were then able to reject for six of the seven currencies in the 1970s and for five out of six currencies in the

1920s period. To some extent the choice of variables to be included in x_t and hence the information set is fairly arbitrary and Hansen and Hodrick (1980) include the obvious candidates such as lagged forecast errors. A summary of some of the results from Hansen and Hodrick (1983) is presented in Table 6.4.

A further analysis of this type has been conducted by Hsieh (1984) who allows for the presence of conditional heteroskedasticity by considering the OLS estimator and taking an asymptotic covariance matrix estimated from

$$V = n(X'X)^{-1}\left(\sum_{t=1}^{n} \hat{u}_t^2 x_t x_t'\right)(X'X)^{-1}$$

When conditional homoskedasticity is assumed

$$\tilde{V} = n\hat{\sigma}^2 (X'X)^{-1}$$

Hsieh (1984) shows that the difference between the two covariance matrices

$$V - \tilde{V} = n(X'X)^{-1}\left(\sum_{t=1}^{n} (\hat{u}_{t+1}^2 - \hat{\sigma}^2)x_t x_t'\right)(X'X)^{-1}$$

goes to zero asymptotically when $x_t x_t'$ and u_{t+1}^2 are uncorrelated. Hsieh points out that V is a consistent estimate of the true asymptotic covariance matrix and is the appropriate one to use for inferential purposes. Hsieh is able to find strong evidence against the UEE hypothesis from using his method.

6.6   Simultaneous equation tests of the unbiased efficient expectations hypothesis with overlapping data

An alternative approach to testing the UEE hypothesis on overlapping data, is to consider the spot and forward exchange rates as constituting some joint process. They can be regarded as being separate components of a vector containing other variables evolving over time and linked through approximate interest parity relationships to other monetary and real variables.

The appropriate vector of variables will be denoted by y_t, a g dimensional vector with the logarithms of the spot and forward rates being the first two elements of y_t. Then

$$y_t' = (s_t f_t y_{3t} \dots y_{gt})$$

On assuming y_t to be a linear non-deterministic jointly covariance stationary process, it follows from the multivariate analogue of Wolds decomposition (see Hannan 1970, pp. 65–71), that y_t will have the unique

Table 6.4 Hansen and Hodrick's (1983) test of the UEE hypothesis with lagged own and other country forecast errors included in the information set.

$$\frac{S_{t+9} - F_{t,9}}{S_t} = a + \sum_{j=1}^{5} b\left(\frac{S_t^j - F_{t-9,9}^j}{S_{t-9}^j}\right) + u_{t+9}$$

Country	$\hat{a}$	$\hat{b}_1$	$\hat{b}_2$	$\hat{b}_3$	$\hat{b}_4$	$\hat{b}_5$	F
France	0.297	−0.165	−0.003	0.252	−0.122	−0.173	6.738
	(0.320)	(0.142)	(0.116)	(0.151)	(0.008)	(0.225)	0.759
Japan	0.428	−0.287	0.204	0.463	0.090	−0.596	20.303
	(0.420)	(0.162)	(0.148)	(0.162)	(0.126)	(0.272)	0.999
Switzerland	0.328	−0.102	0.067	0.626	−0.113	−0.853	16.100
	(0.414)	(0.292)	(0.161)	(0.161)	(0.155)	(0.325)	0.993
U.K.	0.568	0.014	−0.055	0.214	0.190	−0.406	8.390
	(0.381)	(0.199)	(0.097)	(0.112)	(0.132)	(0.182)	0.864
West Germany	.328	−0.281	−0.051	0.417	−0.034	−0.323	9.462
	(0.341)	(0.167)	(0.123)	(0.162)	(0.108)	(0.194)	0.908

Weekly data from February 5, 1976 to December 29, 1980.
F is a test of $H_0: b_j = 0$; $H_1: H_0$ is incorrect.

infinite moving average representation

$$y_t = \sum_{j=0}^{\infty} B_j \varepsilon_{t-j} \tag{6.6.1}$$

where $E(\varepsilon_t) = 0$,

$$E(\varepsilon_t \varepsilon_s') = \begin{cases} \Omega & s = t \\ 0 & s \neq t \end{cases}$$

and $B_0 = 1$.

For a suitable value of p, the model (6.6.1) can then be approximated by the vector autoregressive model, VAR(p)

$$y_t = \sum_{j=1}^{p} A_j y_{t-j} + \varepsilon_t \tag{6.6.2}$$

where the A_j are $g \times g$ coefficient matrices. As noted earlier, such VAR models have been popularised in econometric work by Sims (1980) and others and have the attractive interpretation of being dynamic reduced form equations from a linear structural econometric model. One advantage with consideration of vector autoregressions is that various techniques exist for statistically determining the appropriate order of the maximal lag p, i.e. the extent of lagged information worthy of consideration. Hence it is important in any practical implementation of this approach to ensure that the degree of maximum lag p is sufficient to induce the disturbance vector being a close approximation to white noise.

The model (6.6.2) can be represented in companion form as

$$\begin{bmatrix} y_t \\ y_{t-1} \\ \vdots \\ y_{t-p+1} \end{bmatrix} = \begin{bmatrix} A_1 & A_2 & \cdots & A_p \\ I & & & \\ & \ddots & & \\ & & I & 0 \end{bmatrix} \begin{bmatrix} y_{t-1} \\ y_{t-2} \\ \vdots \\ y_{t-p} \end{bmatrix} \begin{bmatrix} \varepsilon_t \\ 0 \\ \vdots \\ 0 \end{bmatrix}$$

Or, $Y_t = AY_{t-1} + \xi_t$ \hfill (6.6.3)

so that the first g rows of the above gives the VAR model (6.6.2) while the remaining rows are identities. The first order representation is very useful for deriving parameter restrictions corresponding to the UEE hypothesis and allows the $g^2 p$ parameters in (6.6.2) to be expressed as

$$\theta' = \text{vec}(N'A)$$

where $N' = (I : 0)$ and is of dimension $g \times gp$ and vec is the row stacking operator.

Under the assumption of ε_t being normally distributed, the application of OLS to each equation will result in asymptotically efficient estimates of the parameters which will have the limiting distribution

$$\sqrt{n}(\hat{\theta} - \theta) \sim N(0, \Omega \otimes M^{-1}) \tag{6.6.4}$$

where n is the number of observations and

$$M = \plim_{n \to \infty} \frac{1}{n} \sum_{t=1}^{n} Y_{t-1} Y'_{t-1}$$

From (6.6.3) it is straightforward to show that

$$Y_{t+l} = \sum_{j=0}^{l-1} A^j \xi_{t+l-j} + A^l Y_t$$

and that

$$Y_{t+l} = \sum_{j=0}^{l+h-1} A^j \xi_{t+l+h-j} + A^{l+h} Y_{t-h} \tag{6.6.5}$$

In terms of testing the UEE hypothesis we are only interested in the first two elements of Y_t and can define a gp dimensional row vector e'_j with zeros everywhere except for unity in the jth element. Then $e'_1 Y_t = s_t$, $e'_2 Y_t = f_t$ and from (6.6.5)

$$s_{t+l} = e'_1 A^{l+h} Y_{t-h} + e'_1 \sum_{j=0}^{l+h-j} A^j \xi_{t+l+h-j} \tag{6.6.6}$$

and $\quad f_t = e'_2 A^h Y_{t-h} + e'_2 \sum_{j=0}^{h-j} A^j \xi_{t+h-j} \tag{6.6.7}$

Since

$$E_t(\xi_{t+j}) = 0 \quad \text{for } j \geq 1, \tag{6.6.8}$$

it follows that the optimal (in the sense of being unbiased and minimising mean squared error) predictions of s_{t+l} and f_t made at time $t - h$, conditional on the information set Y_{t-h} are

$$E_{t-h} s_{t+l} = e'_1 A^{l+h} Y_{t-h}$$

and

$$E_{t-h} f_t = e'_2 A^h Y_{t-h}$$

From (6.6.6) and (6.6.7)

$$s_{t+l} - f_t = r(\theta)' Y_{t-h} + u_{t+l} \tag{6.6.9}$$

where

$$r_h(\theta)' = e_1' A^{l+h} - e_2' A^h$$

and u_{t+l} is the sum of the right hand side components of (6.6.6) and (6.6.7) which are $MA(l+h-1)$ and $MA(h-1)$ processes. From the results of Granger and Morris (1976) it follows that u_{t+l} will also follow an $MA(l+h-1)$ process. On taking expectations at time $t-h$ throughout (6.6.9) it follows that $E_{t-h} u_{t+l} = 0$ and under the UEE hypothesis

$$E_{t-h}(s_{t+l} - f_t) = 0$$

which implies that the above hypothesis is equivalent to imposing the parameter restrictions

$$H_0 : r_h(\theta)' = e_1' A^{l+h} - e_2' A^h = 0 \tag{6.6.10}$$

Hence no information in Y_{t-h} is useful in explaining the forecast error $(s_{t+l} - f_t)$ and (6.6.10) imposes gp restrictions on the $g^2 p$ unrestricted parameters. This shows the basic equivalence between this procedure and that of Hansen and Hodrick (1980); both are testing the superfluousness of information in Y_{t-h}.

The procedure suggested by Baillie et al. (1983) is to estimate the unrestricted model (6.6.2) and to then apply a Wald statistic to test the UEE hypothesis in (6.6.10). The unrestricted estimates $\hat{\theta}$ can be substituted into A to form $r(\hat{\theta})$, and the Wald statistic is then given by

$$W = r_h(\hat{\theta})' [D_h' \operatorname{Cov}(\hat{\theta}) D_h]^{-1} r_h(\hat{\theta})$$

which from (6.6.4) can be expressed as

$$W = r_h(\hat{\theta})' (\hat{D}_h' \hat{\Omega} \otimes \hat{M}^{-1} \hat{D}_h)^{-1} r_h(\hat{\theta}) \tag{6.6.11}$$

and where

$$D_h = \frac{\delta r(\theta)}{\partial \theta} = \begin{bmatrix} \sum_{j=0}^{l+h-1} (e_1' A'^j e_1) A^{l+h-1-j} - \sum_{j=0}^{h-1} (e_1' A'^j e_2) A^{h-1-j} \\ \hline \sum_{j=0}^{l+h-1} (e_2' A'^j e_1) A^{l+h-1-j} - \sum_{j=0}^{h-1} (e_2' A'^j e_2) A^{h-1-j} \\ \vdots \qquad\qquad\qquad \vdots \\ \sum_{j=0}^{l+h-1} (e_g' A'^j e_1) A^{l+h-1-j} - \sum_{j=0}^{h-1} (e_g' A'^j e_2) A^{h-1-j} \end{bmatrix}$$

The estimate $\hat{D}_h$ of D_h is obtained by inserting maximum likelihood estimates of the parameters θ in the various elements of D_h.

The above results on prediction and the expression for the cross derivative matrix D_h are to be found in Schmidt (1974), Baillie (1981) and

Yamamoto (1981). Under the null hypothesis of UEE, W will have an asymptotic chi squared distribution with gp degrees of freedom.

Rather than calculate the Wald test statistic it is also possible to compute the restricted estimates and form a likelihood ratio statistic. Restricted estimates are available from a minimum chi squared estimator, which Rothenberg (1973, pp. 21–23) has shown to be asymptotically equivalent to the restricted maximum likelihood estimator. The estimator $\tilde{\theta}$ is given by

$$\tilde{\theta} = \hat{\theta} - VD_h'(D_h VD_h')^{-1} r_h(\hat{\theta}) \tag{6.6.12}$$

and

$$\sqrt{n}\,(\tilde{\theta} - \theta) \sim N[0, V - VD_h'(D_h VD_h')^{-1} D_h V] \tag{6.6.13}$$

where $V = \Omega \otimes M^{-1}$. The restricted estimator (6.6.12) is essentially an asymptotically efficient two step estimator, based on the principle of scoring, see Harvey (1981b, Chapter 5). That is, the adjustment to $\hat{\theta}$ concerns the information matrix postmultiplied by the efficient score vector, which is the amount by which the constraint is unsatisfied.

A major problem in implementing the above approach concerns the probable non-stationarity of the variables in the y_t vector. As previously described in Chapter 4, the application of unit root tests reveals the fact that spot and forward exchange rate series are in every case analysed, integrated of order one, i.e. I(1).

Hakkio (1981) and Baillie *et al.* (1983) difference the spot and forward rate series to make them stationary.

Then on differencing both sides of (6.2.4):

$$f_t - f_{t-1} = E_t s_{t+l} - E_{t-1} s_{t+l-1}$$

Or, from the law of iterated projections we can write the restrictions at time $t-1$ as

$$\Delta f_t = E_{t-1} \Delta s_{t+l} \tag{6.6.14}$$

The corollary of this is that if Δs_t and Δf_t are used instead of s_t and f_t in the y_t vector in (6.6.1), then the UEE set of parameter restrictions (6.6.10) will still be valid for $h \geqslant 1$. However the restriction at time t, with $h = 0$, i.e.

$$f_t = E_t s_{t+l} \tag{6.6.15}$$

will not be captured by testing the restriction (6.6.14). Clearly (6.6.15) is different and a stronger test than (6.6.14) or

$$E_{t-1}(s_{t+l} - f_t) = 0$$

As noted by Hodrick (1987) a test of (6.6.15) might conceivably lead to a different inference if only mild evidence against the UEE hypothesis had been found. Summaries of the results obtained by Hakkio (1981) and Baillie, Lippens and McMahon (1983) are given in Table 6.5. It can be seen that quite clear rejection of the hypothesis (6.6.14) was obtained for all the currencies considered.

As noted in Chapter 4 the variables s_t and f_f always appear to be non-stationary and I(1), while the forward premium $(f_t - s_t)$ is I(0); so that spot and forward rates are cointegrated in a particularly convenient manner.

On considering (6.2.4) a simple transformation reveals

$$f_t = E_t s_{t+1}$$

implies

$$(f_t - s_t) = E_t(s_{t+1} - s_t)$$

and

$$(f_t - s_t) = E_t \sum_{j=1}^{l} \Delta s_{t+j}$$

Hence if

$$y_t' = [\Delta s_t, (f_t - st), y_{3t} \ldots y_{gt}]$$

the restriction implies

$$E_{t-h}\left(y_{2t} - \sum_{j=1}^{l} y_{1t+j}\right) = 0 \quad h \geqslant 0 \tag{6.6.16}$$

The restriction (6.6.16) can be tested in a straightforward extension of the previous methodology. In particular the unrestricted model is estimated with elements Δs_t and $f_t - s_t$ and the restriction (6.6.10) is replaced from (6.6.16) with

$$r_h(\theta)' = E_{t-h}\left(y_{2t} - \sum_{j=1}^{l} y_{1t+j}\right) = 0$$

which can be expressed in terms of restrictions on VAR parameters as

$$r_h(\theta)' = e_2' A^h - e_1' \sum_{j=1}^{l} A^{h+j} = 0$$

The unrestricted model can again be tested by means of the Wald statistics (6.6.11) with D_h evaluated from

$$D_h = \begin{bmatrix} \sum_{j=0}^{h-1} (e_1' A'^j e_2) A^{h-1-j} - \sum_{k=1}^{l} \sum_{j=0}^{h+k-1} (e_1' A'^j e_1) A^{h+k-1-j} \\ \sum_{j=0}^{h-1} (e_2' A'^j e_2) A^{h-1-j} - \sum_{k=1}^{l} \sum_{j=0}^{h+k-1} (e_2' A'^j e_1) A^{h+k-1-j} \\ \vdots \qquad\qquad\qquad \vdots \\ \sum_{j=0}^{h-1} (e_g' A'^j e_2) A^{h-1-j} - \sum_{k=1}^{l} \sum_{j=0}^{h+k-1} (e_g' A'^j e_1) A^{h+k-1-j} \end{bmatrix} h \geqslant 1$$

and D_0 as:

$$D_0 = \begin{bmatrix} \sum_{k=1}^{l} \sum_{j=0}^{k-1} (e_1' A'^j e_1) A^{k-1-j} \\ \sum_{k=1}^{l} \sum_{j=0}^{k-1} (e_2' A'^j e_1) A^{k-1-j} \\ \vdots \\ \sum_{k=1}^{l} \sum_{j=0}^{k-1} (e_g' A'^j e_1) A^{k-1-j} \end{bmatrix}$$

It should be noted that the restrictions (6.6.10) and (6.6.16) are both of the form

$$r_h'(\theta) = r_{h-1}'(\theta) A \qquad (6.6.17)$$

So that provided A is non-singular it is possible by post-multiplication through (6.6.17) by A or A^{-1} to successively obtain the restrictions at any previous or subsequent time period. In fact the informational content of the restrictions is summarised by the value of $r(\theta)$ at any h. While it is possible to recover all the restricted vectors at different time periods, there does not appear to be a simple relationship between the computed Wald test statistics given. Hence it may be possible to reject the hypothesis conditional on information available at one time period, but not at another.

A rather more detailed description of the testing of these types of restrictions and their relationship to moving average coefficients is available in Baillie (1987, 1989).

The application of the above methodology critically depends upon the order p of the VAR being sufficiently large to guarantee a good approximation to the infinite moving average representation (6.6.1). The main requirement is that the vector of residuals are a good approximation to white noise. Baillie et al. (1983) uses likelihood ratio tests of different bivariate autoregressions on the spot and forward exchange rates and also use diagnostic tests of autocorrelation. Under a null hypothesis that the disturbance of the ith equation is white noise, Ljung and Box (1979) have shown that the modified Box–Pierce statistic

$$Q_i(m) = n(n+2) \sum_{j=1}^{m} \frac{1}{(n-j)} r_{ij}^2, \quad i = 1 \ldots g$$

where r_{ij} is the residual autocorrelation coefficient of lag j from the ith equation, will have an asymptotic χ^2 distribution with $m - p$ degrees of freedom. To test a null hypothesis that the disturbances constitute a multivariate white noise process the Hosking (1980) multivariate

Table 6.5 Tests of $E_{t-h}(s_{t+1} - f_t) = 0$ based on VARMA (p,q) models

Author	Sample period	Country	Transformation	Number of observations	p	q	h = 0 LR	h = 0 Wald	h = 1 LR	h = 1 Wald
Hakkio (1981)	Apr 24 1973 to May 5 1977	Holland	$\Delta s_t, \Delta f_t$	212	4	0	—	—	29.78[a]	—
,,	,,	West Germany	,,	212	4	0	—	—	26.55[a]	—
,,	,,	Canada	,,	212	4	0	—	—	72.25[a]	—
,,	,,	Switzerland	,,	212	4	0	—	—	93.57[a]	—
Baillie, Lippens and McMahon (1983)	Jun 1 1973 to Apr 8 1980	U.K.	$\Delta s_t, \Delta f_t$	362	9	0	—	—	500.89[a]	191.98[a]
,,	,,	West Germany	,,	362	6	0	—	—	—	249.16[a]
,,	,,	Italy	,,	362	10	0	—	—	—	150.59[a]
,,	,,	France	,,	362	6	0	—	—	—	258.87[a]
,,	Dec 1 1977 to May 15 1980	Canada	,,	128	3	0	—	—	—	52.33[a]
,,	,,	Switzerland	,,	128	3	0	—	—	—	69.94[a]
Levy & Nobay (1985)	Jan 1976 to Dec 1981	Switzerland	Δs $(f_t - s_t)$	313	1	4	110.71[a]	60.04[a]	—	11.40[b]
,,	,,	France	$\Delta s_t, f_t - s_t$	313	1	1	—	47.15[a]	—	8.03[b]
,,	,,	U.K.	,,	313	1	1	—	32.90[a]	—	8.65[b]
,,	,,	Canada	,,	313	1	2	—	14.18[a]	—	6.44[b]
,,	,,	West Germany	,,	313	1	2	—	17.09[a]	—	4.06
Baillie & McMahon	Jun 1 1973 to Apr 8 1980	U.K.	$\Delta s_t, f_t - s_t$	362	4	0	110.71[a]	129.84[a]	7.29	7.34
,,	,,	West Germany	$\Delta s_t, f_t - s_t, i_t - i_{t-4}$	362	2	0	141.46[a]	173.88[a]	10.10[b]	10.21[b]
,,	,,	France	,,	362	7	0	146.92[a]	181.30[a]	25.52[b]	26.13[b]
,,	,,	U.K.	,,	362	2	0	127.55[a]	153.53[a]	13.61[b]	13.82[b]
,,	,,	West Germany	$\Delta s_t, f_t - s_t$	362	2	0	142.07[a]	174.78[a]	11.69[b]	11.84[b]
,,	,,	France	,,	362	7	0	146.34[a]	179.70[a]	29.60	30.41
,,	Mar 1 1980 to Jan 28 1985	U.K.	$\Delta s_t, f_t - s_t$	267	4	0	132.79[a]	170.37[a]	16.84[b]	17.31[b]
,,	,,	West Germany	,,	267	1	0	72.96[a]	84.41[a]	0.64	0.64
,,	,,	Japan	,,	267	2	0	86.38[a]	102.67[a]	6.72	6.80
,,	,,	U.K.	$\Delta s_t, f_t - s_t, i_t - i_{t-4}$	267	4	0	137.65[a]	174.01[a]	21.16[b]	21.86[a]
,,	,,	West Germany	,,	267	2	0	83.10[a]	98.06[a]	13.27[b]	13.50[b]
,,	,,	Japan	,,	267	2	0	87.39[a]	104.06[a]	7.36	7.46

Key: 'a' and 'b' denotes significance at the .01 per cent level and .05 per cent level respectively.

Table 6.6 *Unrestricted estimation of a VAR(2) between Δs_t and $f_t - s_t$ for West Germany: weekly data June 1973 to April 1980*

Dependent variable	Δs_{t-1}	Δs_{t-2}	$f_{t-1} - s_{t-1}$	$f_{t-2} - s_{t-2}$	
Δs_t	0.3461	−0.0090	0.3129	−0.2014	$Q_1(2) = 13.48$ (0.76)
	(0.717)	(0.716)	(0.0858)	(0.0854)	
$f_t - s_t$	−0.0544	−0.0833	−0.1506	0.1682	$Q_2 = 13.58$ (0.76)
	(0.0606)	(0.0606)	(0.0725)	(0.0722)	$H(20) = 82.33$ (0.19)
		Restricted parameter estimates at $h = 1$			
Δs_t	0.2127	0.0133	0.2080	−0.0782	
	(0.0469)	(0.0294)	(0.0577)	(0.0322)	
$f_t - s_t$	−0.0581	0.0087	−0.0538	0.0044	
	(0.0351)	(0.0169)	(0.0437)	(0.0223)	

Test statistic	$h = 0$	$h = 1$	$h = 2$
Wald statistic	173.88	10.21[b]	7.92
LR	141.66[a]	10.10[b]	7.86

Key: p percentiles in brackets beside corresponding test statistics portmanteau statistic can be used. The statistic is given by

$$H(m) = n^2 \sum_{j=1}^{m} \frac{1}{(n-j)} \text{trace } C_j C_0^{-1} C_j C_0^{-1}$$

where C_j is the residual autocovariance matrix of lag j and is defined as

$$C_j = \frac{1}{n} \sum_{t=j+1}^{t} \hat{u}_t \hat{u}_{t-j}$$

Hosking's statistic is asymptotically equivalent to a Lagrange Multiplier test that the residuals follow a vector AR or MA process of order m, against the null hypothesis that they are generated by a vector white noise process. For the statistic to be fairly powerful it is necessary that the maximum lag m is chosen as a small proportion of the total sample size; say as $n^{1/2}$.

Other diagnostic statistics of model adequacy used by Baillie *et al.* (1983) included likelihood ratio tests of different values of p and Akaike information criterion tests.

A summary of some of the empirical results in the area is given in Table 6.5. The first sets of results from Hakkio (1981) and Baillie *et al.* (1983) testing the weaker restriction (6.6.14) imposed by information requirements at time $t - 1$ give rise to strong restrictions of the hypothesis. Levy and Nobay (1986) tackle the problem by estimating vector ARMA models which are sometimes more persimonious than the pure VAR models. One of the motivations of their study was to deal with data transformed according to (6.6.16). Their route for deciding on the appropriate transformations was essentially due to using Tiao and Tsay's (1982) extended sample autocorrelation coefficient approach. This transformation has been subsequently justified by the cointegration analysis discussed in Chapter 4. Further results using VARs on variables $\Delta s_t, f_t - s_t$ and $i_t - i_{t-4}$ where i_t is the Eurobond interest rate differential are reported in Table 6.5. A full description of how these types of restrictions can be tested in the face of non-stationarity with possibly cointegrating factors is provided by Baillie (1989). The results are generally consistent across time periods and between countries and clearly indicate that (6.6.16) can be uniformly rejected on information dated at time t, i.e. ($h = 0$) and generally rejected, although less strongly so, on information dated at time $t - 1$ or earlier.

The estimation of the restricted and unrestricted models for West Germany on 1980 to 1985 data are also presented in Table 6.6 as an example of the type of results obtained. Details of the parameter estimates for other models are omitted for reasons of space.

CHAPTER 7

The role of news and the term structure of the forward premium

7.1 Introduction

This chapter considers two further components of the relationship between spot and forward exchange rates, both of which have been hinted at earlier. Firstly, we consider the role of new information and how the forecast error between the future spot rate and current forward rate can be decomposed into unanticipated parts of various fundamentals. The next strand of the chapter looks at the relationships between forward rates of different maturity times. It can be seen from the IRP formula that implicit interest rates can be derived from the forward premia of different maturity times. These implicit interest rates can be expected to obey a classical term structure model. The next section then examines a test of the rational expectations model of the term structure (RETS), which has been derived by Sargent (1979) and subsequently extended by others. It turns out that the test jointly tests the validity of the term structure of the domestic and foreign bond markets and covered IRP. Most empirical evidence is able to reject RETS for the premium, while evidence on the RETS model for bond markets is mixed.

7.2 The role of news in movements of the spot rate

While purchasing power parity (PPP) is at best a long-run phenomenon the asset market approach appears necessary to understand short-run exchange rate movements. The usual posited relationship is to consider the exchange rate determined by fundamentals z_t and by a proportion of the expected percentage change, to give

$$s_t = z_t + \lambda E_t(s_{t+1} - s_t) \tag{7.2.1}$$

which has a forward solution of

$$s_t = \left(\frac{1}{1+\lambda}\right) \sum_{j=0}^{\infty} \left(\frac{\lambda}{1+\lambda}\right)^j E_t z_{t+j} \tag{7.2.2}$$

so that the exchange rate depends on the expected future paths of the fundamentals.

While many of the variables that are included in the fundamentals have relatively smooth time paths, it is noticeable that spot exchange rates decidedly do not. As we have noted previously, the history of floating exchange rates in the 1970s had been characterised by periods of extreme turbulence and volatility. This empirical evidence has led Frenkel (1981) among others to note that the 'key factor affecting exchange rates has been news'. 'News' in this context is taken to mean any new information which is of relevance to the exchange rate and which was unanticipated in the previous period. Thus news will include the current announced U.K. money supply minus its expectation in the previous period, so that this unanticipated component will only be known once a month when an announcement is made. On learning of the actual U.K. money supply the market will assess the sign and size of the unanticipated component, i.e. the news or surprise, and will modify its view on the appropriate price of the pound sterling. This process will then lead to a reaction on foreign exchange trading and to a change in the spot exchange rate for the pound. While news on key variables such as money supplies, real outputs and interest rates will play an important role, news on variables such as oil prices will also be important for currencies like the pound sterling where oil contributes a significant proportion (approximately 30 per cent) of exports. In this context an announcement that OPEC will be meeting sometime in the future may be the crucial piece of new information rather than any subsequent actual change in oil prices. Thus the market may move the spot rate in anticipation of the price of oil changing rather than waiting for the outcome of the OPEC meeting.

It has also been observed that financial markets are generally relatively quiet or stable before the announcement of important information, with a reduced amount of trading taking place. Thus the New York foreign exchange market tends to 'wait' on Thursdays for the announcement of the weekly U.S. money supply figure, leading to an immediate subsequent increase in the amount of trading taking place and changes in the exchange rates.

Given the occurrence of news and its likely effect on traders in financial markets it is interesting to assess the relative importance of news *vis-à-vis* anticipated or expected changes in fundamentals.

Frenkel (1981) has noted that 'periods which are dominated by uncertainties, new information, rumours, announcements and news, which induce frequent changes in expectations, are likely to be periods in which changes in expectations are the prime cause of fluctuations in asset prices'.

We now return to the type of equation that was utilised in the discussion of forward market efficiency, namely

$$(s_{t+1} - s_t) = \beta(E_t s_{t+1} - s_t) + \varepsilon_{t+1}, \tag{7.2.3}$$

where s_t is the logarithm of the spot rate, so that the left hand side reflects the actual one period percentage change while the right hand side is the expected percentage change plus a white noise error ε which includes the various surprise or news components. An analysis of the series $(s_{t+1} - s_t)$ and $(f_t - s_t)$ is given for various currencies by Mussa (1979) and Frenkel (1981). In their analysis f_t the logarithm of the forward rate, is used as a proxy for the expected future spot exchange rate. What emerges in the study by Frenkel (1981) is that for monthly data from the 1970s the variances of the percentage changes in the spot rates exceed the variances of monthly forward premia by a factor in excess of 20. Similarly Mussa (1979) attributes 90 per cent of spot exchange rate fluctuations to new information. This suggests that the majority of changes in the spot rate occur because of new information which could not have been anticipated in the previous period and also begs the question as to why the foreign exchange markets are so volatile. Do they over react to news and, if so, why? It may be that a considerable amount of volatility is due to speculative behaviour or, conversely, may be due to well intentioned but misdirected governments who are secretly intervening in attempts to stabilise currencies but are unwittingly destabilising a nearly efficient market. If the foreign exchange market is close to being efficient, then it may be that the presence of more speculators, rather than less, will be beneficial for price stability. A more formal analysis of the problem is to write equation (6.2.9) as

$$(s_{t+l} - s_t) = (E_t s_{t+l} - s_t) + \gamma \, \text{news}_{t+l} + u_{t+l}, \tag{7.2.4}$$

where news_{t+l} represents the difference between a function of some fundamentals at time $t + l$ and their expected value at time t. In the case of one variable x_t, news would be represented by

$$\text{news}_{t+l} = (x_{t+l} - E_t x_{t+l}) \tag{7.2.5}$$

Under the above definition news will be a function of $l - 1$ innovations that occur in the prediction interval from period $t + 1$ to $t + l$. Hence

$$E(\text{news}_{t+l} \, \text{news}_{t+l+j}) = 0 \quad j \geqslant l$$

so that the news variable can be represented by a moving average process of order $l - 1$, i.e. MA($l - 1$).

An alternative definition of news would be to take

$$\text{news}_{t+l} = \sum_{j=1}^{l} \alpha_j(x_{t+j} - E_t x_{t+j}) \tag{7.2.6}$$

which will be the sum of $l - 1$ independent MA processes of order $1, 2 \ldots l - 1$ respectively. Under the definition given by (7.2.6), news_{t+l} will still have a MA($l - 1$) and will be indistinguishable from (7.2.5). A still further definition would be

$$\text{news}_{t+l} = \sum_{j=1}^{l} \alpha_j (x_{t+j} - E_{t+j-1} x_{t+j})$$

but this does not seem appropriate given the dating of expectations in equation (7.2.4) where interest is focused on news following an expectation conditional on available and relevant information at time t.

7.3   Econometric approaches to estimating news equations

In most studies $E_t s_{t+l}$ is replaced by the forward rate f_t and given equation (7.2.5), equation (7.2.4) becomes

$$s_{t+l} = \beta f_t + \gamma (x_{t+l} - E_t x_{t+l}) + u_{t+l} \tag{7.3.1}$$

Note that u_{t+l} is also MA($l - 1$) so that subsuming the news term with u_{t+l} would give rise to another error process that also follows on MA($l - 1$) process. In all but two studies l has been chosen to be unity and the fundamental problem concerns how best to generate a news variable and subsequently estimate its coefficient γ and standard error. In one study Dornbusch (1980) defined news on current accounts and outputs as the differences between actuals and OECD forecasts. However, OECD forecasts were only available biannually and news seems to be a concept which is only meaningful when defined over a much shorter period of time.

The first attempt at artificially generating news was by Frenkel (1981) who used the method of Barro (1977) to take the residuals from an auxiliary regression as a proxy for news and to use them as a separate regressor in (7.2.4). Specifically Frenkel considered news on the interest rate differential i_t which is likely to be an extremely important variable in determining exchange rate movements from their expected paths. Frenkel estimated the following equation by OLS

$$i_t = b_0 + b_1 i_{t-1} + b_2 i_{t-2} + b_3 f_{t-1} + \eta_t \tag{7.3.2}$$

where η_t is a white noise process. The residuals

$$(i_{t+1} - E_t i_{t+1}) = i_{t+1} - \hat{\imath}_{t+1} = i_{t+1} - \hat{b}_0 - \hat{b}_1 i_t - \hat{b}_2 i_{t-1} - \hat{b}_3 f_t$$

are then used as a proxy for news and used as a regressor in (7.2.4) which was then estimated by 2SLS. It should be noted that there is some ambiguity attached to the sign of γ. In a non-inflationary environment and

Table 7.1 *Estimates of $s_{t+l} = \alpha + \beta f_t + \gamma(i_{t+l} - E_t i_{t+l}) + u_{t+1}$, i_t is the interest rate differential*

Author	Data time period	Frequency	l	Method for generating 'news'	Estimation method	Country compared with U.S. dollar	$\hat{\alpha}$	$\hat{\beta}$	$\hat{\gamma}$
Frenkel (1981)	June 1973 to June 1979	monthly	1	Residuals from OLS regression of 2SLS i_t on i_{t-1}, i_{t-2}, and f_{t-1}	2SLS	U.K.	0.031 (0.017)	0.959 (0.024)	0.432 (0.181)
,,	,,	,,	1	,,	,,	France	−0.246 (0.077)	0.837 (0.051)	0.245 (0.167)
,,	,,	,,	1	,,	,,	West Germany	−0.222 (0.026)	0.972 (0.031)	0.413 (0.347)
Turnovsky & Ball (1983)	Sept. 1974 to Dec. 1981	quarterly	1	,,	OLS	Australia	−0.038 (0.014)	0.746 (0.080)	0.0022 (0.0010)
Rose (1984)	Jan. 1971 to Oct. 1980	daily	22	$i_t = E_t i_{t+1}$	OLS with Hansen & Hodrick adjustment of covariance matrix	Canada	0.001 (0.001)	1.005 (0.015)	−0.001 (0.001)
Baillie (1987)	June 1973 to April 1980	weekly	12	VAR(2) on current and past s_t, f_t and i_t	VAR with cross equation restrictions	West Germany	NA	NA	0.627†

Key: Standard errors are in parenthesis below parameter estimates

† represents the total news coefficient over 12 weeks on a three month forward rate

measuring currencies *vis-à-vis* the numeraire U.S. dollar, a rise in the domestic (U.S.) rate of interest would be expected to lead to an appreciation of the U.S. dollar, i.e. $s_t\downarrow$, according to the data definitions, and hence $\gamma < 0$. This mechanism might work through covered interest parity and a higher forward premium being brought about by $s\downarrow$ to compensate for a rise in the domestic rates of interest. Alternatively, a rise in domestic interest rates would attract foreign capital and lead to a surplus on capital account, and/or restrict domestic expenditure to lead to a surplus on current account.

However, in an inflationary environment, γ may well be positive. A rise in domestic interest rates may be primarily due to inflationary expectations and will lead to a subsequent reduction in the demand for real balances. The current price level will then be too high for asset market equilibrium; thus domestic prices rise and hence from PPP, $s\uparrow$, i.e. exchange rate depreciation (i.e. $r\uparrow \rightarrow m^d\downarrow \rightarrow p\uparrow \rightarrow s\uparrow$). Generally Frenkel found γ to be positive and significant when estimating (7.3.1) from monthly data between 1973 and 1979. Furthermore, the inclusion of the actual interest rate differential i_{t+1}, as well as its 'news', frequently led to an insignificant coefficient while not changing the significance of the 'news' variable. The same approach has been used by Turnovsky and Ball (1983) for quarterly Australian data with ninety day forward rates and interest rates of identical maturity times. They used a similar equation to (7.3.2) for artificially generating the news variable and, in the subsequent regression model, they also found the news coefficient to support the inflationary expectations story. A study by Rose (1984) on the Canadian dollar versus U.S. dollar is of interest since he took daily data and thus had overlapping data with $l > 1$. Rose generated the interest rate differential extremely simply by assuming that $E_t i_{t+l} = i_t$. A summary of the results of the studies is presented in Table 7.1; it should be noted that while Rose's overall results were not significant, he was able to find a significant news coefficient for sub-periods associated with appreciations, depreciations, etc.

One econometric problem concerns the use of residuals as a proxy for news in equation (7.2.4) and the subsequent use of a two step estimator. As previously mentioned, Pagan (1984) has considered the limiting distribution of such an estimator and shown that the subsequent estimate of the disturbance variance is generally downward biased. Another objection that can be made against most of the above studies is that the generation of the news variable is obtained from simple *ad hoc* expectations schemes, rather than an approach more in line with rational expectations.

A different approach has been taken by Baillie (1987) who shows that when the data-generating process can be interpreted as including an equation with an unanticipated or 'surprise' variable, then that equation should be implicit in the unrestricted moving average representation (MAR) of the variables in the system.

When an equation contains an explanatory variable which is the rational expectation of the dependent variable l periods in the future, then the resulting disturbance will be a moving average process of order $l - 1$. Baillie (1987) shows how the disturbance can be regarded as the sum of separate component moving average processes with the interpretation of being 'surprise' or 'news' on different variables. Furthermore, their coefficients in the equation of interest are reparameterisations of the MAR coefficients which are derived from the estimated finite-order vector autoregressions (VAR), vector autoregressive moving average (VARMA) models. The technique can then be applied to obtain parameter estimates and associated standard errors or 'surprise' variables in the equation of interest. The procedure has the properties that:

(a)   It naturally conditions expectations on current and past values of the variables in the process and hence avoids the problem of having to artificially generate expectations or news from a separate regression.

(b)   The technique allows news to be considered more than one period ahead and avoids the need for generalising Pagan's (1984) technique to this situation.

(c)   The estimated parameters of interest and their standard errors can be found without two-step procedures and complicated adjustments of their respective standard errors.

However a potential disadvantage with the technique is that it does require the specification of a complete multivariate time-series model, rather than just being based on single-equation estimation as in previous studies. On estimating a VAR(2) model for the West German Deutschmark/U.S. dollar, corresponding ninety day forward rates and interest rate differentials, Baillie (1987) found a total news coefficient of 0.627 for news on the interest rate differential which also supports the inflationary expectations hypothesis. Further details of the method are to be found in Baillie (1987).

7.4   Edwards' additive news model

Several studies have considered the impact of different types of news on a one period ahead basis. Such a model would take the form

$$s_{t+1} = \alpha + \beta f_t + \sum_{j=1}^{k} (x_{jt+1} - E_t x_{jt+1}) + u_{t+1} \tag{7.4.1}$$

where the x_{jt} represent important fundamental variables such as money supplies, real outputs, interest rates, oil prices etc. Before considering the results of empirical estimation of the above equation it is worthwhile to first examine a model due to Edwards (1983) which provides a justification of equation (7.4.1). Edward's model is a fairly simple extension of the basic monetary model and is given by the following nine equations:

$$i_t - i_t^* = f_t - s_t \tag{7.4.2}$$

$$E_t s_{t+1} = f_t \tag{7.4.3}$$

$$s_t = p_t - p_t^* + \varepsilon_t \tag{7.4.4}$$

$$i_t = r_t + E_t(p_{t+1} - p_t); \quad i_t^* = r_t^* + E_t(p_{t+1}^* - p_t^*) \tag{7.4.5}$$

$$r_t = \rho + w_t; \quad r_t^* = \rho^* + w_t^* \tag{7.4.6}$$

$$m_t - p_t = a y_t - b i_t; \quad m_t^* - p_t^* = a^* y_t^* - b^* i_t^* \tag{7.4.7}$$

$$m_t = m_{t-1} + \lambda + v_t + n_t - n_{t-1};$$
$$m_t^* = m_{t-1}^* + \lambda^* + v_t^* + n_t^* - n_{t-1} \tag{7.4.8}$$

$$y_t = y_0 + g_t + u_t; \quad y_t^* = y_0^* + g_t^* + u_t^* \tag{7.4.9}$$

As usual s, f, p, m and y denote the spot rate, forward rate and domestic prices, money supply and real outputs: all in logarithmic form. The variables i and r are nominal and real rates of interest, asterisks denote foreign quantities, λ, λ^*, ρ and ρ^* are constants; $\varepsilon_t, w_t, w_t^*, v_t, v_t^*, n_t, n_t^*, u_t$ and u_t^* are all mutually uncorrelated white noise processes.

The model thus specifies a pure interest arbitrage condition, and also assumes the forward rate to be an unbiased and efficient predictor of the future spot rate so that no time varying risk premium is present. The third equation assumes deviations from PPP to be a random white noise process, the fourth is the standard Fisher equation while the fifth equation indicates that the real interest rate in each country is equal to a constant plus a white noise term. The last three equations are a demand for real balances equation and specifications for the growth of money supply and real output. It should be noted that money supply is assumed to grow as a random walk process plus permanent and transitory random shocks v_t and n_t respectively.

From equations (7.4.5), (7.4.6) and (7.4.7)

$$bE_t(p_{t+1} - p_t) = bi_t - b\rho - bw_t$$

$$= (ay_t + p_t - m_t) - b\rho - bw_t$$

which gives rise to a standard rational expectations equation

$$p_t = \left(\frac{b}{1+b}\right) E_t p_{t+1} + \left(\frac{1}{1+b}\right) z_t \tag{7.4.10}$$

where
$$z_t = (m_t - ay_t + b\rho + bw_t)$$

From (3.A.33), one solution of (7.4.10) is seen to be

$$p_t = \left(\frac{b}{1+b}\right) \sum_{j=0}^{\infty} \left(\frac{b}{1+b}\right)^j E_t z_{t+j}$$

Or, $$p_t = \left(\frac{1}{1+b}\right) \sum_{j=0}^{\infty} \left(\frac{b}{1+b}\right)^j E_t(m_{t+j} - ay_{t+j} + b\rho + bw_{t+j}) \quad (7.4.11)$$

Solution of this equation requires solving out the appropriate processes for money and real output. Equation (7.4.7) can be written as

$$(1 - L)m_{t+j} = \lambda + v_{t+j} + n_{t+j} - n_{t+j-1}$$

and on using the identity

$$(1 - L) \equiv (1 - L^j)(1 + L + L^2 + \cdots + L^{j-1})^{-1}$$

it follows that

$$(1 - L^j)m_{t+j} = (1 + L + L^2 + \cdots + L^{j-1})(\lambda + v_{t+j} + n_{t+j} - n_{t+j-1})$$

so that

$$m_{t+j} = m_t + j\lambda + \sum_{i=1}^{j} v_{t+i} + n_{t+j} - n_t$$

and hence

$$E_t m_{t+j} = m_t + j\lambda - n_t \quad j \geqslant 1$$

Substitution into (7.4.11) leads to

$$p_t = \left(\frac{1}{1+b}\right)(m_t - ay_0 - ag_t - au_t + b\rho + bw_t)$$

$$+ \left(\frac{1}{1+b}\right) \sum_{j=1}^{\infty} \left(\frac{b}{1+b}\right)^j$$

$$\times (m_t + j\lambda - n_t - ay_0 - agt - agj + b\rho)$$

Noting that

$$\sum_{j=1}^{\infty} \left(\frac{b}{1+b}\right)^j = b \quad \text{and} \quad \sum_{j=1}^{\infty} j\left(\frac{b}{1+b}\right)^j = b(1+b)$$

Then

$$p_t = m_t - \left(\frac{a}{1+b}\right)u_t + \left(\frac{b}{1+b}\right)w_t - \left(\frac{b}{1+b}\right)n_t + \alpha_0$$

where

$$\alpha_0 = [b(\rho - ag) - ay_0 + b\lambda - agt]$$

Since an analogous derivation for p_t^* can also be found, it follows from equation (7.4.4) that

$$s_t = (\alpha_0 - \alpha_0^*) + (m_t - m_t^*)$$
$$-\left(\frac{a}{1+b}\right)u_t + \left(\frac{b}{1+b}\right)w_t - \left(\frac{b}{1+b}\right)n_t$$
$$+\left(\frac{a^*}{1+b^*}\right)u_t^* - \left(\frac{b^*}{1+b^*}\right)w_t^* + \left(\frac{b^*}{1+b^*}\right)n_t^* + \varepsilon_t \qquad (7.4.12)$$

so that the spot rate is seen to be determined by relative money supplies and news on domestic and foreign moneys, real outputs and real interest rates. From equations (7.4.3) and (7.4.12)

$$f_t = E_t s_{t+1} = (\alpha_0 - \alpha_0^*) + E_t(m_{t+1} - m_{t+1}^*)$$
$$= (\alpha_0 - \alpha_0^*) + (m_t - m_t^*)$$
$$+ (\lambda - \lambda^*) - (n_t - n_t^*) \qquad (7.4.13)$$

and since

$$m_t = m_{t+1} - \lambda - v_{t+1} - n_{t+1} + n_t$$

and on substitution into (7.4.13)

$$f_t = (\alpha_0 - \alpha_0^*) + (m_{t+1} - m_{t+1}^*)$$
$$- v_{t+1} + v_{t+1}^* - n_{t+1} + n_{t+1}^*$$

On comparing (7.4.12) at time $t + 1$ with (7.4.13) at time t it can be seen that

$$s_{t+1} = f_t + v_{t+1} + \left(\frac{b}{1+b}\right)w_{t+1} - \frac{a}{1+b}u_{t+1} - v_{t+1}$$
$$+ \left(\frac{a^*}{1+b^*}\right)u_{t+1}^* - \left(\frac{b^*}{1+b^*}\right)w_{t+1}^* + \varepsilon_{t+1} \qquad (7.4.14)$$

Thus the above equation shows quite clearly that, in the confines of the model (7.4.2) to (7.4.9) inclusive, the difference between the current forward rate and future spot rate will be due to news concerning unanticipated changes in money supplies, real incomes and real interest rates.

Table 7.2 Estimates of $s_{t+1} = \alpha + \beta f_t + \gamma_1[(m_{t+1} - m^*_{t+1}) - E_t(m_{t+1} - m^*_{t+1})] + \gamma_2[(y_{t+1} - y^*_{t+1}) - E_t(y_{t+1} - y^*_{t+1})] + \gamma_3$
$[(r_{t+1} - r^*_{t+1}) - E_t(r_{t+1} - r^*_{t+1})] + \varepsilon_{t+1}$

Author	Data time period	Frequency	Method for generating news	Estimation method	Country compared with U.S. dollar	$\hat{\alpha}$	$\hat{\beta}$	$\hat{\gamma}_1$	$\hat{\gamma}_2$	$\hat{\gamma}_3$
Edwards (1982)	June 1973 to Sept. 1979	monthly	AR(3)	SURE	U.K.	-0.024 (0.014)	0.970 (0.020)	0.103 (0.154)	0.006 (0.002)	0.007 (0.018)
"	"	"	AR(3)	"	France	-0.155 (0.113)	0.951 (0.037)	0.359 (0.142)	0.182 (0.123)	-0.005 (0.015)
"	"	"	AR(3)	"	West Germany	0.032 (0.018)	0.957 (0.021)	0.372 (0.182)	0.243 (0.109)	0.011 (0.023)
"	"	"	AR(3)	"	Italy	0.248 (0.119)	0.962 (0.018)	0.084 (0.190)	-0.046 (0.102)	-0.022 (0.010)
Copeland (1984)	Jan. 1973 to May 1983	"	ARIMA	2SLS	U.K.	-0.056 (0.016)	0.927 (0.022)	0.096 (0.280)	0.159 (0.087)	-0.008 (0.003)

7.5   Empirical results on news

The technique of artificially generating news on variables such as relative money supplies, real incomes and interest rates and estimating equations such as (7.4.1) by OLS or 2SLS has been performed by a number of authors. Results are given in Table 7.2 from Edwards (1982) and Copeland (1984). It should be noted that Edwards used *ex post* real rates of interest while Copeland used nominal Treasury bill rates. Several news coefficients turn out to be significant, albeit with the possible problem of downward biased standard errors discussed by Pagan (1984). Edward's results indicate that a 10 per cent unanticipated increase in the money supply differential for France and West Germany will lead to approximately $3\frac{1}{2}$ per cent depreciation of the domestic exchange rate. The other results are generally mixed with many coefficients being insignificant. MacDonald (1983) has also considered the impact of lagged news and some of his results for the 1920s floating period are presented in Table 7.3.

A number of other studies have examined the general impact of money supply announcements, e.g. see Cornell (1983a,b), Urich (1982) and Urich and Wachtel (1981). For further studies on exchange rates, see Edwards (1982a,b) and Rose and Selody (1984).

A further method for estimating the parameters in a news equation has been suggested by Edwards (1983), who fits separate VARs to monthly data on domestic money, real output and *ex post* real interest rates and to their foreign equivalents. Denoting

$$x_t' = (m_t y_t r_t), \quad x_t^{*\prime} = (m_t^* y_t^* r_t^*)$$

$$\eta_t' = (v_t w_t u_t) \quad \text{and} \quad \eta_t^{*\prime} = (v_t^* w_t^* u_t^*)$$

then it is assumed that

$$x_{t+1} = \sum_{j=1}^{6} B_j x_{t+1-j} + \eta_{t+1} \tag{7.5.1}$$

and

$$x_{t+1}^* = \sum_{j=1}^{6} B_j^* x_{t+1-j}^* + \eta_{t+1}^* \tag{7.5.2}$$

Equations (7.5.1) and (7.5.2) are jointly estimated by SURE with the news equation from (7.4.1), i.e.

$$s_{t+1} = \alpha + \beta f_t + \varepsilon_{t+1} \tag{7.5.3}$$

$$\varepsilon_{t+1} = \gamma_1 v_{t+1} + \gamma_2 w_{t+1} + \gamma_3 u_{t+1}$$
$$+ \gamma_4 v_{t+1}^* + \gamma_5 w_{t+1}^* + \gamma_6 u_{t+1}^* \tag{7.5.4}$$

Table 7.3 Estimates of $s_{t+1} = \alpha + \beta f_t + \gamma_4(m_{t+1} - E_t m_{t+1}) + \gamma_5(m^*_{t+1} - E_t m^*_{t+1}) + \gamma_6(y_{t+1} - E_t y_{t+1}) + \gamma_7(y^*_{t+1} - E_t y^*_{t+1}) + \gamma_8(r_{t+1} - E_t r_{t+1}) + \gamma_9(r^*_{t+1} - E_t r^*_{t+1}) + \varepsilon_{t+1}$

Author	Data time period	Frequency	Method for generating news	Estimation method	Country compared with U.S. dollar	$\hat{\alpha}$	$\hat{\beta}$	$\hat{\gamma}_4$	$\hat{\gamma}_5$	$\hat{\gamma}_6$	$\hat{\gamma}_7$	$\hat{\gamma}_8$	$\hat{\gamma}_9$
Copeland (1984)	Jan. 1973 to May 1983	monthly	ARIMA	2SLS	U.K.	-0.059 (0.016)	0.924 (0.022)	0.032 (0.280)	-0.032 (0.280)	0.151 (0.088)	-0.034 (0.450)	0.002 (0.006)	0.013 (0.005)
MacDonald (1983)	July 1922 to May 1925	,,	2SLS on lagged money, income & interest rates	OLS	U.K.	-0.364 (0.142)	1	0.003 (0.003)	0.071 (0.029)				
				OLS	France	0.059 (1.15)	1	-3.854 (7.865)	0.497 (0.469)				
			,,	OLS	U.K.	0.031 (0.029)	1					0.130 (0.058)	-0.050 (0.050)
			,,	OLS	France	0.003 (0.011)	1					-0.018 (0.020)	0.350 (0.179)

Copeland restricts $\gamma_4 = -\gamma_5$, i.e. takes news on a money supply differential variable. MacDonald takes first differences of money growth rather than levels and restricts $\beta = 1$, so that the dependent variable is $(s_{t+1} - f_t)$.

Edwards assumes that the covariance matrices of η_t and η_t^* are diagonal so that there is zero contemporaneous correlation between the various fundamental variables. However, the news terms on the right hand side of (7.5.3) will be correlated with the elements of η_{t+1} and η_{t+1}^*. The application of SURE will require using the error covariance matrix $\Omega \otimes I$ where

$$
\Omega = \begin{bmatrix}
\sigma_{\varepsilon\varepsilon} & \sigma_{\varepsilon v} & \sigma_{\varepsilon w} & \cdots & \sigma_{\varepsilon u^*} \\
\sigma_{\varepsilon v} & \sigma_{vv} & & & \\
\sigma_{\varepsilon w} & & \sigma_{ww} & & 0 \\
\vdots & & & \ddots & \\
\sigma_{\varepsilon u^*} & & 0 & & \sigma_{u^* u^*}
\end{bmatrix}
$$

It is easily seen from equation (7.5.4) that

$$
\sigma_{\varepsilon v} = \gamma_1 \sigma_{vv}, \ldots, \sigma_{\varepsilon u^*} = \gamma_6 \gamma_{u^* u^*}
$$

Given estimates of the residual variances and covariances, which Edwards obtains in the conventional manner from residuals of (7.5.1), (7.5.2) and (7.5.3); then estimates of the news parameters can be obtained as

$$
\hat{\gamma}_1 = \hat{\sigma}_{\varepsilon v} / \hat{\sigma}_{vv} \quad \text{etc.}
$$

The very restrictive assumption of the absence of contemporaneous correlation between and across the disturbances of x_t and x_t^* is necessary to produce this simple estimation technique. A further disadvantage with the method is that standard errors of the estimated γ's are difficult to compute and are not reported by Edwards. Of twenty four estimated news coefficients (six in each of four equations estimated by SURE) only eight turn out to have the expected sign. However, many of the coefficients, particularly those attached to money supply and real interest rates, are relatively large in magnitude.

In general the empirical evidence on the importance of different types of news is fairly mixed with inconsistency of results between different authors findings. It is important to note that news is essentially something by definition that is uncorrelated with the forward rate in a regression of future spot rates on current forward rates. Thus the exclusion of news variables will not bias the coefficient estimate of the forward rate variable; it will at most raise the variance of the disturbance. The relative importance of different types of news still seems an open question and a number of econometric problems will need to be settled before progress can be made.

One particularly interesting avenue for research in this area is the consideration of transmission of news between different markets, both spatially and temporally. Hogan and Sharpe (1984) present evidence on how the closing price of the Australian dollar *vis-à-vis* the U.S. dollar on the New York market affects the initial price of the same currency on the Australian foreign exchange market when it opens a few hours after the New York market has closed. The relationship between the impact of news on different financial markets is also interesting, together with the issue of whether markets respond symmetrically to news.

7.6   The term structure of the forward premium

One of the fundamental theories regarding exchange rate behaviour is the covered interest rate parity relationship

$$\frac{F_t - S_t}{S_t} = \frac{r_t^d - r_t^f}{1 + r_t^f},$$

which implies that the forward premium or discount equals a type of interest rate differential. The formula is required to hold for forward rates and domestic and foreign interest rates of exactly the same maturity times. This implies that the forward premium is an implicit interest rate, and standard term structure theory of interest rates behaviour should be expected to apply to forward premia of different maturity times. Given forward rates of maturity times one and n periods, denoted by F_t' and F_t^n respectively, the corresponding implicit interest rates will be given by

$$r_t = \frac{F_t' - S_t}{S_t} \tag{7.6.1}$$

and

$$R_t = \frac{F_t^n - S_t}{S_t}, \tag{7.6.2}$$

The classical expectations hypothesis of the term structure between interest rates r_t and R_t^n is generated from a competitive equilibrium condition and is expressed as

$$(1 + R_t^n)^n = \prod_{i=0}^{n-1} (1 + E_t r_{t+i}), \tag{7.6.3}$$

where E_t is the standard rational expectations operator. The theory assumes that agents are profit maximisers, that there are zero transaction costs and taxes, and a high degree of substitutability between bonds of different maturity periods. This implies that there is a zero liquidity premium, which is analogous to a zero time varying risk premium in the UEE hypothesis.

Given knowledge at time t of two current interest rates of maturity times

n and $n - 1$, the n period maturity forward rate is implied from the equation

$$(1 + R_t^n)^n = (1 + R_t^{n-1})^{n-1}(1 + E_t r_{t+n})$$
$$= (1 + R_t^{n-1})^{n-1}(1 + f_t^n)$$

so that

$$f_t^n = E_t r_{t+n} \tag{7.6.4}$$

The validity of equation (7.6.3) is dependent on a joint hypothesis that the rational expectations model of the term structure is valid for both domestic and foreign bond markets and that covered interest parity is maintained. Rejection of the hypothesis is consistent with a failure of one or more of the three separate above hypotheses.

In order to test the rational expectations model of the term structure it is usual to take a linear approximation to equation (7.6.3) (see Begg 1982, p. 212). This gives the equation

$$R_t^n = \frac{1}{n}(r_t + E_t r_{t+1} + \cdots + E_t r_{t+n-1}) \tag{7.6.5}$$

and on conditioning on information dated at time $t - h$:

$$E_{t-h} R_t^n = \frac{1}{n} \sum_{l=0}^{n-1} E_{t-h} r_{t+l} \tag{7.6.6}$$

This restriction is clearly extremely similar to that of the UEE hypothesis given by (6.4.1) and involves a linear combination of forward looking expectations on the two variables. Tests of the rational expectations model of the term structure have been previously derived in the context of the domestic bond market by Sargent (1979) and implemented for forward premia by Hakkio (1981) and Baillie and McMahon (1985). It should be noted that a wide and extensive literature has developed over the years on testing expectations models of the term structure (see Melino 1987). Many of the tests have involved the so called volatility tests associated with Shiller (1979) and LeRoy and Porter (1981). For a critical review of these tests, see Flavin (1983) and Melino (1987). This section is confined to dealing with a general treatment of the cross equation restriction method as implemented by Hakkio (1981b) and Baillie and McMahon (1985).

As in the case of testing the UEE hypothesis the short and long-term forward premia can be regarded as the first two elements of a vector y_t, such that

$$y_t = (r_t R_t^n y_{3t} \cdots y_{gt})$$

and is again modelled as a VAR(p) as in equation (6.5.8)

$$y_t = \sum_{j=1}^{p} A_j y_{t-j} + \varepsilon_t,$$

with the first order representation

$$Y_t = AY_{t-1} + \eta_t$$

where

$$Y_t = (y_t y_{t-1} \dots y_{t-p+1}), \quad \eta_t = (\varepsilon_t 0 \dots 0)$$

$$A = \begin{bmatrix} A_1 A_2 \dots A_{p-1} & A_p \\ \hline I & 0 \end{bmatrix}$$

On utilising the results and approach taken in equations (6.5.9) to (6.5.14) inclusive, it is easily seen that (7.6.6) implies the gp parameter restrictions

$$r_h(\theta)' = e_2' A^h - \frac{1}{n} e_1' \sum_{l=0}^{n-1} A^{l+h} = 0 \quad h = 0, 1, 2 \dots \tag{7.6.7}$$

where e_j is the null vector, save for unity in its j element.

Maximum likelihood estimation of the unrestricted VAR(p) model will realise parameter estimates $\hat{\theta}$, with the limiting distribution (6.6.4) and allows computation of the Wald test statistic

$$W_h = r_h(\hat{\theta})' [D_h'(\hat{\Omega} \otimes M^{-1}) D_h]^{-1} r_h(\hat{\theta})$$

where

$$D_0 = -\frac{1}{n} \begin{bmatrix} \sum_{l=0}^{n-1} \sum_{j=0}^{l-1} (e_1' A'^j e_2) A^{l-1-j} \\ \sum_{l=0}^{n-1} \sum_{j=0}^{l-1} (e_2' A'^j e_1) A^{l-1-j} \end{bmatrix}$$

and

$$D_h = \frac{\partial r_h(\theta)}{\partial \theta}$$

$$= \begin{bmatrix} \sum_{j=0}^{h-1} (e_1 A'^j e_2) A^{h-1-j} - \frac{1}{n} \sum_{l=0}^{n-1} \sum_{j=0}^{l+h-1} (e_1' A'^j e_2) A^{l+h-1-j} \\ \sum_{j=0}^{h-1} (e_2' A'^j e_1) A^{h-1-j} - \frac{1}{n} \sum_{l=0}^{n-1} \sum_{j=0}^{l+h-1} (e_2' A'^j e_1) A^{l+h-1-j} \end{bmatrix}$$

$$h = 1, 2 \dots$$

Under the null hypothesis given by (7.6.7), W_h will have an asymptotic chi squared distribution with gp degrees of freedom. Analogous to equations (6.6.10) and (6.6.16) the parameters estimates subject to restrictions (7.6.7) are obtained by the asymptotically efficient two step estimator

$$\tilde{\theta}_h = \hat{\theta} - (\Omega \otimes M^{-1}) D_h [D_h'(\Omega \otimes M^{-1}) D_h]^{-1} r_h(\hat{\theta})$$

which facilitates calculation of likelihood ratio test statistics. Under the null hypothesis the restricted parameter estimates $\tilde{\theta}$ will have the limiting distribution

$$\sqrt{n}(\tilde{\theta}_h - \theta) \sim N(0, P_h)$$

where

$$P = (\Omega \otimes M^{-1}) - (\Omega \otimes M^{-1})D_h[D_h'(\Omega \otimes M^{-1})D_h]^{-1}D_h(\Omega \otimes M^{-1})$$

Table 7.4 presents some of the results from testing the rational expectations model of the term structure; although only the articles by Hakkio (1981b) and Baillie and McMahon (1985) specifically relate to forward premia. Apart from Attfield and Duck (1982), all the above papers chose $g = 2$ so the y_t vector only contained short and long rates. Full details of the VAR models fitted to thirty and ninety day forward premia, on monthly data from 1973 to 1980 and estimated subject to restrictions at time t, $t - 1$ and $t - 2$, are given in Table 7.5 and are more detailed versions of the results presented by Baillie and McMahon (1985). It should be noted that each pair of variables, for each currency were approximately covariance stationary in levels, i.e. I(0).

Overall, however, the results give rise to an unambiguous rejection of the model and further results by Lippens (1987) suggest the cause of such rejections is most probably due to a failure of the term structure models in the domestic and foreign bond markets. This suggests the need for developing an appropriate model of time varying liquidity premia. Currently, research is taking place on using the ARCH type time dependent conditional variance models discussed in Chapter 4 for this purpose (see Engle, Lillien and Robins 1987).

7.7   Modelling the time varying risk premium

The fact that the unbiased efficient expectations (UEE) hypothesis can be clearly rejected on foreign exchange market data begs the question as to the cause of the rejection. Since it is hard to accept the possibility of agents freely engaging in sub-optimal behaviour when forming expectations and since most of the requirements of perfect capital markets have been well approximated in recent years by the floating foreign exchanges, the empirical evidence therefore suggests the presence of a time varying risk premium. While competition between traders should be expected to keep the risk premium small, the extreme volatility of exchange rates, together with the clear rejection of UEE, suggests otherwise. Grauer *et al.* (1976) derived a theoretical asset pricing model (APM) to explain risk in foreign exchange and subsequent authors have attempted to give the theory

Table 7.4 *Tests of rational expectations model of the term structure from VAR models*

Authors	Data series considered	Frequency	Data time period	Transformation	h	p	Likelihood ratio	Wald
Sargent (1979)	Salomon Brothers 3 month T bills and 5 yr. U.S. government bonds	quarterly	1953 QII to 1971 QIV	First differences	1	4	8.58 (0.)	—
Attfield & Duck (1982)	U.K. 3 month and 10 year rates of interest	"		"	1	4		4.85 (0.10)
Melino (1983)	Salomon Brothers 3 month T bills and 5 yr. U.S. government bonds	"	1953 QII to 1971 QIV	"	0	4	—	0.40 (0.00)
	"	"	"	"	1	4	8.97 (0.)	10.42 (0.24)
Hakkio (1981)	Forward premium for West Germany against U.S. with one and six month forward rates	"	March 1973 to December 1976	"	1	4	11.13 (0.19)	21.84 (0.01)
	Forward premium for Canada against U.S. with one and six month forward rates	"	"	"	1	4	20.84 (0.01)	42.11 (0.00)
Baillie & McMahon (1985)	Forward premium for U.K. against U.S. with one & three month forward rates	monthly	June 1973 to April 1980	levels	1	2	34.71 (0.00)	15.28 (0.00)
	Forward premium for West Germany against U.S. with one and three month forward rates	"	"	"	1	2	14.25 (0.00)	151.53 (0.00)
	Forward premium for Italy against U.S. with one and three month forward rates	"	"	"	1	2	92.47 (0.00)	

Key: *p* percentiles in brackets beside test statistics.

Table 7.5 Details of estimated VAR models applied to monthly data on 30 day and 90 day forward premia

U.K. unrestricted model

Coefficient estimates of:

1st equation

r_{t-1}	r_{t-2}	R^n_{t-1}	R^n_{t-2}
−0.1085 (0.1059)	−0.0705 (0.1064)	0.2472 (0.1022)	0.1572 (0.1044)

2nd equation

r_{t-1}	r_{t-2}	R^n_{t-1}	R^n_{t-2}
−0.1067 (0.1083)	−0.0041 (0.1089)	0.4591 (0.1045)	0.2329 (0.1068)

U.K. restricted h = 0 model

Coefficient estimates of:

1st equation

r_{t-1}	r_{t-2}	R^n_{t-1}	R^n_{t-2}
−0.6282 (0.0363)	−0.1193 (0.0255)	2.5394 (0.0408)	−0.5744 (0.0363)

2nd equation

r_{t-1}	r_{t-2}	R^n_{t-1}	R^n_{t-2}	Wald	LR
−0.4596 (0.1016)	0.3235 (0.0974)	1.6202 (0.0925)	−0.4890 (0.0930)	667.24 (0.00)	211.84 (0.00)

U.K. restricted h = 1 model

Coefficient estimates of:

1st equation

r_{t-1}	r_{t-2}	R^n_{t-1}	R^n_{t-2}
−0.1533 (0.1052)	−0.0811 (0.1014)	0.3376 (0.1011)	0.0945 (0.0968)

2nd equation

r_{t-1}	r_{t-2}	R^n_{t-1}	R^n_{t-2}	Wald	LR
−0.0800 (0.0404)	−0.0224 (0.0262)	0.1846 (0.464)	0.0540 (0.0319)	42.11 (0.00)	34.71 (0.00)

Table 7.5 *continued*

U.K. restricted h = 2 model

Coefficient estimates of:

1st equation

r_{t-1}	r_{t-2}	R^n_{t-1}	R^n_{t-2}	2nd equation				Wald	LR
				r_{t-1}	r_{t-2}	R^n_{t-1}	R^n_{t-2}		
-0.1030	-0.1208	0.2401	0.0822	-0.1886	-0.0309	0.0034	0.3102	35.50 (0.00)	30.97 (0.00)
(0.1013)	(0.1048)	(0.1026)	(0.0987)	(0.0287)	(0.0145)	(0.0422)	(0.0174)		

West Germany unrestricted model

Coefficient estimates of:

1st equation

r_{t-1}	r_{t-2}	R^n_{t-1}	R^n_{t-2}	2nd equation			
				r_{t-1}	r_{t-2}	R^n_{t-1}	R^n_{t-2}
0.0620	-0.0917	0.2606	-0.0385	-0.1298	-0.0312	0.3137	0.3536
(0.1081)	(0.1073)	(0.1395)	(0.1445)	(0.0815)	(0.0809)	(0.1015)	(0.1090)

West Germany restricted h = 0 model

Coefficient estimates of:

1st equation

r_{t-1}	r_{t-2}	R^n_{t-1}	R^n_{t-2}	2nd equation				Wald	LR
				r_{t-1}	r_{t-2}	R^n_{t-1}	R^n_{t-2}		
-0.5263	-0.0069	2.7351	-0.8063	-0.2933	0.1179	1.0700	-0.1585	358.14 (0.00)	147.86 (0.00)
(0.0222)	(0.0178)	(0.0401)	(0.0360)	(0.0774)	(0.0758)	(0.0964)	(0.0990)		

All the test statistics in the above table have asymptotic X^2_4 distributions and X^2_4 (0.01) = 13.28.

West Germany restricted h = 1 model

Coefficient estimates of:

1st equation

r_{t-1}	r_{t-2}	R^n_{t-1}	R^n_{t-2}
-0.1872 (0.0502)	-0.0438 (0.0295)	0.2921 (0.0613)	0.1407 (0.0469)

2nd equation

r_{t-1}	r_{t-2}	R^n_{t-1}	R^n_{t-2}	Wald	LR
0.0148 (0.1047)	-0.1189 (0.0901)	0.3624 (0.1334)	0.2453 (0.1237)	15.28 (0.00)	14.25 (0.00)

West Germany restricted h = 2 model

Coefficient estimates of:

1st equation

r_{t-1}	r_{t-2}	R^n_{t-1}	R^n_{t-2}
0.0192 (0.1030)	-0.0379 (0.1009)	0.3808 (0.1355)	0.0707 (0.1185)

2nd equation

r_{t-1}	r_{t-2}	R^n_{t-1}	R^n_{t-2}	Wald	LR
-0.0886 (0.0368)	0.0045 (0.0325)	0.1460 (0.0612)	-0.0053 (0.0316)	15.32 (0.00)	14.32 (0.00)

Italy unrestricted model

Coefficient estimates of:

1st equation

r_{t-1}	r_{t-2}	R^n_{t-1}	R^n_{t-2}
-0.1734 (0.1116)	-0.1601 (0.1116)	0.3949 (0.0724)	0.0091 (0.0769)

2nd equation

r_{t-1}	r_{t-2}	R^n_{t-1}	R^n_{t-2}
-0.1387 (0.1796)	-0.1679 (0.1796)	-0.7140 (0.1165)	0.1790 (0.1238)

Table 7.5 continued

Italy restricted h = 0 model

Coefficient estimates of:

	1st equation				2nd equation				Wald	LR
	r_{t-1}	r_{t-2}	R^n_{t-1}	R^n_{t-2}	r_{t-1}	r_{t-2}	R^n_{t-1}	R^n_{t-2}		
	-0.090 (0.0684)	-0.1007 (0.0516)	1.5737 (0.0452)	0.0352 (0.0449)	-0.7276 (0.1311)	0.5962 (0.1032)	2.6649 (0.0677)	-0.6884 (0.0652)	827.38 (0.00)	239.62 (0.00)

Italy restricted h = 1 model

Coefficient estimates of:

	1st equation				2nd equation				Wald	LR
	r_{t-1}	r_{t-2}	R^n_{t-1}	R^n_{t-2}	r_{t-1}	r_{t-2}	R^n_{t-1}	R^n_{t-2}		
	-0.1648 (0.1060)	-0.0982 (0.1040)	0.3194 (0.0700)	0.1905 (0.0717)	-0.0752 (0.0410)	-0.0217 (0.0228)	0.1204 (0.0382)	0.0392 (0.0209)	151.53 (0.00)	92.47 (0.00)

Italy restricted h = 2 model

Coefficient estimates of:

	r_{t-1}	r_{t-2}	R^n_{t-1}	R^n_{t-2}	Wald	LR
1st equation	-0.2117 (0.1088)	1.1670 (0.1077)	0.3018 (0.0678)	0.1263 (0.0761)		
2nd equation	0.0088 (0.0130)	-0.1088 (0.0101)	0.1878 (0.0226)	0.1794 (0.0120)	57.80 (0.00)	44.91 (0.00)

empirical content. However, econometric estimation of any model that is at all realistic has so far proved difficult and work in this area is currently fairly tentative. In order to develop a theoretically sound model of risk it is necessary to appeal to the finance literature and in particular the discrete time APM of Rubenstein (1976), Lucas (1978) and others. In this model investors are assumed to maximise their expected utility, subject to consecutive budget constraints. In equilibrium the product of the asset price and the conditional expectation of the marginal utility of some consumption good are equal to the conditional expectation of the product of marginal consumption l periods in the future and the l period return on the asset. All prices are in terms of some numeraire good. Expressed in terms of nominal returns the equilibrium condition on the APM amounts to

$$E_t(Y_{Mt+l}R_{t+l,l}) = 1$$

where Y_{Mt+l} is the marginal rate of substitution of money between $t + l$ and t and $R_{t+l,l}$ is an l period nominal return. If an l period nominal risk free asset is available at time t then

$$E_t Y_{Mt+l} = (R_{t+l,l})^{-1} \tag{7.7.1}$$

In the foreign exchange market, $(S_{t+l} - F_t)$ can be regarded as the profit from assuming a long position in the forward market and, since no investment is required at time t, it follows that the conditional expectation of the marginal utility of the nominal profit from contracting in the forward market must be zero. Hence

$$E_t[Y_{Mt+l}(S_{t+l} - F_t)] = 0 \tag{7.7.2}$$

and

$$\mathrm{Cov}_t(Y_{Mt+l}S_{t+l}) + E_t(Y_{Mt+l})E_t S_{t+l} = F_t E_t Y_{Mt+l},$$

and on dividing through by the marginal rate of substitution between t and $t + l$ and rearranging gives

$$(F_t - E_t S_{t+l}) = \frac{\mathrm{cov}_t(Y_{Mt+l}S_{t+l})}{E_t Y_{Mt+l}} \tag{7.7.3}$$

The term on the right hand side of the above describes the risk premium and will only be zero if individuals are risk neutral and/or the distributions of the future spot rate and the marginal rate of substitution are uncorrelated.

One of the earliest attempts at measuring foreign exchange market risk and indeed to utilise the APM of Grauer et al. (1976) was by Roll and Solnik (1977). In an earlier paper, Solnik (1973) showed that one of the equilibrium conditions in a theory of international asset pricing is that

$$r_n - r_i = \mu_{ni} + b_i \sum_{j=1}^{N} w_j(r_n - r_j - \mu_{nj})$$ (7.7.4)

where r_j is a riskless interest rate for country j, b_i is constant, w_j are the weights for country j, and μ_{nj} is the expected rate of change of the spot rate S_{jt} for country j, i.e.

$$\mu_{nj} = \frac{E_t(S_{jt+1} - S_{jt})}{S_{jt}}$$

Then Roll and Solnik (1977) show that

$$\frac{E_t(S_{it+1} - F_{it})}{S_{it}} = b_i \sum_{j=1}^{N} w_j \left[\frac{E_t(S_{jt+1} - F_{jt})}{S_{jt}} \right]$$

$$\text{for} \quad i = 1, 2 \ldots N \quad (7.7.5)$$

where there are N countries in total. In order to operationalise the model the expected rate of change of the spot rate is replaced with the extraordinary exchange return for country j, i.e.

$$R_{jt+1} = \frac{S_{jt+1} - F_{jt}}{S_{jt}}$$

so that equation (7.7.5) reduces to

$$R_{it} = a_i + b_i \sum_{j=1}^{N} w_j R_{jt} + \varepsilon_{it}$$ (7.7.6)

where ε_{it} is a white noise error process, b_i is the exchange risk factor. The approach taken by Roll and Solnik (1977) is to estimate equation (7.7.6) for eight countries based on monthly data between July 1971 and January 1975. A major problem in the empirical analyses is the choice of weights w_j and Roll and Solnik (1977) proxied them with real GNP and unweighted averages of 1/7 for all j. The estimates of equation (7.7.5) reported by Roll and Solnik generally gave rise to significant b coefficients, although the economic interpretation of their signs is not always clear. They carried out a further test of the CAPM pricing model by regressing the *ex post* observed return for country j on its associated estimated risk measure b_j.

Although an interesting and novel approach, the work of Roll and Solnik only partially clarifies the issue of risk and is obscured by many econometric difficulties along the way.

Hansen and Hodrick (1983) considered several ways of modelling the marginal rate of substitution Y_{Mt+1} and hence of quantifying the role of risk in (7.7.3). The lognormal model arises out of assuming that $s_t = \ln S_t$ and $f_t = \ln F_t$ form a jointly covariance stationary process. On taking logarithms through (7.7.3) and the first order terms of a Taylor series expansion it is easily shown that

$$E_t s_{t+1} - f_t = -\tfrac{1}{2} \text{Var}_t \, s_{t+1} - \text{cov}_t(s_{t+1} y_{Mt+1}). \qquad (7.7.7)$$

where $y_{Mt+1} = \ln Y_{Mt+1}$. However, under the stationarity assumption the right hand side of (7.7.7) must be independent of time and hence a constant. Thus under the joint stationarity assumption the lognormal model implies a constant rather than a time varying risk premium. Hansen and Hodrick (1983) attempted to test this model by applying the methodology discussed in their (1980) paper, as discussed in Chapter 6. Hence OLS is used to consistently estimate the parameters a and ψ in the model

$$(s_{t+1} - f_t) = a + \psi' x_t + u_{t+1},$$

with the appropriate estimate (6.5.4) being taken of the asymptotic covariance matrix. As before, x_t contains any information which is available at time t and b is the constant risk premium.

The data set used by Hansen and Hodrick corresponds to 512 semi-weekly observations from February 1976 to December 1980 with Tuesday thirty day forward rates predicting Thursday spot rates and Friday thirty day forward rates predicting Monday spot rates. For the jth currency, Hansen and Hodrick estimated the regression

$$s_{jt+9} - f_{jt} = a_j + \sum_{i=1}^{5} b_{ji}(s_{jit} - f_{it-9})$$

$$+ \sum_{i=1}^{5} c_{ji}(f_{it} - s_{it}) + u_{t+9}$$

so that multi-country forecast errors and forward premiums are included in the information set. Under the hypothesis of constant risk aversion the coefficients ψ, that is the b_{ji}'s and c_{ji}'s should all be zero. Hansen and Hodrick found this hypothesis could be clearly rejected for each of the five currencies considered. Furthermore, the constant term a_j was generally not significant. Thus, although the theoretic argument for a constant risk premium has been advanced by a number of authors, e.g. Stockman (1978) and Frenkel and Razin (1980), the theory is not satisfied in empirical work.

A further approach followed by Hansen and Hodrick (1983) was to consider variation over time in expected profits in the forward market and to use a Nominal Risk Free Return Model. Thus the proportional change in the forward premium is used instead of the forward premium in (7.7.3) to give

$$E_t\left(\frac{S_{jt+l} - F_{jt}}{S_{jt}}\right) = -\frac{\text{Cov}_t\left[Y_{Mt+l}\left(\frac{S_{jt+l} - F_{jt}}{S_{jt}}\right)\right]}{E_t Y_{Mt+l}}$$
(7.7.8)

But from (7.7.1)

$$E_t\left(\frac{S_{jt+l} - F_{jt}}{S_{jt}}\right) = b_j R_{t+l,l}$$

where

$$b_j = -\text{Cov}_t\left[\left(\frac{S_{jt+l} - F_{jt}}{S_{jt}}\right)Y_{Mt+l}\right]$$
(7.7.9)

and is assumed to be a constant. By a similar analysis the regression

$$\left(\frac{S_{jt+9} - F_{jt}}{S_{jt}}\right) = a_j + \sum_{i=1}^{5} b_{ji}\left(\frac{S_{it} - F_{it-9}}{S_{it-9}}\right)$$
$$+ c_j R_{t+9,9} + u_{t+9}$$

is estimated by OLS, the adjusted parameter estimates covariance matrix calculated and under the hypothesis that model (7.7.8) is appropriate we would expect $a_j = b_{j1} = b_{j2} + \cdots = b_{j5} = 0$ and c_j to be significantly different from zero. Unfortunately, the data fail to support this model since the c_j are insignificantly different from zero and the hypothesis, that the other coefficients are zero, is overwhelmingly rejected.

Thus given the detailed econometric work of Hansen and Hodrick there seems little support for the risk premium being constant or the Nominal Risk Free Return model.

A further interesting approach has recently been provided by Cosset (1984), who represents the marginal rate of substitution Y_{Mt+l} as

$$Y_{Mt+l} = (B + I^{-1}W)^{\gamma-1}I^{-1},$$
(7.7.10)

where I^{-1} is a world price deflator, W is world nominal wealth; both denominated in the reference country, B is a constant invariant with the numeraire and $1 - \gamma$ is the world's risk tolerance. In this model the risk premium is a function of the covariance between the future spot exchange rate and real world wealth scaled by the world price deflator. Cosset proxies world aggregate wealth with a value weighted world market index composed of national stock price indices. On using monthly data from March 1973 to February 1980 the covariance term

$$\text{Cov}_t\left[\frac{S_{t+1}(B + I^{-1}W)^{\gamma-1}I^{-1}}{E_t(B + I^{-1}W)^{\gamma-1}}\right]$$
(7.7.11)

was computed over six and twelve month periods. For all fifteen currencies considered the risk premium (7.7.10) changes sign over a short period of time and random behaviour of the risk premium cannot be rejected by the runs test. Furthermore, Cosset was unable to reject the hypothesis that the mean of the risk premium is zero and concluded that the covariance terms (7.7.11) may fail to exist due to the non-stationarity of the exchange rates. In order to simplify analysis of the covariance term, Cosset (1984), next assumed that the covariance between individual assets could be ignored and that the covariance could be explained completely with reference to a single market index. This type of assumption follows Sharpe (1963) where similar assets are related through common relationships with an index of market performance. Thus a volatile exchange risk premium must depend on a common element of variance, in order to justify the single index model of Sharpe (1963). This proposition has been tested by Cosset using the multivariate method of principal components and he finds that as much as 61 per cent of the variance is explained by the first principal component, suggesting a strong market element within most currencies. However, the correlation between the first principal component and the proxy for world wealth is only 0.29, suggesting that other common factors must be the cause of the volatility of the exchange risk premium.

Several other approaches have also been considered in an attempt to model time varying risk premia. Domowitz and Hakkio (1985) have applied Engle's (1982) autoregressive conditional heteroskedasticity (ARCH) process to model the forecast error $(s_{t+1} - f_t)$. They too find the risk premium frequently changes sign, but find evidence for the existence of the risk premium rather mixed. One problem associated with this is relative lack of volatility and ARCH effects when using monthly data: see Baillie and Bollerslev (1989b), Boothe and Glassman (1985), Diebold and Nerlove (1986) etc. Kaminsky and Perugia (1986) have used the Lucas (1978) asset pricing model for risk premia with domestic and foreign prices and consumption included. The use of monthly data for consumption and prices and of necessity exchange rates, thus reduces the importance of ARCH effects. In an attempt to circumvent these problems Baillie and Bollerslev (1987c) used weekly data and for the ith currency estimated a model of the form

$$s_{it+1} - f_{it} = \beta_{i0} + c_{it+1} + \sum_{j=1}^{l} \theta_j \varepsilon_{jt+1-j}$$

$$+ \sum_{j=1}^{g} a_j \operatorname{Var}_t s_{jt+1} \qquad (7.7.12)$$

$$+ \sum_{j=1}^{g} b_{ij} \operatorname{Cov}_t s_{it+1} s_{jt+1} \qquad i \neq j$$

$$\Delta s_{jt} = \varepsilon_{jt} + b, \qquad j = 1, .. g$$

$$\varepsilon_t | \Omega_{t-1} \sim N(0, H_t)$$

where

$$\varepsilon_t' = (\varepsilon_{1t} \dots \varepsilon_{gt}), \quad |H_t| > 0.$$

With thirty day forward rates and four currencies used $g = l = 4$. The main problem with this type of approach is to find a simple parameterisation of the conditional covariance matrix H_t: see Engle, Bollerslev and Wooldridge (1987). Baillie and Bollerslev (1989c) assumed that each conditional variance term follows a GARCH $(1, 1)$ model of the form

$$h_{iit} = \alpha_{ii0} + \alpha_{ii}\varepsilon_{it-1}^2 + \beta_{ii}h_{iit-1}$$

while the conditional covariances are defined as

$$h_{ijt} = \rho_{ij}h_{it}^{1/2}h_{jt}^{1/2}, \quad \text{where } \rho_{ij} = \text{Correlation}(\varepsilon_{it}\varepsilon_{jt} | \Omega_{t-1})$$

is assumed constant. The multivariate GARCH model turns out to be a satisfactory representation of the second moment properties of the data, but the estimated GARCH in mean parameters a_j and b_{ij} which proxy the risk premia are generally insignificant. Similarly to Nerlove and Diebold (1986) who used a multivariate ARCH Framework, Baillie and Bollerslev were unable to identify particular variables as explaining the risk premium.

If the model is well specified so that nominal exchange rates follow a random walk process, and the risk premium is constant then the total variation in $(s_{it+4} - f_{it})$ should be due to the third term on the right hand side of (7.7.12) which is a moving average process of order 4. Since s_{it} are Martingales it is possible to evaluate the θ_j coefficients. Under this assumption Baillie and Bollerslev show that the variance of $(s_{it+4} - f_{it})$ is 2.833 times greater than the total variation in ε_{1t+4}. The sample values of the latter quantity for the U.K., West Germany, Switzerland and France are 2.99, 3.15, 3.21 and 3.36 respectively. This suggests that the presence of the risk premium only adds marginal variability to that explained by the MA(4) process. In conclusion, while the risk premium may well be an important element of exchange rates, its modelling and subsequent estimation is still an open issue for further research and its total impact on the variance of $(s_{it+l} - f_{it})$ appears relatively small.

CHAPTER 8

Estimation and testing of exchange rate models

8.1   Introduction

Chapter 3 developed the theoretical properties of some of the main models of exchange rate determination and it is the estimation, testing and forecasting from such models with which this chapter is concerned. Since Chapter 3 we have considered the empirical evidence on quantifying various aspects of foreign exchange market theory and have in many cases found some of these simplifying assumptions to be inappropriate. Despite the fact that some crucial assumptions may be lacking it still seems worthwhile to consider the work that has taken place on estimating models of exchange rate behaviour. This is because the assumptions may in some instances still be reasonable approximations and because subsequent improvements in technique and methodology can be usefully learnt from the initial work.

This chapter focuses on some empirical studies that have been concerned with testing short and long-run versions of PPP and of estimating the basic monetary model, with and without dynamics in the demands for real balances equations, and a variant of the monetary model, due to Frankel (1979a) known as the real interest rate differential model. The number of studies considered is fairly small since not a lot of satisfactory econometric work has taken place on estimating the models strictly within their original formulation. Thus, although a number of large-scale macromodels contain exchange rate equations which are based on fairly sound econometric techniques, much of this work falls outside the scope of this chapter since they are frequently solely concerned with finding a good fitting real exchange rate equation with estimated coefficients that make some sense economically. A good example of this is the U.K.'s National Institute of Economic and Social Research's (NIESR) macromodel. Hall (1983) discusses the types of exchange rate models used by NIESR and makes the following observation:

> In trying to explain the movement in the exchange rate a fairly eclectic standpoint has been chosen. Rather than try to derive a restrictive theoretical equation or engage in extensive hypothesis testing the aim has been to estimate a reasonably satisfactory equation which yields sensible properties when included in the macromodel.

The final equation reported by Hall (1983) and used in the NIESR model consisted of the change in the real exchange rate explained in terms of current and lagged real interest rate differentials, real current balances, changes in domestic to world prices and a variable measuring the price of North Sea oil. The equation was estimated from quarterly data and is fairly typical of similar exchange rate equations used in other macromodels. More recent macromodels now attempt to base exchange rate equations on more precise theories. For example, the updated NIESR exchange rate equation uses an explicit maximising model of risk averse investors. For a detailed study of modelling changes in the U.K. real exchange rate see Davidson (1985).

8.2   Purchasing power parity

In Section 3.2 we discussed various formulations of purchasing power parity (PPP) theory, both in the short and long runs. Since the work of Cassel (1922) the theory has been the attention of extensive empirical investigation, with fairly mixed results. A major debate has concerned the choice of the most appropriate price indices with which to test the theory. Some of the points were discussed in 3.2, and a very detailed treatment and survey is provided by Officer (1976). Rather than pursuing these points in further detail, this section will deal with some of the econometric evidence and an interpretation in the light of the concept of cointegration introduced in Chapter 4.

On taking logarithms of equation (3.2.1) the absolute, short-run PPP theory can be stated as

$$s_t = p_t - p_t^* \tag{8.2.1}$$

where the lower case letters denote logarithms of the variables concerned. Many authors have attempted to test the theory by estimating models of the form

$$s_t = \alpha + \beta(p_t - p_t^*) + u_t \tag{8.2.2}$$

and testing whether $\alpha = 0$, $\beta = 1$, and u_t is white noise. It should be noted that in addition to the general controversy over the correct formulation of PPP as originally motivated by Cassel (1922), even the inclusion of the disturbance term u_t has provoked discussion. Samuelson (1964, p. 153) notes that 'unless very sophisticated indeed, PPP is a misleading, pretentious doctrine, promising us what is rare in economics, detailed numerical predictions'. Holmes (1967) has pointed out that Cassel (1922) himself had doubts about the extreme form of the theory (3.2.1). Apart from the debate over whether a stochastic disturbance term should be added, it has also been proposed by Hodgson and Phelps (1975) among others, that the right hand side of equation (8.2.2) should be replaced with a distributed lag of past relative price variables.

However, many studies have attempted to test the basic relationship (8.2.2) by the application of OLS or by IVE to alleviate the problem of joint endogeneity between relative prices and the exchange rate. In particular, Frenkel (1978) and Genberg (1978) used monthly data from the 1920s and 1970s and generally found support for the theory. They used WPI series for the relative price variables.

A more recent study by Hakkio (1984) has estimated dynamic versions of (8.2.2) jointly for several countries by 3SLS. Hakkio's results generally favour the proposition of long-run PPP, although he also includes an AR(1) disturbance term in several equations. It should be noted that in many cases the estimated autoregressive parameter is close to unity, suggesting the possibility that the variables in the equation are not cointegrated and that it is not a proper long-run relationship. Since no formal tests for this were reported, the above statement is at best, a reasonable guess.

Some authors such as King (1977) have tested a relative version of PPP by estimating the model

$$\Delta s_t = \alpha + \beta \Delta(p_t - p_t^*) + \varepsilon_t \qquad (8.2.3)$$

and generally find that the restrictions $\alpha = 0$ and $\beta = 1$ cannot be rejected. Pigott and Sweeney (1985) have estimated a pooled version of (8.2.3) and allowed the intercept term to vary across countries. They conclude (p. 82) that 'changes in the means of the processes generating exchange rate changes and relative inflation rates have contributed to statistical results that have been misleadingly interpreted as showing a relationship between Δs_t and $\Delta(p_t - p_t^*)$ that is not there.'

While there is some controversy about the validity of PPP as a short-run relationship, there is generally a more widely held belief that some variant of PPP may well hold in the long run. Analysis of s_t and $(p_t - p_t^*)$ on monthly data from March 1973 to December 1983 (where relative prices are based on consumer price indices), reveal that both variables are I(1) in

Table 8.1 *Tests of unit roots in relative price series*

Country	Dickey Fuller statistic	Value of p
U.K.	−2.01	1
Japan	0.47	0
West Germany	−1.71	2
Canada	0.66	4
France	1.21	3

The Dickey Fuller statistic is the t statistic on β in the OLS regression

$$\Delta(p_t - p_t^*) = \beta(p_t - p_t^*) + \sum_{j=1}^{p} \gamma_j \Delta(p_{t-j} - p_{t-j}^*) + u_t$$

where p is minimised subject to u_t being white noise. At the 1% and 5% significance levels, the Dickey Fuller statistic is −1.95 and −2.60 respectively.

terms of their degree of integration (see Table 8.1). A borderline rejection of the I(1) hypothesis for relative prices, could however be obtained for the U.K. The technique of testing for cointegration is again useful in determining whether or not a linear combination of the high variance components of nominal exchange rates and relative prices effectively balance out each other and leave a disturbance term which is stationary. Using the same data set, Baillie and Selover (1987), estimated (8.2.2) by OLS and imposed the standard Dickey Fuller statistics to test for a unit root in the estimated residuals of $\hat{u}_t$. The results are reported in Table 8.2 and show that the hypothesis $\hat{u}_t$ is I(1) can only be rejected for France; implying that no cointegrating relationship, or evidence of long-run PPP can be found for the other four countries. Hence the exchange rates and relative prices will apparently drift apart without bounds. Similar results have also been obtained by Patel (1987) and Adler and Lehman (1983) who find evidence that the real exchange rate is a random walk. This amounts to showing that u_t will be I(1) in (8.2.2) if $\alpha = 0$ and $\beta = 1$ is imposed.

Hence it does seem that permanent departures from PPP can arise, some detailed discussion of this is provided by Officer (1976) and Pigott and Sweeney (1985). Converseley, Taylor and McMahon (1988) cannot reject PPP for 1920s data.

8.3   Estimation of the monetary model

The theory behind the basic monetary model has been previously developed in 3.3 and can be expressed by the five equations

$$s_t = p_{t.} - p_t^* \tag{8.3.1}$$

Table 8.2 *Tests of cointegration between exchange rates and relative prices*

OLS estimates of $s_t = \alpha + \beta(p_t - p_t^*) + u_t$

Country	$\hat{\alpha}$	β	DF statistic
U.K.	0.6251	0.0119	−1.17
	(50.49)	(9.47)	
Japan	−5.51	0.0049	−1.49
	(−462.71)	(3.40)	
West Germany	−8.002	0.0031	−1.31
	(−52.55)	(2.52)	
Canada	−0.0522	0.0173	−1.35
	(−6.94)	(10.32)	
France	−1.5847	0.0248	−2.23
	(−198.11)	(21.43)	

DF is the Dickey Fuller statistic to test for a unit root in $\hat{u}_t$; the OLS residuals. The t statistics are in parentheses.

$$m_t - p_t = k + \phi y_t - \lambda r_t \tag{8.3.2}$$

$$m_t^* - p_t^* = k^* + \phi_t^* y_t^* - \lambda^* r_t^* \tag{8.3.3}$$

$$r_t - r_t^* = f_t - s_t \tag{8.3.4}$$

$$f_t = E_t s_{t+1} \tag{8.3.5}$$

For estimation purposes the model can be most usefully expressed as

$$s_t = -(k - k^*) + (m_t - m_*) - \phi(y_t - y_t^*) + \lambda(r_t - r_t^*) \tag{8.3.6}$$

and alternatively as

$$s_t = z_t + \left(\frac{1}{1+\lambda}\right) E_t s_{t+1} \tag{8.3.7}$$

$$s_t = \left(\frac{1}{1+\lambda}\right) \sum_{j=0}^{\infty} \left(\frac{\lambda}{1+\lambda}\right)^j E_t z_{t+j} \tag{8.3.8}$$

where

$$z_t = \left(\frac{1}{1+\lambda}\right)(m_t - m_t^*) - \left(\frac{\phi}{1+\lambda}\right)(y_t - y_t^*) + c \tag{8.3.9}$$

Initial empirical studies by Frenkel (1976), Bilson (1978) and Kohlhagen (1979) generally estimated variants of equation (3.3.6), such as

$$s_t = \beta_0 + \beta_1(m_t - m_t^*) + \beta_2(y_t - y_t^*) + \beta_3(r_t - r_t^*) + \varepsilon_t$$

Table 8.3 *Estimation of the real interest rate differential model for West Germany*

Author	Sample period	Estimation method	n	Constant	$(m_t - m_t^*)$	$(y_t - y_t^*)$	$(r_t - r_t^*)$	$(\pi_t - \pi_t^*)$	$(p_t - p_t^*)$	$\hat{\rho}$
Frankel (1979a and b)	July 1974 Feb. 1980	OLS	44	1.33 (0.10)	0.87 (0.17)	-0.72 (0.22)	-1.55 (1.94)	28.65 (2.70)		
Frankel	„	CORC	43	0.80 (0.19)	0.31 (0.25)	-0.33 (0.20)	-0.26 (1.96)	7.72 (4.47)		0.98
Frankel	„	IVE with AR(1)	41	1.39 (0.12)	0.97 (0.21)	-0.52 (0.22)	-5.40 (2.04)	29.40 (3.33)		0.46
Driskill & Sheffrin (1981)	„	CORC	41	-4.75 (0.54)	0.37 (0.27)	-0.36 (0.19)		0.014 (0.01)	-0.66 (0.88)	0.98 (0.03)
Haynes & Stone (1981)	July 1974 April 1980	CORC	44	-4.08 (23.40)	-0.57 (1.89)	0.02 (0.08)	0.22 (0.13)	13.33 (3.57)		0.77

Author	Sample period	Estimation method	n	Constant	m_t	m_t^*	y_t	y_t^*	r_t	r_t^*	π_t	π_t^*	$\hat{\rho}$
Haynes and Stone (1981)	July 1974 April 1980	CORC		1.86 (1.65)	0.24 (0.84)	-1.84 (3.95)	0.20 (0.77)	0.56 (2.20)	0.02 (0.01)	-2.50 (1.29)	2.62 (0.67)	3.53 (0.75)	0.59
Haynes and Stone	„	CORC		-1.64 (1.31)	$(m_t - m_t^*)$ -0.65 (1.90)		-0.38 (1.23)	-0.13 (0.44)	-7.28 (2.29)	-1.95 (0.79)	13.73 (2.98)	-9.04 (1.66)	0.62
Frankel (1981)	Feb. 1974 Nov. 1980	IVE		2.45 (1.22)	$(m_t - m_t^*)$ -0.50 (0.34)		-0.17 (0.32)	-0.22 (0.29)	$(r_t - r_t^*)$ -1.47 (0.52)		7.24 (2.08)	-4.88 (0.76)	0.66
Frankel	„	IVE		3.81 (1.84)	1.00 (constrained)		0.14 (0.39)	-0.67 (0.41)	-2.12 (0.65)		11.31 (3.09)	-5.10 (1.32)	0.82

Key: CORC denotes the use of the Cochrane Orcutt method, so that the disturbance process is assumed to be AR(1). Standard errors are in parentheses underneath parameter estimates.

Or, in some cases $(r_t - r_t^*)$ is replaced by the forward premium $(f_t - s_t)$. Most of the above studies found evidence which was in favour of the monetary model. However, the use of the interest rate differential, or forward premium as an explanatory variable, is a potential problem because of simultaneous equation bias resulting from the joint endogeneity of these variables with the nominal exchange rate.

A model which has attracted a lot of attention in the literature is the relationship

$$s_t = \beta_1(m_t - m_t^*) + \beta_2(y_t - y_t^*)$$
$$+ \beta_3(r_t - r_t^*) + \beta_4(\pi_{t+1} - \pi_{t+1}^*) + u_t \qquad (8.3.10)$$

where π_{t+1} and π_{t+1}^* the expected next periods rate of domestic and foreign inflation respectively. It can easily be seen that (8.3.10) is a rearrangement of the Frankel (1979) real interest rate differential model (3.6.9) and contains a number of other models nested within itself. In general it would be expected that $\beta_1 = 1$, $\beta_2 < 0$ and $\beta_4 > 0$. The sign of β_3 is unclear; in the traditional Keynesian model, a rise in domestic interest rates leads to a currency appreciation and implies a negatively signed β_3, while a rise in r_t due to inflationary expectations would lead to β_3 being positive. In Dornbusch's (1976a and b) sticky price model $\beta_3 = 0$ and $\beta_4 > 0$.

In his original study Frankel (1979) proxied the expected rate of inflation by a long-term interest rate or consol rate and estimated the model from monthly data between July 1974 and February 1978 for the Deutschmark against the U.S. dollar. Frankel's estimates, given in Table 8.3, were initially quite supportive of the theory and seemed to account for the depreciating Deutschmark during this period. Subsequent results obtained by Driskill and Sheffrin (1981) and Haynes and Stone (1981) are also presented in Table 8.3. Driskill and Sheffrin use IVE to allow for the possible endogeneity of the short-term interest rate differential, while Haynes and Stone estimated by relaxing the constraint of unity elasticity of the money supply differential and equal and oppositely signed elasticities on real outputs. Tables 8.4 and 8.5 are taken from Baillie and Selover (1987) and provide updated estimates from data between March 1973 and December 1983 for the U.K., Japan, West Germany, Canada and France vis-à-vis the U.S. dollar. Although generally unsupportive of the model it should also be noted that each equation contains strong autocorrelation with an estimated AR(1) parameter near unity. Overall the results are qualitatively very similar to those obtained by Driskill and Sheffrin (1981), Haynes and Stone (1981) and Boothe and Glassman (1987) for the West German Deutschmark. Table 8.6 presents the same model estimated jointly for the five countries by SURE with a diagonal vector

Table 8.4 OLS estimation of equation (3.3.1)

Country	Constant	$(m_t - m_t^*)$	$(y_t - y_t^*)$	$(r_t - r_t^*)$	$(\pi_{t+1} - \pi_{t+1}^*)$	R^2	$\hat{\sigma}_u$	Durbin–Watson
U.K.	−1.1222	0.6691	0.4762	0.0102	−0.0020	0.44	0.1164	0.102
	(3.881)	(5.899)	(1.827)	(2.078)	(0.248)			
Japan	−7.1967	−0.3137	0.2769	0.0102	0.0286	0.59	0.0889	0.204
	(11.938)	(2.618)	(1.587)	(3.042)	(3.806)			
West Germany	−0.1855	−1.1404	−0.4806	0.0135	0.0080	0.51	0.0969	0.369
	(2.118)	(8.213)	(1.641)	(3.096)	(1.434)			
Canada	2.2580	−0.9289	−1.4435	0.0086	−0.0015	0.56	0.0600	0.343
	(6.253)	(6.439)	(9.531)	(2.830)	(0.119)			
France	−1.2366	0.6886	−1.4285	0.0276	0.0559	0.68	0.1105	0.416
	(32.86)	(6.533)	(4.292)	(5.834)	(4.542)			

Parameter estimates of:

t statistics are in parentheses

Table 8.5 *Estimation of equation (8.3.1) with an AR(1) disturbance* $u_t = pu_{t-1} + \varepsilon_t$

Country	Constant	Parameter estimates of:				R^2	$\hat{\rho}$	$\hat{\sigma}_\varepsilon$
		$(m_t - m_t^*)$	$(y_t - y_t^*)$	$(r_t - r_t^*)$	$(\pi_{t+1} - \pi_{t+1}^*)$			
U.K.	0.2067	0.1618	−0.2278	−0.0002	0.0003	0.2053	0.9819	0.0289
	(0.576)	(1.300)	(1.720)	(0.099)	(0.054)			
Japan	−6.0163	−0.0969	0.1298	−0.0044	0.0055	0.9209	0.9675	0.0323
	(15.12)	(1.254)	(0.627)	(1.692)	(0.755)			
West Germany	−0.9294	0.0589	−0.0975	−0.0023	−0.0094	0.2274	0.9794	0.0334
	(7.556)	(0.629)	(0.610)	(1.339)	(1.163)			
Canada	−0.1883	0.0340	0.1039	−0.0038	0.0074	0.0534	0.9896	0.0130
	(1.399)	(0.751)	(1.266)	(2.198)	(2.333)			
France	−1.7967	−0.1011	−0.0714	−0.0007	−0.0021	0.1417	0.9940	0.0327
	(7.032)	(1.054)	(0.558)	(0.279)	(0.327)			

t statistics are in parentheses.

Table 8.6 Estimation of equation (8.3.1) by SURE with diagonal VAR(1)

Country	Constant	Parameter estimates of:				$\hat{\rho}$
		$(m_t - m_t^*)$	$(y_t - y_t^*)$	$(r_t - r_t^*)$	$(\pi_{t+1} - \pi_{t+1}^*)$	
U.K.	-2.0828	1.0424	0.3093	0.0050	0.0214	
	(9.743)	(12.56)	(1.831)	(1.510)	(3.762)	0.938
Japan	-5.2835	0.0648	0.4577	0.0053	0.0355	
	(10.52)	(0.650)	(3.308)	(1.970)	(5.794)	0.913
West Germany	-0.5737	-0.4657	-0.0469	0.0072	0.0067	
	(8.757)	(4.482)	(0.243)	(2.547)	(1.524)	0.911
Canada	2.3546	-0.9675	-1.4316	0.0101	-0.0028	
	(7.268)	(7.478)	(10.39)	(3.673)	(0.262)	0.802
France	-1.2083	0.8288	-0.9313	0.0133	0.0499	
	(34.33)	(8.453)	(3.100)	(3.129)	(4.497)	0.840

t statistics in parentheses.

autoregressive error process. Again the presence of near unit roots in the autoregressive error process suggests a lack of cointegration.

The results of applying Augmented Dickey Fuller tests, discussed in Chapter 4, to each of the variables in (8.3.10) are presented in Table 8.7. The hypothesis of a unit root in any autoregression is tested by means of applying OLS to

$$\Delta x_t = \beta x_{t-1} + \sum_{j=1}^{p} \gamma_j \Delta x_{t-j} + \varepsilon_t$$

and testing

$$H_0 : \beta = 0 \quad \text{versus} \quad H_A : \beta > 0$$

For a sample size of 100 the appropriate test statistic at the 1 per cent, 5 per cent and 10 per cent significance levels are -3.51, -2.89 and -2.58 respectively (see Fuller 1976, p. 373). While p is chosen sufficiently large that ε_t closely approximates white noise. Some general conclusions can be tentatively reached, namely, monthly nominal exchange rates, relative money supplies (excluding the U.K.) and nominal long-term interest rate differentials are generally I(1). Real output differentials, excluding Japan and possibly the U.K., and short-term interest rate differentials excluding West Germany, are I(0). Since the variables in (8.3.10) possess different orders of integrability, it follows that (8.3.10) cannot exist as a meaningful long-run equilibrium relationship.

An attempt at finding a cointegrating relationship of the form of (8.3.10) has indirectly already been obtained through the OLS estimates of (8.3.10) reported in Table 8.3. The fact that two variables, real output and short-term interest rate differentials are I(0) is basically superfluous to the search for a cointegrating relationship between the remaining I(1) variables. Applying Augmented Dickey Fuller tests to the residuals of (8.3.10), Table 8.8 shows that the unit root hypothesis could not be rejected for any of the equations. Hence, there is no empirical evidence of (8.3.10) existing as a long-run relationship for any of the five countries considered.

8.4   Estimation of the monetary model under rational expectations

An alternative to working with the monetary model in terms of (3.3.6) or (8.3.10) is provided by directly modelling the future expected exchange rate in equations (3.3.13) and (3.3.14). That is

$$s_t = \left(\frac{1}{1+\lambda} \right) \sum_{j=0}^{\infty} \left(\frac{\lambda}{1+\lambda} \right)^j E_t z_{t+j} \tag{8.4.1}$$

Table 8.7 Tests of unit roots in fundamental variables

Country	s_t	$(m_t - m_t^*)$	Variables $(y_t - y_t^*)$	$(r_t - r_t^*)$	$(\pi_{t+1} - \pi_{t+1}^*)$
U.K.	−1.74	−.251 (1)	−1.85	−2.72 (2)	−0.88 (2)
Japan	−0.44	−0.54 (2)	−1.19 (2)	−2.03 (1)	−0.11 (1)
West Germany	−0.36	−0.39 (2)	−2.42	−1.72 (2)	−0.34 (1)
Canada	0.62	−0.23 (1)	−2.09	−2.23 (1)	−1.32 (2)
France	1.77	2.53 (2)	−2.21 (1)	−2.45 (1)	−1.30 (2)

The 1% and 5% significance levels of the above test statistics are −1.95 and −2.60 respectively. The number in parentheses beside the statistic is the number of lags in the Augmented Dickey Fuller test. When omitted it is zero.

Table 8.8 *Tests of cointegration between the exchange rate and fundamental variables*

Country	DF statistic
U.K.	-0.75
Japan	-1.41
West Germany	-1.28
Canada	-0.80
France	-0.61

where

$$z_t = \left(\frac{1}{1+\lambda}\right)[(m_t - m_t^* - \phi(y_t - y_t^*)] \tag{8.4.2}$$

The work of Hoffman and Schlagenhauf (1983) provides the first attempt at estimating (3.3.14) directly and appears a substantial advance in terms of econometric methodology over previous studies. As mentioned in Chapter 3, one major problem with the estimation of monetary type models concerns the incorporation of the rational expectations assumption. The approach adopted by Hoffman and Schlagenhauf (1983) is to assume that a typical variable, say x_t contained in the fundamentals z_t is generated by the ARIMA $(1, 1, 0)$ process

$$\Delta x_t = \rho \Delta x_{t-1} + \varepsilon_t \tag{8.4.3}$$

On noting that

$$(1 - L^j) \equiv (1 + L + L^2 + \cdots + L^{j-1})(1 - L)$$

it follows that any process x_t can be expressed as

$$x_{t+j} - x_t = \sum_{i=1}^{j-1} \Delta x_{t+i}$$

and hence

$$E_t x_{t+j} = x_t + \sum_{i=1}^{j} E_t \Delta x_{t+i} \tag{8.4.4}$$

However, from (8.4.3)

$$\Delta x_{t+i} = \rho^i \Delta x_t + \sum_{h=0}^{i-1} \rho^h \varepsilon_{t+i-h}$$

and $\quad E_t \Delta x_{t+i} = \rho^i \Delta x_t$

On substituting back into (8.2.2)

$$E_t x_{t+j} = x_t + \left(\sum_{i=1}^{j} \rho^i \right) \Delta x_t$$

$$E_t x_{t+j} = x_t + \frac{\rho(1-\rho^j)}{(1-\rho)} \Delta x_t \tag{8.4.5}$$

On assuming that each fundamental m, m^*, y and y^* follows (8.4.1) albeit with different parameters, ρ_m, ρ_m^*, ρ_y and ρ_y^* respectively, then substituting into the forward expectations solution (8.4.3) gives

$$s_t = \left(\frac{1}{1+\lambda} \right) \sum_{j=0}^{\infty} \left(\frac{\lambda}{1+\lambda} \right)^j \left[m_t + \frac{\rho_m(1-\rho_m^j)}{1-\rho_m} \Delta m_t - m_t^* - \frac{\rho_m^*(1-\rho_m^{*j})}{1-\rho_m^*} \Delta m_t^* \right.$$

$$\left. - \phi y_t - \frac{\phi \rho_y(1-\rho_y^j)}{1-\rho_y} \Delta y_t + \phi y_t^* + \frac{\phi \rho_y^*(1-\rho_y^{*j})}{1-\rho_y^*} \Delta y_t^* \right] \tag{8.4.6}$$

On noting that

$$\sum_{j=0}^{\infty} \left(\frac{\lambda}{1+\lambda} \right)^j = (1+\lambda)$$

and

$$\sum_{j=0}^{\infty} \left(\frac{\lambda}{1+\lambda} \right)^j \frac{\rho(1-\rho)^j}{(1-\rho)} = \left(\frac{\rho}{1-\rho} \right) \sum_{j=0}^{\infty} \left(\frac{\lambda}{1+\lambda} \right)^j (1-\rho)^j$$

$$= \left(\frac{\rho}{1-\rho} \right) \left[(1+\lambda) + \frac{(1+\lambda)}{(1+\lambda-\lambda\rho)} \right] = \rho\lambda(1+\lambda)/(1+\lambda-\lambda\rho)$$

it is then easily shown that the spot exchange rate equation (8.4.6) is given by

$$s_t = c + (m_t - m_t^*) - \phi(y_t - y_t^*) + \frac{\rho_m \lambda}{1+\lambda-\lambda\rho_m} \Delta m_t$$

$$- \frac{\rho_m^* \lambda}{1+\lambda-\lambda\rho_m^*} \Delta m_t^* - \frac{\phi\rho_y \lambda}{1+\lambda-\lambda\rho_y} \Delta y_t$$

$$+ \frac{\phi\rho_y^* \lambda}{1+\lambda-\lambda\rho_y^*} \Delta y_t^* \tag{8.4.7}$$

which is now an equation purely in observables with all expectations eliminated. Equation (8.4.7) can be compared with the equations

$$s_t = k + m_t - m_t^* - \phi(y_t - y_*)$$

$$+ \theta_1 \Delta m_t + \theta_2 \Delta m_t^* + \theta_3 \Delta y_t + \theta_4^* \Delta y_t^* \tag{8.4.8}$$

and

$$s_t = k + \theta_5 m_t + \theta_6 m_t^* + \theta_7 y_t + \theta_8 y_t^*$$
$$+ \theta_1 \Delta m_t + \theta_2 \Delta m_t^* + \theta_3 \Delta y_t + \theta_4^* \Delta y_t^* \qquad (8.4.9)$$

The first equation (8.4.8) imposes the usual monetary model restrictions of unit elasticity of money supplies and equal income elasticities for domestic and foreign countries, but imposes three restrictions implied by the generation of expectations from equation (8.4.7). The implied restrictions are

$$\theta_1(\rho_m^* \theta_2 - \theta_2 - \rho_m^*) = \theta_2(\rho_m \theta_1 - \theta_1 + \rho_m)$$
$$\theta_1(\rho_y \theta_3 - \theta_3 - \phi \rho_y) = \theta_3(\rho_m \theta_1 - \theta_1 + \rho_m) \qquad (8.4.10)$$

and

$$\theta_1(\rho_y^* \theta_4 - \theta_4 - \phi \rho_y^*) = \theta_4(\rho_m \theta_1 - \theta_1 + \rho_m)$$

Apart from the above three expectations restrictions, equation (8.4.9) also imposes the standard monetary model assumptions of

$$\theta_5 = 1$$
$$\theta_6 = -1$$

and

$$\theta_7 = -\theta_8$$

Hoffman and Schlagenhauf (1983) estimated (8.4.7) jointly with (8.4.3) for each of the four fundamental variables and also carried out estimations for the restricted versions corresponding to (8.4.8) and (8.4.9). Likelihood ratio tests for the two sets of restrictions are given in Table 8.9 and the restricted parameter estimates corresponding to (8.2.5) are given in Table 8.10. While the expectations restrictions are satisfied, the monetary model restrictions can only be rejected for West Germany and not for France or the U.K. The estimates obtained by Hoffman and Schlagenhauf (1983) seem to provide fairly strong evidence in favour of the monetary model, although we know from previous chapters that many of the underlying assumptions of the model, especially that of short-run PPP, are invalid.

Although the above study of Hoffman and Schlagenhauf was very detailed and complex to carry out, there are several further complexities to be considered if watertight evidence for the monetary model is to be provided. Although there is some empirical support for assuming (8.4.3) as the appropriate process for each fundamental variable, the ARIMA (1, 1, 0) assumption is really a way of forming extrapolative expectations rather

Table 8.9 *LR tests reported by Hoffman and Schlagenhauf*

	West Germany	France	UK
Tests of rational expectations	0.64 (0.88)	4.36 (0.22)	6.38 (0.10)
Tests of rational expectations and coefficient restrictions implied by monetary model	1.05 (0.99)	6.10 (0.41)	6.59 (0.36)

Key: The test statistics in the first row have asymptotic χ_3^2 distributions and in the second row they have asymptotic χ_6^2 distributions.

Table 8.10 *Hoffman and Schlagenhaufs estimates of the monetary model*

	West Germany	France	UK
λ	1.784 (0.82)	1.108 (0.54)	1.782 (1.06)
ϕ	1.507 (0.24)	0.969 (0.17)	0.508 (0.14)
ρ_m	0.813 (0.07)	0.810 (0.07)	0.821 (0.06)
ρ_m^*	0.269 (0.10)	0.652 (0.08)	0.526 (0.09)
ρ_y	0.714 (0.07)	0.704 (0.07)	0.755 (0.08)
ρ_{y*}	−0.180 (0.11)	−0.309 (0.10)	−0.144 (0.12)

Asymptotic standard errors are in brackets below corresponding parameter estimates.

than rational expectations. A second potential problem concerns the use of seasonally adjusted data. It is well-known that most seasonal adjustment filters distort relationships between time series (see Sims 1974 and Wallis 1974). However, in this type of study the presence of seasonal ARIMA processes of possible order 12 would considerably complicate the nature of the restrictions and make estimation and testing of the model considerably more complex. Anderson (1985) has also investigated the effect of differencing the spot exchange rate and considered how this may effect empirical results. Thus Hoffman and Schlagenhauf (1983) do not actually estimate (8.4.9), but a differenced version

$$\Delta s_t = \theta_5 \Delta m_t + \theta_6 \Delta m_t^* + \theta_7 \Delta y_t + \theta_8 \Delta y_t^*$$
$$+ \theta_1 \Delta^2 m_t + \theta_2 \Delta^2 m_t^* + \theta_3 \Delta^2 y_t + \theta_4 \Delta^2 y_t^* + v_t$$

Anderson presents some evidence that this equation was over differenced and on imposing alternative specifications to (8.4.3) for the fundamental variables, Anderson is able to reject most of the restrictions in the monetary model.

An even more detailed econometric analysis of the monetary model is to be found in Woo (1985) who extended the monetary model to include a Goldfeld (1973) type partial adjustment in the demand for real balances. Hence equations (3.3.2) and (3.3.3) are replaced with

$$(m_t - m_t^*) - (p_t - p_t^*) = (k - k^*) + \phi(y_t - y_t^*) + \alpha(m_{t-1} - m_{t-1}^*)$$
$$- \alpha(p_{t-1} - p_{t-1}^*) - \lambda(r_t - r_t^*) + \varepsilon_t \quad (8.4.11)$$

where ε_t is a serially uncorrelated, independent, identically distributed disturbance and the various parameters in (8.4.11) are assumed identical between the domestic and foreign countries. On maintaining equations (3.3.1), (3.3.4) and (3.3.5) and substituting s_t from (3.3.1) into (8.4.11), it follows that

$$s_t = \left(\frac{\beta}{1+\beta}\right) E_t s_{t+1} + \left(\frac{\alpha}{1+\beta}\right) s_{t-1} + \frac{1}{1+\beta} x_t \quad (8.4.12)$$

where

$$x_t = (m_t - m_t^*) - \alpha(m_{t-1} - m_{t-1}^*) - \phi y_t + \theta y_t^* (k - k^*) - \varepsilon_t$$

On taking expectations at time $t - 1$ throughout (8.4.12)

$$\left(\frac{\beta}{1-\beta}\right) E_{t-1} s_{t+1} - E_{t-1} s_t + \left(\frac{\alpha}{1+\beta}\right) s_{t-1} = \frac{1}{1+\beta} E_{t-1} x_t \quad (8.4.13)$$

which is extremely similar to the forward rational expectations equation (3.4.20) for the Dornbusch Sticky Price monetary model. On following the same method of solution as with equation (3.4.20), we have to consider the characteristic equation of (8.4.12) namely

$$\beta F^2 - (1+\beta)F + \alpha = 0$$

which has solutions

$$\xi = (1+\beta) \pm \frac{\sqrt{(1+\beta)^2 - 4\alpha\beta}}{2\beta}$$

which gives roots of $\xi_1 < 1$ and $\xi_2 > 1$; so that as for the Dornbusch model under rational expectations, one solution corresponds to a stable solution path, and the other to an unstable path.

The solution of (8.4.13) is then

$$s_t = \xi_1 s_{t-1} - (\beta \xi_2)^{-1} \sum_{j=0}^{\infty} \xi_2^{-j} E_{t-1} x_{t+j} + \varepsilon_t \qquad (8.4.14)$$

which, as expected, is extremely similar to (3.4.22). Woo (1985) estimates (8.4.14) jointly with a VAR model of order 5 for the three exogenous variables included in x_t; namely $(m_t - m_t^*)$, y_t and y_t^* and estimates the parameters of the VAR model and (8.4.14) by a non-linear approximate ML routine. The results of the estimation for West Germany and the U.S. are reasonable and appear to give rise to plausible parameter values. Woo also found that the cross-equation restrictions generated by the theory could not be rejected. In order to avoid the problem of non-stationary fundamentals Woo first regressed seasonally adjusted versions of $(m_t - m_t^*)$, y_t and y_t^* on time, time squared and a constant and took the residuals. It is unclear as to exactly how such data transformations effect estimation of (8.4.14). Similar transformations have been shown by Nelson and Kang (1984) to have undesirable properties. However, as has been noted previously, stable solutions to forward looking rational expectations generally require covariance stationary exogenous variables.

In conclusion, we should note that estimation of nominal exchange rate determination models has been largely unsatisfactory with little support forthcoming for standard theories. Meese and Rogoff (1983) have shown that the random walk is at least as good a predictor as more complicated structural models. Overall there are many challenges for future work to provide a sound theoretical model for the determination of nominal exchange rates which cannot be econometrically rejected.

Bibliography

Abel, A. B. and F. S. Mishkin (1983), On the econometric testing of rationality–market efficiency, *Review of Economics and Statistics*, **63**, 318–23.

Adler, M. and B. Dumas (1976), Portfolio choice and the demand for forward exchange, *American Economic Review*, **66**, 332–9.

(1983), International portfolio choice and corporation finance: a survey, *Journal of Finance*, **38**, 925–84.

Adler, M. and B. Lehmann (1983), Deviations from purchasing power parity in the long run, *Journal of Finance*, **38**, 1471–87.

Agmon, T. and S. Bronfeld (1975), The international mobility of short-term covered arbitrage capital, *Journal of Business Finance and Accounting*, **2**, 269–78.

Akaike, H. (1973), Information theory and an extension of the maximum likelihood principle. In B. N. Petrov and F. Csáki (eds.), *2nd International Symposium on Information Theory Budapest*; Akadémia Kiado, 267–81.

Alexander, D. and L. R. Thomas (1987), Monetary/asset models of exchange rate determination. How well have they performed in the 1980's? *International Journal of Forecasting*, **3**, 53–64.

Alexander, S. S. (1964), Price movements in speculative markets: trends or random walks. In P. H. Cootner (ed.), *The Random Character of Stock Prices*, Cambridge, Mass.: MIT Press.

Aliber, R. Z. (1973), The interest rate parity theorem: a reinterpretation, *Journal of Political Economy*, **81**, 1451–9.

(1975), Monetary independence under floating exchange rates, *Journal of Finance*, **30**, 365–76.

(1978), The integration of national financial markets: a review of theory and findings, *Weltwirtschaftliches Archiv*, 114, 448–80.

Andersen, T. M. (1984), Some implications of the efficient capital market hypothesis, *Journal of Post Keynesian Economics*, **I**, 281–94.

Anderson, R. G. (1985), Testing the monetary model of exchange rates under rational expectations, Ohio State University, Dept. of Economics, Working Paper.

Arnold, B. C. and S. J. Press (1983), Bayesian inference for pareto populations, *Journal of Econometrics*, **21**, 287–306.

Artus, J. R. and J. H. Young (1979), Fixed and flexible exchange rates: a renewal of the debate, *IMF Staff Papers*, **26**, 4, 654–98.

Attfield, C. L. F. and N. W. Duck (1982), Tests of the rational expectations model of the term structure of U.K. interest rates, *Economic Letters*, **10**, 115–21.

237

Attfield, C. L. F., D. Demery and N. W. Duck (1985), *Rational Expectations in Macroeconomics, an Introduction to Theory and Evidence*, Oxford: Basil Blackwell.

Bachelier, L. J. B. A. (1900), *Théorie de la speculation*, Paris: Gauthier-Villars.

Bailey, R. W., R. T. Baillie and P. C. McMahon (1984), Interpreting econometric evidence on efficiency in the foreign exchange market, *Oxford Economic Papers*, **36**, 67–85.

Baillie, R. T. (1981), Prediction from the dynamic simultaneous equation model with vector autoregressive errors, *Econometrica*, **49**, 1331–7.

(1987), Inference in dynamic models containing 'surprise' variables, *Journal of Econometrics*, **35**, 101–17.

(1989), Econometric tests of rationality and market efficiency, *Econometric Reviews*, **8**, 151–86.

Baillie, R. T. and T. Bollerslev (1989a), Common stochastic trends in a system of exchange rates, *Journal of Finance*, **44**, 167–81.

(1989b), The message in daily exchange rates: a conditional variance tale, *Journal of Business and Economic Statistics*, **7**, 297–305.

(1989c), A multivariate generalized ARCH approach to modelling risk premia in forward foreign exchange rate markets, *Journal of International Money and Finance*, forthcoming.

Baillie, R. T., R. E. Lippens and P. C. McMahon (1983), Testing rational expectations and efficiency in the foreign exchange market, *Econometrica*, **51**, 553–63.

Baillie, R. T. and P. C. McMahon (1984), Empirical evidence on interest rate parity, University of Birmingham Discussion Paper.

(1985), Some joint tests of market efficiency: the case of the forward premium, *Journal of Macroeconomics*, **7**, 137–50.

Baillie, R. T. and D. D. Selover (1987), Cointegration and models of exchange rate determination, *International Journal of Forecasting*, **3**, 43–52.

Balassa, B. (1964), The purchasing power parity doctrine: a reappraisal, *Journal of Political Economy*, **72**, 584–96.

Ball, R. and P. Brown (1968), An empirical evaluation of accounting income numbers, *Journal of Accounting Research*, **6**, 159–78.

Bank of International Settlements, Annual Reports, 1976, 1977, Basle.

Barro, R. J. (1977), Unanticipated money growth and unemployment in the United States, *American Economic Review*, **67**, 101–15.

Baumol, W. J. (1957), Speculation, profitability, and stability, *Review of Economics and Statistics*, **39**, 263–71.

Beenstock, Michael (1978), *The Foreign Exchanges. Theory, Modelling and Policy*, London: MacMillan.

Begg, D. K. H. (1982), *The Rational Expectations Revolution in Macroeconomics*, Oxford: Philip Allan.

Bell, G. (1974), Bank speculators: once bitten, twice shy? *The Times*, 15 May, 27.

Bergstrand, J. H. (1983), Is exchange rate volatility 'excessive'?, *Federal Reserve Bank of Boston New England Economic Review*, 5–14.

Berndt, E. K., B. H. Hall, R. E. Hall and J. A. Hausman (1974), Estimation and inference in nonlinear structural models, *Annals of Economic and Social Measurement*, **4**, 653–65.

Bilson, J. F. O. (1981), The speculative efficiency hypothesis, *Journal of Business*, **54**, 435–51.

(1978), Rational expectations and exchange rates, in J. A. Frenkel and H. G. Johnson, *The Economics of Exchange Rates: Selected Studies*, 75–96.

(1979), Recent developments in monetary models of exchange rate determination, *IMF Staff Papers*, **26**, 201–23.

Black, S. W. (1972), The use of rational expectations in models of speculation, *Review of Economics and Statistics*, **54**, 161–5.

Blanchard, O. J. (1979), Speculative bubbles, crashes and rational expectations, *Economics Letters*, **3**, 387–9.

Bollerslev, T. (1986), Generalised autoregressive conditional heteroskedasticity, *Journal of Econometrics*, **31**, 307–28.

(1987), A conditional heteroskedastic time series model for security prices and rates of return data, *Review of Economics and Statistics*, **69**, 542–7.

Bomhoff, E. J. and P. Korteweg (1983), Exchange rate variability and monetary policy under rational expectations: some Euro-American experiences 1973–1979, *Journal of Monetary Economics*, **11**, 169–206.

Boothe, P. and P. Glassman (1985), The statistical distribution of exchange rates: empirical evidence and economic implications, *Journal of International Economics*, **22**, 297–319.

Box, G. E. P. and G. M. Jenkins (1970), *Time Series Analysis: Forecasting and Control*, San Francisco: Holden Day.

Box, G. E. P. and D. A. Pierce (1970), Distribution of residual autocorrelations in autoregressive integrated moving average time series models, *Journal of the American Statistical Association*, **65**, 1509–26.

Branson, W. H. (1969), The minimum covered interest differential needed for international arbitrage activity, *Journal of Political Economy*, **77**, 1028–34.

(1977), Asset markets and relative prices in exchange rate determination, *Sozialwissenschaftliche Annalen*, 69–89.

Brillembourg, A. and S. M. Schadler (1979), A model of currency substitution in exchange rate determination, 1973–78, *IMF Staff Papers*, **26**, 513–42.

Brittain, B. (1981), International currency substitution and the apparent instability of velocity in some western European economies and the United States, *Journal of Money Credit and Banking*, **13**, 135–55.

Browne, F. X. (1983), Departures from interest rate parity, further evidence, *Journal of Banking and Finance*, **7**, 253–72.

Burt, J., F. R. Kaen and G. G. Booth (1977), Foreign exchange market efficiency under flexible exchange rates, *Journal of Finance*, **32**, 1325–30.

Cagan, P. (1956), The monetary dynamics of hyperinflation. In M. Friedman (ed.), *Studies in the Theory of Money*, Chicago, 25–117.

Canterbury, E. R. (1975), The modern theory of foreign exchange and the net speculative residual, *Southern Economic Journal*, **41**, 182–7.

Cassel, G. (1919), The depreciation of the German Mark, *Economic Journal*, **29**, 496–6.

(1922), *Money and Foreign Exchange After 1914*, London: Constable and Co.

Caves, D. W. and E. F. Feige (1980), Efficient foreign exchange markets and the monetary approach to exchange rate determination, *American Economic Review*, **70**, 120–34.

Charest, G. (1978), Dividend information, stock returns and market efficiency, *Journal of Financial Economics*, **6**, 293–330.

Cooley, T. F. and F. C. Prescott (1976), Estimation in the presence of stochastic parameter variation, *Econometrica*, **44**, 167–84.

Cootner, P. H. (ed.) (1964), *The Random Character of Stock Market Prices*, Cambridge, Mass.: MIT Press.

Copeland, L. S. (1984), The pound sterling/U.S. dollar exchange rate and the 'news', *Economic Letters*, **15**, 109–13.

Cornell, B. (1977), Spot rates, forward rates, and exchange market efficiency, *Journal of Financial Economics*, **5**, 56–65.

(1983a), Money supply announcements and interest rates: another view, *Journal of Business*, **56**, 1–23.

(1983b), The money supply announcements puzzle: review and interpretation, *American Economic Review*, **73**, 644–57.

Cornell, W. B. and J. K. Dietrich (1978), The efficiency of the foreign exchange market under floating exchange rates, *Review of Economics and Statistics*, **60**, 111–20.

Cossett, J. C. (1984), On the presence of risk premium in foreign exchange markets, *Journal of International Economics*, **16**, 139–54.

Cowles, A. (1960), A revision of previous conclusions regarding stock price behaviour, *Econometrica*, **28**, 909–15.

Cumby, R. E. and M. Obstfeld (1981), Exchange rate expectations and nominal interest differentials: a test of the Fisher hypothesis, *Journal of Finance*, **36**, 697–704.

David, H. A., H. O. Hartley and E. S. Pearson (1954), The distribution of the ratio in a single normal sample of range to standard deviation, *Biometrika*, **41**, 482–93.

Davidson, J. (1985), Econometric modelling of the sterling effective exchange rate, *Review of Economic Studies*, **41**, 231–40.

Demsetz, H. (1968), The cost of transacting, *Quarterly Journal of Economics*, **82**, 33–53.

Dickey, D. A. and W. A. Fuller (1979), Distribution of the estimates for autoregressive time series with a unit root, *Journal of the American Statistical Association*, **74**, 427–32.

(1981), Likelihood ratio statistics for autoregressive time series with a unit root, *Econometrica*, **49**, 1057–72.

Diebold, F. X. and M. Nerlove (1986), The dynamics of exchange rate volatility: a multivariate larent factor ARCH model, University of Pennsylvania, Econometrics Discussion Paper.

Domowitz, I. and C. S. Hakkio (1985), Conditional variance and the risk premium in the foreign exchange market, *Journal of International Economics*, **19**, 47–66.

Dooley, M. P. and J. Shafer (1976), Analysis of short-run exchange rate behavior, March 1973 to September 1975, International Finance Discussion Paper No. 76, Federal Reserve Board (mimeo).

Dornbusch, R. (1976a), Expectations and exchange rate dynamics, *Journal of Political Economy*, **84**, 1161–76.

(1976b), Exchange rate expectations and monetary policy, *Journal of International Economics*, **6**, 231–44.

(1980a), Exchange rate economics: where do we stand?, *Brookings Paper on Economic Activity*, **9**, 143–205.

(1980b), *Open Economy Macroeconomics*, New York: Basic Books, Inc.

Dornbusch, R. and S. Fischer (1980), Exchange rates and the current account, *American Economic Review*, **70**, 960–71.

Driskill, R. A. (1981), Exchange-rate dynamics: an empirical investigation, *Journal of Political Economy*, **89**, 357–71.

Driskill, R. A. and S. M. Sheffrin (1981), On the mark: comment, *American Economic Review*, **71**, 1068–74.

Edwards, S. (1982a), Exchange rates and 'news': a multi-currency approach, *Journal of International Money and Finance*, **1**, 211–24.

(1982b), Exchange rate market efficiency and new information, *Economic Letters*, **9**, 377–82.

(1983), Floating exchange rates, expectations and new information, *Journal of Monetary Economics*, **11**, 321–36.

Einzig, P. (1967), *A Dynamic Theory of Forward Exchange*, 2nd ed., London: MacMillan.

Engle, R. F. (1982), Autoregressive conditional heteroskedasticity with estimates of the variance of U.K. inflation, *Econometrica*, **50**, 987–1008.

Engle, R. F. and T. Bollerslev (1986), Modelling the persistence of conditional variances, *Econometric Review*, **5**, 1–50.

Engle, R. F. and C. W. J. Granger (1987), Cointegration and error correction: representation, estimation and testing, *Econometrica*, **55**, 251–76.

Engle, R. F., D. F. Hendry and J. F. Richard (1983), Exogeneity, *Econometrica*, **51**, 277–304.

Engle, R. F., D. M. Lilien and R. P. Robins (1987), Estimating time varying risk premia in the term structure: the ARCH M model, *Econometrica*, **55**, 391–400.

Evans, G. and S. Honkapohja (1986), A complete characterisation of ARMA solutions to linear rational expectations models, *Review of Economic Studies*, **L111**, 227–39.

Fama, E. F. (1963), Mandelbrot and the stable Paretian hypothesis, *Journal of Business*, **36**, 420–9.

(1965), The behaviour of stock market prices, *Journal of Business*, **38**, 34–105. 34–105.

(1970), Efficient capital markets: a review of theory and empirical work, *Journal of Finance*, **25**, 383–417.

(1976), *Foundations of Finance: Portfolio Decisions and Security Prices*, New York: Basic Books Inc.

Fama, E. F. and M. E. Blume (1966), Filter rules and stock market trading, *Journal of Business*, **39**, 226–41.

Fama, E. F. and A. Farber (1979), Money, bonds and foreign exchange, *American Economic Review*, **69**, 639–49.

Fama, E. F., L. Fisher, M. Jensen and R. Roll (1969), The adjustment of stock prices to new information, *International Economic Review*, **10**, 1–21.

Fama, E. F. and R. Roll (1968), Some properties of symmetric stable distributions, *Journal of the American Statistical Association*, **63**, 817–36.

(1971), Parameter estimates for symmetric stable distributions, *Journal of the American Association*, **63**, 817–36.

Farber, A. L., R. Roll and B. Solnik (1977), An empirical study of risk under fixed and flexible exchange, in Karl Brunner and Allan H. Meltzer (eds.), *Stabilization of the Domestic and International Economy*, Amsterdam, 235–67.

Feiger, G. M. (1978), Divergent rational expectations in a dynamic market model of futures markets, *Journal of Economic Theory*, **17**, 164–78.

Feldstein, M. S. (1968), Uncertainty and forward exchange speculation, *Review of Economics and Statistics*, **50**, 182–92.

Fieleke, N. S. (1975), Exchange rate flexibility and the efficiency of the foreign exchange markets, *Journal of Financial and Quantitative Analysis*, **10**, 409–26.

Figlewski, S. (1978), Market 'efficiency' in a market with heterogeneous information, *Journal of Political Economy*, **86**, 581–97.

Finn, F. J. (1974), Stock splits: prior and subsequent price relationships, *Journal of Business Finance and Accounting*, **1**, 93–108.

Firth, M. A. (1977), The investment performance of unit trusts in the period 1965–75, *Journal of Money, Credit and Banking*, **9**, 597–604.

Flavin, M. A. (1983), Excess volatility in the financial markets: a reassessment of the empirical evidence, *Journal of Political Economy*, **91**, 929–56.

Fleming, M. J. (1962), Domestic financial policies under fixed and flexible exchange rates, *IMF Staff Papers*, **9**, 369–79.

Flood, R. P. and P. M. Garber (1980), Market fundamentals versus price-level bubbles – the first tests, *Journal of Political Economy*, **88**, 745–76.

Frankel, J. A. (1979a), On the mark: theory of floating exchange rates based on real interest rate differentials, *American Economic Review*, **69**, 610–22.

  (1979b), The diversibility of exchange risk, *Journal of International Economics*, **9**, 379–93.

  (1981), On the mark: comment, *American Economic Review*, **71**, 1075–82.

  (1982), In search of the exchange risk premium: a six-currency test assuming mean-variance optimisation, *Journal of International Money and Finance*, **1**, 255–74.

Frenkel, J. A. (1973), Elasticities and the interest parity theory, *Journal of Political Economy*, **81**, 741–7.

  (1976), A monetary approach to the exchange rate: doctrinal aspects and empirical evidence, *Scandinavian Journal of Economics*, **78**, 200–24; reprinted in J. A. Frenkel and H. G. Johnson (eds.), *The Economics of Exchange Rates: Selected Studies*, Reading 1978, 1–25.

  (1977), The forward exchange rate, expectations, and the demand for money: the German hyperinflation, *American Economic Review*, **67**, 653–70.

  (1978), Purchasing power parity: evidence from the 1920's, *Journal of International Economics*, **8**, 161–91.

  (1979), Further evidence on expectations and the demand for money during the German hyperinflation, *Journal of Monetary Economics*, **5**, 81–96.

  (1980), Exchange rates, prices and money: lessons from the 1920's, *American Economic Review*, Papers and Proceedings, **70**, 235–42.

  (1981), The collapse of PPP in the 1970's, *European Economic Review*, **16**, 145–65.

Frenkel, J. A. and R. M. Levich (1975), Covered interest arbitrage: unexploited profits, *Journal of Political Economy*, **83**, 325–38.

  (1977), Transaction costs and interest arbitrage: tranquil versus turbulent periods, *Journal of Political Economy*, **85**, 1209–26.

Frenkel, J. A. and M. L. Mussa (1980), The efficiency of foreign exchange markets and measures of turbulence, *American Economic Review*, Papers and Proceedings, **70**, 374–81.

Frenkel, J. A. and Razin, A. (1980), Stochastic prices and tests of efficiency of foreign exchange markets, *Economic Letters*, **6**, 165–70.

Friedman, D. and S. Vandersteel (1982), Short-run fluctuations in foreign exchange rates: evidence from the data 1973–9, *Journal of International Economics*, **13**, 171–86.

Friedman, M. (1953), The case for flexible exchange rates, in M. Friedman (ed.), *Essays in Positive Economics*, Chicago, Ill.: University of Chicago Press, 157–203.

(1957), *A Theory of the Consumption Function*, Princeton, N.J.: Princeton University Press.

Friedman, B. M. (1979), Optimal expectations and the extreme information assumptions of rational expectations macromodels, *Journal of Monetary Economics*, **5**, 23–41.

Friend, I. (1972), The economic consequences of the stock market, *American Economic Review*, **62**, 212–19.

Fuller, W. A. (1976), *Introduction to Statistical Time Series*, New York: Wiley.

Genberg, H. (1978), Purchasing power parity under fixed and flexible exchange rates, *Journal of International Economics*, **8**, 247–76.

Geweke, J. and E. Feige (1979), Some joint tests of the efficiency of markets for forward exchange, *The Review of Economics and Statistics*, **61**, 334–41.

Giddy, I. H. (1976), An integrated theory of exchange rate equilibrium, *Journal of Financial and Quantitative Analysis*, **11**, 883–92.

Giddy, I. and G. Dufey (1975), The random behaviour of flexible exchange rates: implications for forecasting, *Journal of International Business Studies*, 1–32.

Girmes, D. and A. Benjamin (1975), Random walk hypotheses for 543 stocks and shares registered on the London Stock Exchange, *Journal of Business Finance and Accounting*, 134–45.

Girmes, D. and D. Damant (1974), Charts and the random walk, *Investment Analyst*, **41**, 16–19.

Glahe, F. R. (1966), Professional and nonprofessional speculation, profitability and stability, *Southern Economic Journal*, **33**, 443–55.

Gnedenko, B. V. and A. N. Kolmogorov (1954), *Limit Distributions for Sum of Independent Random Variables*, translated by K. L. Chung, Cambridge, Mass.: Addison-Wesley Mathematical Series.

Godfrey, L. G. (1978), Testing against general autoregressive and moving average error models when the regressions include lagged dependent variables, *Econometrica*, **46**, 1293–302.

Goldfeld, S. (1973), The demand for money revisited, *Brookings Papers on Economic Activity*, **3**, 577–638.

Goodman, S. H. (1979), Foreign exchange rate forecasting techniques: implications for business and policy, *Journal of Finance*, **34**, 415–27.

Gourieroux, C., J. J. Laffont and A. Monfort (1982), Rational expectations in dynamic linear models: analysis of the solutions, *Econometrica*, **50**, 409–26.

Granger, C. W. J. (1969), Investigating causal relations by econometric models and cross-spectral methods, *Econometrica*, **37**, 428–38.

(1986), Developments in the study of cointegrated economic variables, *Oxford Bulletin of Economics and Statistics*, **48**, 213–28.

Granger, C. W. J. and A. P. Anderson (1978), *An Introduction to Bilinear Time Series Models*, Göttingen: Springer Verlag.

Granger, C. W. J. and O. Morgenstern (1963), Spectral analysis of New York stock market prices, *Kyklos*, **16**, 1–27.

(1964), The random walk hypothesis of stock market behaviour, *Kyklos*, **17**, 1–30.

(1970), *Predictability of Stock Market Prices*, Lexington, Mass.: Heath Lexington Books.

Granger, C. W. J. and M. J. Morris (1976), Time series modelling and interpretation, *J. Royal Statist. Soc.*, *A*, **139**, 246–57.

Grauer, F. L. A., R. H. Litzenberger and R. E. Stehle (1976), Sharing rules and equilibrium in an international trade capital market under uncertainty, *Journal of Financial Economics*, **4**, 233–56.

Gregory, A. W. and M. R. Veall (1985), Formulating Wald tests of nonlinear restrictions, *Econometrica*, **53**, 1465–8.

Grossman, S. J. and J. E. Stiglitz (1976), Information and competitive price systems, *American Economic Review*, **66**, 246–53.

(1980), On the impossibility of informationally efficient markets, *American Economic Review*, **70**, 393–408.

Group of Thirty (1980), *Foreign Exchange Markets Under Floating Rates: A Study in International Finance*, New York: World Trade Centre, Park Avenue.

(1985), *The foreign exchange markets in the 1980s*, New York.

Grubel, H. G. (1963), A multicountry model of forward exchange: theory, policy, and empirical evidence 1955–1962, *Yale Economic Essays*, **3**, 105–69.

(1979), The Peter principle and the efficient market hypothesis, *Financial Analysts Journal*, 72–5.

Haas, R. D. (1974), More evidence on the role of speculation in the Canadian forward exchange market, *Canadian Journal of Economics*, **7**, 496–501.

Hahn, F. H. (1982), *Money and Inflation*, Oxford: Basil Blackwell.

Hakkio, C. S. (1981a), Expectations and the forward exchange rate, *International Economic Review*, **22**, 663–78.

(1981b), The term structure of the forward premium, *Journal of Monetary Economics*, **8**, 41–58.

(1984), A reexamination of purchasing power parity: a multi country and multi period study, *Journal of International Economics*, **17**, 265–77.

Hall, S. G. (1983), The exchange rate, National Institute of Economic and Social Research, Discussion Paper No. 57.

Hannan, E. J. (1970), *Multiple Time Series Analysis*, London: Wiley.

Hansen, L. P. and Hodrick, R. J. (1980), Forward exchange rates as optimal predictors of future spot rates: an econometric analysis, *Journal of Political Economy*, **88**, 829–53.

(1983), Risk averse speculation in forward exchange markets: an econometric analysis, in J. A. Frankel (ed.), *Exchange Rates and International Macroeconomics*, Chicago: University of Chicago Press.

Harvey, A. C. (1981a), *The Econometric Analysis of Times Series*, Oxford: Philip Allan.

(1981b), *Times Series Models*, Oxford: Philip Allan.

Hayashi, F. and C. A. Sims (1983), Nearly efficient estimation of time series models with predetermined but not exogenous instruments, *Econometrica*, **51**, 783–98.

Haynes, S. E. and J. A. Stone (1981), On the mark: comment, *American Economic Review*, **71**, 1060–71.

Helpman, E. and A. Razin (1982), Dynamics of a floating exchange rate regime, *Journal of Political Economy*, **90**, 728–54.

Henfrey, A., B. Albrecht and P. Richards (1977), The U.K. stock market and the efficient market model, *Investment Analyst*, **48**, 5–24.

Hirschleifer, J. and J. G. Riley (1979), The analytics of uncertainty and information – an expository survey, *Journal of Economic Literature*, **27**, 1375–421.

Hodgson, J. S. and P. Phelps (1975), The distributed impact of price level variation on floating exchange rates, *Review of Economics and Statistics*, **57**, 58–64.

Hodrick, R. (1987), The empirical evidence on the efficiency of forward and futures foreign exchange markets, London: Harwood Academic Publishers.

Hodrick, R. and S. Srivastava (1984), An investigation of risk and return in forward foreign exchange, *Journal of International Money and Finance*, **3**, 5–30.

Hoffman, D. L. and P. Schmidt (1981), Testing the restrictions implied by the rational expectations hypothesis, *Journal of Econometrics*, **15**, 265–87.

Hoffmann, D. L. and D. E. Schlagenhauf (1983), Rational expectations and monetary models of exchange rate determination, *Journal of Monetary Economics*, **11**, 247–60.

Hogan, W. P. and I. G. Sharp (1984), On the relationship between the New York closing spot U.S. \$/\$A exchange rate and the Reserve Bank of Australia's official rate, *Economic Letters*, **14**, 73–9.

Holmes, A. R. and F. H. Schott (1965), *The New York Foreign Exchange Market*, New York.

Holmes, J. M. (1967), The purchasing power parity theory: in defence of Gustav Cassel as a modern theorist, *Journal of Political Economy*, **75**, 686–95.

Hooper, P. and J. Morton (1978), Summary measures of the dollars foreign exchange value, *Federal Reserve Bulletin*, **64**, 783–9.

Hosking, J. R. M. (1980), The multivariate portmanteau statistic, *Journal of the American Statistical Association*, **75**, 602–8.

Hsieh, D. A. (1985), The statistical properties of daily foreign exchange rates: 1974–1983, University of Chicago, Graduate School of Business, Manuscript.

Huang, R. D. (1981), The monetary approach to exchange rates in an efficient foreign exchange market: tests based on volatility, *Journal of Finance*, **36**, 31–41.

International Monetary Fund (1974), Guidelines for the management of floating exchange rates, *Annual Report*, 122–6.

(1975), *Annual Report*.

International Financial Statistics, OECD Country Reports, various issues.

Jacobs, R. L., E. E. Leamer and M. P. Ward (1979), Difficulties with testing for causation, *Economic Inquiry*, **17**, 401–13.

Jensen, M. C. (1968), The performance of mutual funds in the period 1945–64, *Journal of Finance*, **23**, 389–416.

(1978), Some anomalous evidence regarding market efficiency, *Journal of Financial Economicsk*, **6**, 95–101.

Kaminsky, G. and R. Peruga (1987), Risk premium and the foreign exchange market, UCSD Department of Economics discussion paper.

Kaserman, D. L. (1973), The forward exchange rate: its determination and behaviour of the future spot rate, *Proceedings of the American Statistical Association*, 417–22.

Katz, S. I. (1975), *'Managed Floating' as an Interim International Exchange Rate Regime, 1973–1975*, New York.

Kemp, M. C. (1963), Speculation, profitability and price stability, *Review of Economics and Statistics*, **45**, 185–9.

Kendall, M. G. (1953), The analysis of economic time series – Part I: prices, *Journal of the Royal Statistical Society* (Series A), **96**, 11–25.

Kendall, M. G. and A. Stuart (1966), *The Advanced Theory of Statistics*, 3: *Design and Analysis and Time Series*, London: Charles Griffin & Company Ltd.

Kesselman, J. (1971), The role of speculation in forward rate determination, *Canadian Journal of Economics*, **4**, 279–98.

Keynes, J. M. (1924), A tract on monetary reform, *The Collected Writings of John Maynard Keynes*, IV, London: Macmillan.

(1927), Some aspects of commodity markets, *Manchester Guardian Commercial*, European Reconstruction Series.

(1936), *The General Theory of Employment, Interest and Money*, London: Macmillan.

Kindleberger, C. P. (1976), Lessons of floating exchange rates, in K. Brunner and A. H. Meltzer, *Institutional Arrangements and the Inflation Problem*, *Carnegie–Rochester Conference Series on Public Policy*, **3**, 51–77.

Kohlhagen, S. W. (1975), The performance of the foreign exchange markets: 1971–1974, *Journal of International Business Studies*, **6**, 33–8.

(1978), *The Behaviour of Foreign Exchange Markets – a Critical Survey of the Empirical Literature*, New York University Monograph Series in Finance and Economics, 1988-3 New York University No. 3 Salomon Brothers Center.

König, H. and W. Gaab (1982), Smooth exchange rates by central bank intervention, in *Experience and Problems of the International Monetary System*, 177–96, Economic Notes, Monte dei Paschi di Siena.

Kouri, P. J. K. (1976), The exchange rate and the balance of payments in the short-run and in the long-run, a monetary approach, *Scandinavian Journal of Economics*, **78**, 280–304.

(1983), Balance of payments and the foreign exchange market: a dynamic partial equilibrium model, in J. S. Bhandari, B. H. Putnam and J. H. Levine, *Economic Interdependence and Flexible Exchange Rates*, MIT Press.

Kouri, P. J. K. and J. B. de Macedo (1978), Exchange rates and the international adjustment process, *Brookings Papers on Economic Activity*, **1**, 111–50.

Le Roy, S. and R. Porter (1981), The present value relation: tests based on implied variance bounds, *Econometrica*, **49**, 555–74.

Levich, R. (1978), Further results on the efficiency of markets for foreign exchange, in *Managed Exchange Rate Flexibility: The Recent Experience*, Federal Reserve Bank of Boston, 20, 58–80.

(1979), On the efficiency of markets for foreign exchange, in R. Dornbusch and J. Frenkel (eds.), *International Economic Policy, Theory and Evidence*, John Hopkins, 246–67.

Levi, M. D. (1978), The weekend game: clearing houses versus federal funds, *Canadian Journal of Economics*, **11**, 750–7.

(1983), *International Finance, Financial Management and the International Economy*, New York: McGraw-Hill.

Levy, E. and A. R. Nobay (1986), The speculative efficiency hypothesis, a bivariate analysis, *Economic Journal, Annual Supplement*, 109–21.

Lintner, J. (1965), The valuation of risk assets and the selection of risky investments in stock portfolios and capital budgets, *Review of Economics and Statistics*, **47**, 13–37.

Lippens, R. E. (1987), Multi maturity efficient market hypothesis: sorting out rejections in international interest and exchange rate models, *International Journal of Forecasting*, **3**, 149–58.

Ljung, G. M. and G. E. P. Box (1978), On a measure of lack of fit in time series models, *Biometrika*, **65**, 297–303.

Lloyd-Davies, P. and M. Canes (1978), Stock prices and the publication of second-hand information, *Journal of Business*, **51**, 43–56.

Logue, D. E. and R. J. Sweeney (1977), 'White noise' in imperfect markets: the case of the franc/dollar exchange rate, *Journal of Finance*, **32**, 761–8.

Logue, D. E., R. J. Sweeney and T. D. Willett (1978), Speculative behaviour of foreign exchange rates during the current float, *Journal of Business Research*, **6**, 159–74.

Longworth, D. (1981), Testing the efficiency of the Canadian–U.S. exchange market under the assumption of no risk premium, *Journal of Finance*, **36**, 43–9.

Lorie, J. and M. Hamilton (1973), *The Stock Market: Theories and Evidence*, Homewood, Ill.: R. D. Irwin Inc.

Lorie, J. and V. Niederhoffer (1968), Predictive and statistical properties of insider trading, *Journal of Law and Economics*, **11**, 35–53.

Lucas, R. C. (1978), Asset prices in an exchange economy, *Econometrica*, **46**, 1429–45.

Lutkepohl, H. (1982), Discounted polynomials for multiple time series model building, *Biometrika*, **69**, 107–15.

Macdonald, R. (1983), Some tests of the rational expectations hypothesis in the foreign exchange market, *Scottish Journal of Political Economy*, **30**, 235–50.

Mandelbrot, M. (1963), The variation of certain speculative prices, *Journal of Business*, **36**, 394–419.

  (1966), Forecasts of future prices, unbiased markets and martingale model, *Journal of Business*, **39**, 242–55.

  (1969), Long-run linearity, locally Gaussian process H-spectra and infinite variances, *International Economic Review*, **10**, 82–111.

McMahon, P. C. (1987), Risk, expectations and uncertainty in the foreign exchange market; a reinterpretation of the empirical evidence, University of Birmingham, manuscript.

  (1988), Forward rates and expected future spot rates, Bank of England, manuscript.

McCallum, B. T. (1977), The role of speculation in the Canadian forward exchange market: some estimates assuming rational expectations, *Review of Economics and Statistics*, **59**, 145–51.

  (1979), Testing for the roles of speculation in the forward exchange market: a reply, *Review of Economics and Statistics*, **61**, 611–12.

McCulloch, J. H. (1975), Operational aspects of the Siegel Paradox, *Quarterly Journal of Economics*, **89**, 170–2.

McCurdy, T. H. and I. G. Morgan (1987), Tests of the martingale hypothesis for foreign currency with time varying volatility, *International Journal of Forecasting*, **3**, 131–48.

McFarland, J. W., R. R. Pettit and S. K. Sung (1982), The distribution of foreign exchange price changes: trading day effects and risk measurement, *Journal of Finance*, **37**, 693–715.

McKinnon, R. I. (1976), Floating foreign exchange rates 1973–1973: the emperor's new clothes, in K. Brunner and A. Meltzer (eds.), *Institutional Arrangements and the Inflation Problem*, **3**, *Carnegie–Rochester Conference Series on Public Policy*, supplement to the *Journal of Monetary Economies*, 315–425.

  (1979), *Money in International Exchange: The Convertible Currency System*, Oxford: Oxford University Press.

(1982), Currency substitutions and instability in the world dollar market, *American Economic Review*, **72**, 320–33.

Messe, R. A. (1986), Testing for bubbles in exchange markets: a case of sparkling rates? *Journal of Political Economy*, **94**, 345–73.

Meese, R. A. and R. Rogoff (1983), Empirical exchange rate models of the seventies: do they fit out of sample?, *Journal of International Economics*, **14**, 3–24.

Meese, R. A. and K. J. Singleton (1982), On unit roots and the empirical modeling of exchange rates, *Journal of Finance*, **37**, 1029–35.

Melino, A. (1983), Estimation of a rational expectations model of the term structure, in *Essays on Estimation and Inference in Linear Rational Expectations Models*, unpublished Ph.D. Dissertation, Harvard University.

(1987), The term structure of interest rates: evidence and theory, *Journal of Monetary Economics* (forthcoming).

Milhoj, A. (1987), A conditional variance model for daily deviations of an exchange rate, *Journal of Business and Economic Statistics*, **5**, 99–103.

Minford, P. and Peel, D. A. (1983), *Rational Expectations and the New Macroeconomics*, Oxford: Martin Robertson.

Minot, W. G. (1974), Tests for integration between major western European capital markets, *Oxford Economic Papers*, **26**, 424–39.

Mishkin, F. S. (1978), Efficient markets theory: implications for monetary policy, *Brookings Papers on Economic Activity*, **3**, 707–52.

(1981), Are market forecasts rational? *American Economic Review*, **71**, 295–306.

(1983), *A Rational Expectations Approach to Macroeconomics*, Chicago, Ill.: University of Chicago Press.

Moore, A. B. (1964), Some characteristics of changes in common stock prices, in P. H. Cootner (ed.), *The Random Character of Stock Market Prices*, Cambridge, Mass.: MIT Press.

Mundell, R. A. (1961), Flexible exchange rates and employment policy, *Canadian Journal of Economics and Political Science*, **27**, 509–17.

(1968), *International Economics*, New York: MacMillan.

Mussa, M. L. (1974), A monetary approach to balance of payments analysis, *Journal of Money, Credit and Banking*, **6**, 333–51.

(1976), The exchange rate, the balance of payments and monetary and fiscal policy under a regime of controlled floating, *Scandinavian Journal of Economics*, **78**, 229–54.

(1979), Empirical regularities in the behavior of exchange rates and theories of the foreign markets, in K. Brunner and A. H. Meltzer (eds.), *Policies for Employment, Prices and Exchange Rates, Carnegie–Rochester Conference Series on Public Policy*, supplement to the *Journal of Monetary Economics*, 9–57.

Muth, J. F. (1960), Optimal properties of exponentially weighted forecasts, *Journal of the American Statistical Association*, **55**, 299–306.

(1961), Rational expectations and the theory of price movements, *Econometrica*, **29**, 315–35.

Nelson, C. R. and Kang, H. (1984), Spurious periodicity in inappropriately detrended time series, *Econometrica*, **40**, 741–51.

Newey, K. N. and K. D. West (1987), A simple, positive semi-definite heteroskedasticity and autocorrelation consistent covariance matrix, *Econometrica*, **55**, 703–8.

Niederhoffer, V. and M. F. M. Osborne (1966), Market making and reversal on the stock exchange, *Journal of the American Statistical Association*, **61**, 897–916.

Niehans, J. (1975), Some doubts about the efficacy of monetary policy under flexible exchange rates, *Journal of International Economics*, **5**, 275–82.

(1979), Monetary policy and overshooting exchange rates, *Aussenwirtschaft*, **34**, 199–219.

Nurkse, R. (1944), *International Currency Experience*, League of Nations, Geneva.

Officer, L. (1976), The purchasing power parity theory of exchange rates: a review article, *IMF Staff Papers*, **23**, 1–60.

Officer, L. H. and T. D. Willett (1970), The covered-arbitrage schedule: a critical survey of recent developments, *Journal of Money, Credit and Banking*, **2**, 247–57.

Osborne, M. F. M. (1959), Brownian motion in the stock market, *Operation Research*, **7**, 145–73, reprinted.

OECD (1986), Main Economic Indicators, Paris.

Pagan, A. R. (1984), Econometric issues in the analysis of regressions with generated regressors, *International Economic Review*, **25**, 221–47.

Pantula, S. G. (1984), Autoregressive conditionally heteroskedastic models, North Carolina State University, Dept. of Statistics, Working Paper.

Perron, P. (1986), Tests of joint hypothesis for time series regression with a unit root, Université de Montreal, C.R.D.E., cahier de recherche No. 2086.

Perron, P. and P. C. B. Phillips (1987), Does GNP have a unit root? A re-examination, *Economics Letters*, **23**, 139–45.

Pesaran, M. H. (1985), Formation of inflation expectations in British manufacturing industries, *Economic Journal*, **95**, 948–75.

Phillips, P. C. B. (1987), Time series regression with a unit root, *Econometrica*, **55**, 277–301.

Phillips, P. C. B. and Perron, P. (1986), Testing for a unit root in time series regression, Cowles Foundation Discussion Paper No. 795, Yale University.

Pigott, C. and R. J. Sweeney (1985), Testing the exchange rate implications of two popular monetary models, in S. W. Arnott, R. J. Sweeney and T. D. Willet (eds.), *Exchange Rates, Trade and the US Economy*, Ballinger Publications.

Pippenger, J. E. (1973), The case for freely fluctuating exchange rates: some evidence, *Western Economic Review*, **11**, 314–26.

(1978), Interest arbitrage between Canada and the United States: a new perspective, *Canadian Journal of Economics*, **11**, 183–93.

Plosser, C. I. and G. W. Schwert (1977), Estimation of a non-invertible moving average process: the case of overdifferencing, *Journal of Econometrics*, **6**, 199–224.

Poole, W. (1967a), Speculative prices as random walks: an analysis of ten time series of flexible exchange rates, *Southern Economic Journal*, **33**, 468–78.

(1967b), The stability of the Canadian flexible exchange rate, 1950–1962, *Canadian Journal of Economics and Political Science*, 205–17.

Prachowny, F. J. (1970), A note on interest parity and the supply of arbitrage funds, *Journal of Political Economy*, **78**, 540–6.

Praetz, P. D. (1976), On the methodology of testing for independence in futures prices, *Journal of Finance*, **31**, 977–9.

(1979), A general test of a filter effect, *Journal of Financial and Quantitative Analysis*, **14**, 385–94.

(1979), Testing for a flat spectrum on efficient market price data, *Journal of Finance*, **34**, 645–58.

Revankar, N. S. (1980), Testing of the rational expectations hypothesis, *Econometrica*, **48**, 1347–64.

Richards, P. H. (1978), Sharpe performance among pension funds? *Investment Analyst*, **51**, 9–14.

Rogalski, R. J. and J. D. Vinso (1977), Price level variations as predictors of flexible exchange rates, *Journal of International Business Studies*, **8**, 71–82.

(1980), Empirical properties of foreign exchange rates, *Journal of International Business Studies*, 69–79.

Roll, R. and B. Solnik (1977), A pure foreign exchange asset pricing model, *Journal of International Economics*, **7**, 161–79.

Roper, D. E. (1975), The role of expected value analysis for speculative decisions in the forward currency market: comment, *Quarterly Journal of Economics*, **89**, 157–69.

Rose, A. K. (1984) Testing for news in foreign exchange markets, *Economics Letters*, **14**, 369–76.

Rose, A. K. and J. G. Selody (1984), Exchange market efficiency: a semi-strong test using multiple markets and daily data, *Review of Economics and Statistics*, **66**, 669–72.

Rothenberg, T. J. (1973), *Efficient Estimation with A Priori Information*, New Haven: Yale University Press.

Rozeff, M. (1974), Money and stock prices, market efficiency and the lag in the effect of monetary policy, *Journal of Financial Economics*, **1**, 245–302.

Rubinstein, M. (1976), The valuation of uncertain income streams and the pricing of options, *Bell Journal of Economics and Management Science*, **7**, 407–25.

Salemi, M. K. (1979), Adaptive expectations, rational expectations and money demand in hyperinflation Germany, *Journal of Monetary Economics*, **5**, 593–604.

Samuelson, P. A. (1964), Theoretical notes on trade problems, *Review of Economics and Statistics*, **46**, 145–54.

(1965), Proof that properly anticipated prices fluctuate randomly, *Industrial Management Review*, **6**, 41–9.

Sargent, T. J. (1973), Rational expectations, the real rate of interest and the natural rate of unemployment, *Brookings Papers on Economic Activity*, **2**, 429–72.

(1979), A note on maximum likelihood estimation of the rational expectations model of the term structure, *Journal of Monetary Economics*, **5**, 133–43.

Sawa, T. (1978), Information criteria for discriminating among alternative regression model, *Econometrica*, **42**, 303–9.

Schadler, S. (1977), Sources of exchange rate variability: theory and empirical evidence, *IMF Staff Papers*, **24**, 428–41.

Schmidt, P. (1973), The asymptotic distribution of dynamic multipliers, *Econometrica*, **41**, 161–4.

(1974), The asymptotic distribution of forecasts in an econometric model, *Econometrica*, **42**, 303–9.

Schwarz, G. (1978), Estimating the dimension of a model, *Annals of Statistics*, **6**, 461–4.

Sharpe, W. (1963), A simplified model for portfolio analysis, *Management Science*, **9**, 277–93.

(1964), Capital asset prices: a theory of market equilibrium under conditions of risk, *Journal of Finance*, **19**, 425–42.

Shiller, R. J. (1979), The volatility of long-term interest rates and expectations models of the term structure, *Journal of Political Economy*, **87**, 1190–219.

(1981), Alternative tests of rational expectations models: the case of the term structure, *Journal of Econometrics*, **16**, 71–81.

Shiller, R. J. and Perron, P. (1985), Testing the random walk hypothesis: power versus frequency of observation, *Economic Letters*, **18**, 381–6.

Siegel, J. J. (1972), Risk interest rates and the forward exchange, *Quarterly Journal of Economics*, **89**, 173–5.

(1975), Reply–risk interest rates and the forward exchange, *Quarterly Journal of Economics*, **89**, 173–5.

Sims, C. (1974), Seasonality in regression, *Journal of the American Statistical Association*, **69**, 618–25.

(1980), Macroeconomics and reality, *Econometrica*, **48**, 1–48.

Smith, P. N. and M. R. Wickens (1984), An empirical investigation into the causes of failure of the monetary model of the exchange rate, *Journal of Applied Econometrics*, **1**, 143–62.

Solnik, B. H. (1973), Equilibrium in an international capital market under uncertainty, *Journal of Economic Theory*, **8**, 506–24.

(1973), *European Capital Markets: Towards a General Theory of International Investment*, Lexington, Mass.: London.

(1974), An equilibrium model of the international capital market, *Journal of Economic Theory*, **8**, 500–24.

(1978), International parity conditions and exchange risk: a review, *Journal of Banking and Finance*, **2**, 281–93.

Solt, M. E. and P. J. Swanson (1981), On the efficiency of the markets for gold and silver, *Journal of Business*, **54**, 453–78.

Spraos, J. (1953), The theory of forward exchange and recent practice, *Manchester School of Economics and Social Studies*, **21**, 87–117.

Startz, R. (1982), Do forecast errors on term premia really make the difference between long and short-term rates? *Journal of Financial Economics*, **10**, 323–9.

Stein, J. L. (1961), Destabilizing speculative activity can be profitable, *The Review of Economics and Statistics*, **43**, 301–2.

(1962), The nature and efficiency of the foreign exchange market, *International Finance Section*, New Jersey: Princeton University.

(1965), The forward rate and the interest parity, *Review of Economics and Statistics*, **32**, 113–26.

(1968), Illiquidity and limits to interest arbitrage: reply, *Journal of Finance*, **23**, 670–1.

(1980), The dynamics of spot and forward prices in an efficient foreign exchange market with rational expectations, *American Economic Review*, **70**, 565–83.

Stein, J. L. and E. Tower (1967), The short-run stability of the foreign exchange market, *Review of Economics and Statistics*, **49**, 173–85.

Stiglitz, J. E. (1983), Futures markets and risk: a general equilibrium approach, in M. E. Streit (ed.), *Futures Markets, Modelling, Managing and Monitoring Futures Trading*, Oxford: Basil Blackwell.

Stock, J. H. (1987), Asymptotic properties of least squares estimators of cointegrating vectors, *Econometrica*, **55**, 1,035–56.

Stockman, A. C. (1978), Risk, information and forward exchange rates, in J. A.

Frenkel and H. G. Johnson (eds.), *The Economics of Exchange Rates*, Reading, Mass., 159–78.

(1980), A theory of exchange rate determination, *Journal of Political Economy*, **88**, 673–98.

Stoll, H. R. (1968), An empirical study of the forward exchange market under fixed and flexible exchange rates systems, *Canadian Journal of Economics*, **1**, 55–78.

(1972), Causes of deviation from interest–rate parity: a comment, *Journal of Money, Credit and Banking*, **1**, 113–17.

Stulz, R. M. (1981), A model of international asset pricing, *Journal of Financial Economics*, **9**, 383–406.

Taylor, M. P. (1987), Covered interest-rate parity: a high frequency, high quality data study, *Economica*, **54**, 429–438.

Taylor, M. P. and P. C. McMahon (1988), Long-run purchasing power parity in the 1920s, *European Economic Review*, **32**, 179–97.

(1980), Conjectured models for trends in financial prices, tests and forecasts, *Journal of the Royal Statistical Society*, A, **143**, 338–62.

Taylor, S. (1982), Tests of the random walk hypothesis against a price trend hypothesis, *Journal of Financial and Quantitative Analysis*, **17**, 37–61.

Tiao, G. C. and Guttman, I. (1980), Forecasting contemporeal aggregates of multiple time series, *Journal of Econometrics*, **12**, 219–30.

Tiao, G. C. and Tsay, R. S. (1983), Multiple time series modelling and extended sample cross correlations, *Journal of Business and Economic Statistics*, **1**, 43–56.

Tsiang, S. C. (1959), The theory of forward exchange and effects of government intervention on the forward exchange market, *IMF Staff Papers*, **7**, 75–106.

Turnovsky, S. J. and K. M. Ball (1983), Covered interest parity and speculative efficiency: some empirical evidence for Australia, *Economic Record*, 271–80.

Upson, R. B. (1972), Random walk and forward exchange rates: a spectral analysis, *Journal of Financial and Quantitative Analysis*, **7**, 1897–905.

Urich, T. J. (1982), The information content of weekly money announcements, *Journal of Monetary Economics*, **10**, 73–88.

Urich, T. J. and P. Wachtel (1981), Market responses to the weekly money supply announcements in the 1970s, *Journal of Finance*, **36**, 1064–72.

Van Belle, J. J. (1973), A neglected aspect of the modern theory of forward exchange, *Southern Economic Journal*, **39**, 117–19.

Verrechia, R. E. (1982), Information acquisition in a noisy rational expectations economy, *Econometrica*, **50**, 1415–30.

Wallace, N. (1979), Why markets in foreign exchange are different from other markets, Federal Reserve Bank of Minneapolis, *Quarterly Review*, **3**, 1–7.

Wallis, K. F. (1974), Seasonal adjustment and relations between variables, *Journal of the American Statistical Association*, **69**, 18–31.

(1980), Econometric implications of the rational expectations hypothesis, *Econometrica*, **48**, 49–72.

Westerfield, J. M. (1977), An examination of foreign exchange risk under fixed and floating regimes, *Journal of International Economics*, **7**, 181–200.

White, H. (1980), A heteroskedasticity consistent covariance matrix estimator and a direct test of heteroskedasticity, *Econometrica*, **48**, 817–38.

Whiteman, C. H. (1983), *Linear Rational Expectations Models: A Users Guide*, Minneapolis: University of Minnesota Press.

Whitman, M. (1975), Global monetarism and the monetary approach to the balance of payments, *Brookings Papers in Economic Activity*, **3**, 491–536.

Whitman, M. (1984), Assessing greater variability in exchange rates: a private sector perspective, *American Economic Review Papers and Proceedings*, **74**, 2, 298–304.

Whittle, P. (1963), *Prediction and Regulation by Linear Least Squares Methods*, London: English Universities Press.

Wickens, M. R. (1984), Rational expectations and exchange rate dynamics, in T. Peters, P. Praet and P. Reding (eds.), *International Trade and Exchange Rates in the Late Eighties*.

Williamson, J. (1983), *IMF Conditionality*, Cambridge, Mass.: MIT Press.

Williamson, P. J. (1972), Measuring mutual fund performance, *Financial Analysts Journal*, November–December.

Woo, W. T. (1985), The monetary approach to exchange rate determination under rational expectations, *Journal of International Economics*, **18**, 1–16.

Working, H. (1958), A theory of anticipatory prices, *American Economic Review*, 188–99.

Yamamoto, T. (1981), Predictions of multivariate autoregressive moving average models, *Biometrika*, **68**, 485–92.

Zellner, A. (1979), Causality and econometrics, in K. Brunner and A. H. Meltzer (eds.), *Carnegie–Rochester Conference Series*, **10**, 9–54.

Index